D0759137

Dan Nimmo is professor of political science at the University of Tennessee. His teaching and research efforts center on American government, political communication, public opinion, and voter behavior. The current editor of *Communication Yearbook,* he is the author of *The Political Persuaders, Popular Images of Politics,* and several other books.

James E. Combs is professor of political science at Valparaiso University. His main professional interests are political theory and American politics. He is the author of *Dimensions of Political Drama* and co-editor of *Drama in Life.*

Dan Nimmo/James E. Combs

SUBLIMINAL
POLITICS
MYTHS
& MYTHMAKERS
IN AMERICA

A SPECTRUM BOOK

PRENTICE-HALL, INC., Englewood Cliffs, N.J. 07632

Library of Congress Cataloging in Publication Data

Nimmo, Dan D
    Subliminal politics.

    (A Spectrum Book)
    Includes index.
    1. United States—Politics and government.
2. Communication in politics—United States.
3. Public relations and politics. 4. Myth.
I. Combs, James E., joint author. II. Title.
JK1726.N53   320.9'73   79–25468
ISBN 0-13-859116-4
ISBN 0-13-85108-3 pbk.

JK1726
N53

Editorial production/supervision
  and interior design by Heath Silberfeld
Manufacturing buyer: Barbara A. Frick
Cover design by Michael Freeland

Printed in the United States of America

10 9 8 7 6 5 4 3 2 1

PRENTICE-HALL INTERNATIONAL, INC., *London*
PRENTICE-HALL OF AUSTRALIA PTY. LIMITED, *Sydney*
PRENTICE-HALL OF CANADA, LTD., *Toronto*
PRENTICE-HALL OF INDIA PRIVATE LIMITED, *New Delhi*
PRENTICE-HALL OF JAPAN, INC., *Tokyo*
PRENTICE-HALL OF SOUTHEAST ASIA PTE. LTD., *Singapore*
WHITEHALL BOOKS LIMITED, *Wellington, New Zealand*

109394

Persons attempting to find a motive in this narrative will be prosecuted; persons attempting to find a moral in it will be banished; persons attempting to find a plot in it will be shot.

By Order of the Author

MARK TWAIN
Huckleberry Finn

CONTENTS

PREFACE

Given the market glut, there is scarcely room for yet another book purporting to describe what people know about American politics. This is not such a book. There is, however, ample reason for a book discussing what people *think* they know about American politics. This is that book. Specifically, our topic is the taken-for-granted set of assumptions, conceptions, and ideas about American politics that lies below the threshold of consciousness, that substantial realm of dramatic accounts whose accuracy and plausibility go largely unquestioned. In short, this is a book about myths of American politics and the persons who make and help plant them in our subconscious—politicians, political press agents, popular entertainers, journalists, pollsters, and political scientists.

Two points about our topic and our treatment of it warrant emphasis. First, we avoid the all-too-easily-voiced view that myths by their very nature are false ideas. For us myth is a nonperjorative term. A myth may be true, false, or both. The key characteristic of myth, however, is that it is a dramatic representation of past, present, or future events that people *believe.*

Second, we identify and discuss the actors in the American political drama who we regard as key mythmakers. We describe the myths they make and how they do it. Our intent is not to demean, degrade, or disparage. Rather it is to remind. Myth is so common in American politics, and mythmaking so pervasive, that the creation and communication of mythical accounts has become subliminal, that is, people engage in it without even realizing it happens, just as they accept the credibility of those accounts unthinkingly. By reminding ourselves that all manner of political actors engage in mythmaking—including the authors of this book along with other political scientists—we hope to alert readers to the mythical components of what passes for political knowledge and make those who deny that they do so more circumspect in their mythmaking.

In the process of generating, organizing, and articulating the ideas in this presentation, each of the authors had occasion to test out those thoughts on unsuspecting students in lecture and seminar courses. For their patience and radical skepticism we are thankful. Dorothy Herscher did an admirable job in typing early drafts of the manuscript, and Paulette Acres—certainly one of the most reliable of persons at her task—typed the final version. The completion of the work was facilitated by financial assistance provided through Dean Howard Peters and Vice President John Strietelmeier of Valparaiso

University. Jan Trice and Karen Johnson of the University of Tennessee provided helpful proofing of the manuscript. Heath Silberfeld guided the work skillfully through production for Spectrum Books. Again it was a pleasure to work with Spectrum's Director, Michael Hunter. Finally, and foremost, this book is dedicated to Jackie Combs, mother of one of the authors.

SUBLIMINAL POLITICS

PART I

NOT LIVING BY BREAD ALONE

THE NATURE OF AND NECESSITY FOR POLITICAL MYTHS

CHAPTER 1

The Unicorn
Is A Mythical Beast
And There Are
A Lot Of Unicorns
In Politics

Four decades ago, the late James Thurber, one of America's wittiest writers, published a tale entitled "The Unicorn in the Garden." It went like this:

One morning as a man was having breakfast he looked out his window and saw a white unicorn with a golden horn munching roses in the garden. The man arose, went to the bedroom, awakened his sleeping wife and told her of the unicorn. "The unicorn is a mythical beast," she retorted, then went back to sleep. The man turned, went downstairs, and out into the garden. There was the unicorn, now eating tulips. The man pulled up a lily, gave it to the unicorn, and the lily too was consumed. Back the man went to his wife, roused her, and explained what had happened. Whereupon the wife pronounced her husband a "booby" that should be put in the "booby hatch." This upset the man. He returned to the garden. But, lo, the unicorn had gone, so the man sat down among the flowers and went to sleep. Meanwhile his wife arose, dressed, and telephoned the police and a psychiatrist. She demanded they bring a strait jacket. The police and psychiatrist arrived and the wife related the story—how her husband "saw a unicorn this morning," how it had eaten a lily, and had a golden horn on its forehead. Suddenly the police seized the wife and after a terrific struggle, subdued her, placing her in the strait jacket. Just then the man entered the house to find his wife trussed up. "Did you tell your wife you saw a unicorn?" asked the psychiatrist. "Of course not," replied the husband. "The unicorn is a mythical beast." The psychiatrist apologized, informed the husband that the wife was "crazy as a jay bird," and off the police went with her. The husband, reported Thurber, lived happily ever after. The moral? Don't count your boobies until they are hatched![1]

Like most of Thurber's fables, this one teaches an important lesson, caught ironically in the statement, "The unicorn is a mythical beast." For that "nonexistent" beast, in an important sense, did exist. The beast had reality and consequences. The unicorn was real in the sense that someone believed, or believed that other people believed, in its existence. And the reality of the beast had consequences in that its existence resulted in a sudden change in a marital situation. The unicorn was decidedly not a mythical beast.

If people define situations as real, a noted social scientist said, they are real in their consequences.[2] The moral of Thurber's tale and the sociologist's dictum imply that if people believe something to be so, in an important way, it is. Now this runs against commonplace views about reality. We like to think that there is a clear distinction between the real and the imaginary, that our experience can be relied on, and that valid knowledge of the world "out there" is possible. But the world is more complicated than that, and our easy knowledge of it is not as sure as we might like to think.

At the risk of sounding philosophical, we may ask ourselves the age-old question: What, after all, do we really know? We are mortal, finite, limited beings who exist in a particular space and time, culture and personality. The amount of knowledge—in whatever form—available to us in any situation is limited, as are the capacity of our brains and the willingness of our personalities to accept certain things. Nevertheless, we have to cope with the onrush of experience, the necessity of choice, the desire to understand. And so we *define* situations as real and act upon that knowledge. We use our imaginations to extend our experience. We build our image of the world by making connections, constructions, and pictures of reality *as if* they were true. We impute an order and meaning to the world by importing into our images of the world a variety of symbolic structures to which we give reality, including unicorns.

For example, take an individual life. We live in a crucible of experience and a fund of consciousness. One develops an image of one-self that changes as time goes by. That image may be distorted by attributing qualities to ourselves that we do not possess. Through memory, we may distort past events in our lives, giving them characteristics of value they did not have (in, say, the transformation of childhood into a Golden Age one would now like to recapture). Similarly, we can project great expectations into a future through images of what we desire to be (as into career fulfillment). Our imaginations add to our immediate sensible experience, extending our vistas and the quality of our lives beyond what is immediate, palpable, and real.

So it is with our image of politics. "The world we have to deal with politically is out of reach, out of sight, out of mind," said Walter Lippman, one of this nation's foremost political analysts.[3] Yet there are clearly things we believe about the political world, even though we have not directly experienced them. We believe there was a presidential election in 1976, that there is an administration in Washington, and that there is a possibility of nuclear war with the Russians. These are facts of the contemporary political reality. There are probably ways to check some facts for their accuracy. Most of the time we do not; we simply accept those facts as true. Thus, in the dynamics of political situations, we have to rely on a jumble of images, most of which are not sensible to our immediate situation, to build a mosaic of what is happening. Such images are a shifting combination of facts, prejudices, values, pictures, memories, and projections. Taken together, they constitute what we shall argue in this book are the mythical beasts of politics.

We, the authors of this book, may be accused by readers of being—like the husband in Thurber's tale—a couple of boobies. We see a lot of mythical beasts in the rose garden of American politics. We see them in America's political past and in the present, and we most assuredly think that they will be with us in the future. And we see a lot of people feeding flowers to those mythical beasts: politicians and their publicity agents, the purveyors of popular culture, journalists and pollsters, and even our colleagues—the social, political, and behavioral scientists. Are we crazy as jay birds? Perhaps. That is for our readers to decide.

A LINGERING FASCINATION WITH UNICORNS
Or What Politicians and Scholars Have Said About Myth

"Mythology distracts us everywhere—in government as in business, in politics as in economics, in foreign affairs as in domestic policy. . . . The great enemy of the truth is very often not the lie—deliberate, contrived, and dishonest—but the myth, persistent, persuasive, and unrealistic. Too often we hold fast to the clichés of our forbears. We subject all facts to a prefabricated set of interpretations. We enjoy the comfort of opinion without the discomfort of thought."[4]

The time was June 11, 1962. The place was Yale University. The address was entitled "Myths Respecting American Government." The speaker was the president of the United States, John F. Kennedy. Many are the politicians who exploit myths for a variety of reasons, both self-serving and altruistic. But few have been those to speak directly about the nature of myth and the role of myths in American political life. In doing so in his Yale address, Kennedy (who became the legendary figure in a Camelot myth of his own and others' making) called attention to three questions about myths, political myths included, that warrant consideration:

What are myths, especially political myths, and why do people of intelligence, education, and alleged breeding so often dismiss the assertions of some other persons as mere myths, obviously the concoctions of boobies and jay birds?

What are the characteristics of myths? Are they, as Kennedy suggested, "unrealistic," or might those unicorns not be instead the very core of our realities, our political realities?

Why do we have myths, especially among a people as enlightened by science and technology as are Americans? Perhaps W.C. Fields was right when he supposedly said, "Ahh, yes! A man has to believe in something, and I believe I'll have another drink." Are our myths about politics but a bit of libation?

What are myths? Answers to the first of our three questions have been posed by classicists, philosophers, anthropologists, linguistic scholars, social scientists, even folklorists. The resulting assertions provide a plethora of definitions, theories, and schools of thought. Consider the following clues to the character of a myth.

The Common Sense School

Drop what you're doing, go where a lot of people gather, say, a fast food restaurant. As you stand in line to order your Big Mac, Colonel Sanders, or one of the seeming infinity of ice cream flavors, strike up a conversation with the person behind you. Politely suggest that the food at this establishment does not differ in quality from that of any other fast food chain. Say, for instance, "It's a myth that a Big Mac is better than a Whopper; they're just alike." With such a statement, you have captured the essentials of a common sense approach to myth —that is, a myth has no foundation in fact; it is simply another word for illusion.

The common sense school of myths has many members, some of them lifelong students of myths. For example, two historians, Patrick Gerster and Nicholas Cords, have written a fascinating text that challenges a very high proportion of the beliefs taught in American schools and colleges as being mythical.[5] We will discuss a few of their ideas more in Chapter 2. Here, however, it suffices to note that they define a myth as a false belief that is traditionally accepted as true and taken to be real.

A renowned European philosopher, Ernst Cassirer, probably did more than any other modern theorist to explore the place of myths in contemporary politics.[6] His view of myths also emphasized the illusory, distorted quality of such beliefs. Cassirer drew a distinction between what he called the mythical consciousness of primitive peoples and the scientific consciousness of modern persons. Members of primitive cultures, he wrote, conceive things in immediate, concrete ways and endow objects and events with unique personalities. Death, for example, is a personalized force that "comes," "stalks," and "goes." Rivers are not just bodies of water; they have minds of their own, as when they *refuse* to rise. Old Ben intoning, "May the Force be with you" in the popular film *Star Wars* exemplified what Cassirer was writing about, a mythical outlook on the world that could explain cause and effect as flowing from a vital force. But, in contrast with primitives, argued Cassirer, the scientific consciousness of modern persons draws a distinction between illusion and fact. Impressions of things and the feelings those things evoke are critically checked against experience and evidence. Emotional attachments to totems, magic, astrology, and ritual are replaced by hard-headed appeals to reason, facts, experiment, and proof.

For Cassirer, then, mythical thinking is a reversion to childlike make-believe, to primitive mysticism. The mythical world-view of prescientific peoples simply could not, or at least should not, exist alongside the empirical, scientific outlook of modern societies. What vexed Cassirer was that myth and science *do* reside side by side in the modern world.[7]

Cassirer's views are a sophisticated version of a common sense approach to myth: At best, myths are simplistic and distorted beliefs based upon emotion rather than rigorous analysis; at worst, myths are dangerous falsifications. Before accepting, rejecting, or modifying the common usage of the term, let us consider other schools of thought.

The Timeless Truth School

Before President Jimmy Carter's brother Billy sought rehabilitation for alcoholism, he was not the only American who liked to drink beer. Seemingly the only thing approaching the gulping multitudes of beer drinkers are the numerous brands of beer. Is one brand superior to all others? There are two myths: first, the myth carefully nurtured by advertisers that "_____ is Good, Better, Best." Just ask the connoisseur. Second, there is the myth implied in "They all taste the same to me"—the myth of no, rather than *vive,* difference. Which myth is true, which false? The common sense school tells us that both are false, and perhaps they are. The timeless truth school would have us think that both may be true, and perhaps they are.

The timeless truth school emphasizes not the substantive facts contained in a myth—not whether or not George Washington did or did not confess to chopping down the famous cherry tree—but whether people believe the myth, regardless of its accuracy. Myths are thus taken to be true in the sense that they are believed. So, to the beer drinker of discriminating palate, Coors, Michelob, Olympia, Löwenbrau, or whatever reigns supreme; to others, "Beer's beer."

Like the common sense school, the timeless truth view has a sophisticated version. Identified with the scholarly writing of Mircea Eliade, it argues that a myth is an account believed to be true, an account that describes an event occurring in the "beginnings of time" that explains the origin of things and, through their origins, how things are now.[8] Hence, myths are timeless truths. Consider, for instance, the myth of Eden. The account states as fact a series of events not demonstrably true or false, but taken on trust by many people. Denied admission to Eden because of the sins of their forebears, the descendants of Adam and Eve wander through the world seeking to recover the perfection of primordial beginnings, to restore the energy, grace, and bliss of things as they were when the world was new.

Possession and denial, loss and recovery, depletion and restoration, death and rebirth—such are the themes common to myths viewed as timeless truths. The timeless truths about beers do not differ. This is particularly evident in the mythmaking televised commercials that identify brands of beers with the purity of primal times and ways (e.g., the land of sky blue waters; clear, babbling brooks and mountain streams; the finest barleys and hops; the brewing art of the ancient masters; etc.). A search for recoverable origins—therein lies the character of myth as timeless truth.

The "What You See Is Not What You Get" School

A third set of views about myths shares something with both the common sense theories and the timeless truths school. With the former, it holds that the surface content of myths is false. With the latter, it agrees that, if we delve beneath the surface, there are realities represented in mythical tales.

What are these "hidden meanings" of myths? The oldest answer goes back to classical antiquity, at least to the Stoics. Myths, they said, should not be read as they stand, but as allegories masking a moral or philosophical lesson. What the precise hidden meaning was of such parables, metaphors, and stories the Stoics and succeeding generations of allegorists could never agree upon. Their interpretations of hidden meanings were arbitrary and presumptuous, for the meaning given a myth by the interpreter was taken for granted as more real or true than any intended by the original mythmaker.

Classical antiquity offered another answer, however—that is, that myths are accounts of past personages or events rather than morality plays. By translating myths, therefore, one could arrive at what really happened in earlier times. The problem with this, the Euhemerist view, differs little from the view of the allegorist. If myths are garbled history, whose deciphering provides the most plausible historical account? And why is one account more authentic than another?

The German idealists of the nineteenth century took another crack at opening the core meaning of myths. For them, people act as they think; change people's ideas, and you change how they lead their lives. Ideas do not change willy-nilly, but in conformity with the logic of an overarching Mind or Spirit guiding historical destiny. Given these assumptions, it is but a small step to argue that myths embody the inner truth of the Spirit, or climate, of the times that binds a people through shared attitudes, opinions, preconceptions, aspirations, hopes, anxieties, and fears.

Perhaps the Spirit of History does move among us, but modern interpreters of myth have had no easier time of identifying its character than did the allegorists or the Euhemerists. Small wonder, then, that they have turned elsewhere in search of the hidden meaning of myths. Although that search has yielded provocative insights into the character of mythical thought generally, if there is a hidden meaning below the surface of particular myths, it remains as lost as the fabled continent of Atlantis. Without belaboring the description of each, here are a few of the theories generated by the searchers after true meanings:

Myth is an ancient form of speech. Like the allegorists and the Euhemerists, these searchers seek the essentials of myths in poetical allusions and metaphors. Unlike their predecessors, however, these mythbreakers argue that *all* myths share a common theme. That theme, according to Henry Tudor's concise analysis, is "the rising and setting of the sun and the daily conflict between light and darkness." Poking fun, Tudor remarks, "It was clear that, with sufficient ingenuity, anything from the song of sixpence to the career of Napoleon could be proved a solar myth—the migration of the sun from east to west, of darkness from west to east."[9]

Myths are primitive explanations of things that spark the curiosities of both savages and civilized persons. This appears identical to Cassirer's view, but there is a difference. Cassirer argued that myth is a childlike world outlook held by primitives. But myths considered as explanations are not Cassirer's *Weltanschauung* covering all reality; they are specific stories invented to account for specific events. Myth is not an isolated province of thought that sharply differs from a scientific worldview; rather, myth is the science of the primitive and what Frazer, in his classic study of magic and religion in human culture, *The Golden Bough,* called "the bastard-sister of science."[10]

Myth is ritual. This view, too, is a variation of the ratio that myth is to science as primitive is to modern. Here is the reasoning: Primitives developed rituals (rites, prayers, dances, incantations, etc.) to help them secure from the gods and nature the necessities of health, food, water, children, and so on. As means of emotional outlet, rituals have two sides: physical act (e.g., dancing) and verbal utterance. It is in the verbal utterance that myths are born—as parables, tales, narratives, and stories.

The Symbolic School

The reader can be forgiven for thinking that theories about myth overlap. A brief account of three theories purporting to describe what myths symbolize beyond the content of the myths themselves makes the overlap even more apparent.

Dreams are the stuff that myths are made of. In this day and age, we have come to expect a Freudian theory of everything, and myths are no exception. The theory derives from Freud's view that dreams are made up of symbols representing unfulfilled wishes. Through dreams, the wishes are symbolically fulfilled. Since many symbols that occur in dreams also occur in myths, myths, like dreams, are products of fantasy, of the unconscious. But individuals have dreams, whereas whole societies have myths. How can something personal and private be so collectivized? The Swiss psychologist Carl Jung suggested an answer: Below the surface of each individual's *per-*

sonal unconscious is a deeper *collective* unconscious, what Jung called "archetypes" or "universal images" that are suprapersonal and are shaped by everybody in society.[11] The hidden meaning of myths (sometimes called "mythemes," for universal mythical themes) is that they symbolize these archetypes.

Myth as social glue. The quest for the real meaning of myths has also goaded sociologists and anthropologists. Three characterizations emerge. First, *myths are collective representations*—that is, catchall accounts encompassing a society's doctrines, ideologies, ideas, and interests. Even if embodied in a single leader, as was the racial myth of Aryan superiority by Hitler for the Nazis, the myth and its embodiment form a collective representation that is essentially impersonal—a part of a group member's being, much like one's language. Second, the idea of *myths as functional requisites* derives from the extensive work of cultural anthropologist Bronislaw Malinowski and his followers.[12] The theory assumes that people and societies have basic needs that must be fulfilled if they are to survive. Functions are defined as activities undertaken to satisfy such needs. Key social needs are to assure and enhance group solidarity and to legitimize the authority of some members of society to act and others to follow. Myths symbolize codes of approved beliefs, values, and behavior and thus function to legitimize authority. Finally, there is the theory that *myths symbolize underlying structures.* The science of structural linguistics, from which this theory derives, posits that language is governed by laws—or structures—imposed on the unconscious mind, laws or structures that cannot be violated by speakers of that language. Extending that assumption beyond language leads to the proposition that all institutions and activities are governed by unconscious, underlying structures. To understand the activities, therefore, their hidden structures must be uncovered. Such is also the case with myths; that is, below the manifest content of myths (which often seems silly, foolish, false, and contradictory) are coherent, lawful structures guiding human conduct.

Myths as political ploys. To this juncture, we have already reviewed the theories of two writers that suggest what myths symbolize in politics: Cassirer's view that political myths operate as emotional, primitive world-views that endanger rational decision making and Malinowski's thesis that myths symbolize and legitimize political authority. Tangential to the first is the political science proposition that myths are symbols used by political elites to arouse and command the popular support of the masses, thus rationalizing and advancing elitist interests in the name of the public good. Think, for example, of how many American politicians invoked the myths surrounding 1776 during the 1976 election-year bicentennial celebration of independence; were the orations always altruistic? The Malinowski thesis also has support from political scientists. Long before he achieved notoriety as President Jimmy Carter's chief foreign policy advisor, for instance, Zbigniew Brzezinski co-authored a major study of totalitarian dictatorship which argued that a myth is a story about a nation's past events used to reinforce the authority of the existing regime.[13] Similarly the noted French political sociologist, Jacques Ellul, speaks of myths as public illusions that mask the real distribution of power and benfits in society.[14] Students of politics, then, also assume that there is something more to myth than a simple fairy tale.

YOU CAN'T GO HOME AGAIN
Therein Lies the Nature of Myth

With these ideas borrowed from scholarly schools of thought before us, we can now fashion answers to the three questions posed earlier: What are myths, what is their character, and why do we have them?

Looking Backward

George Herbert Mead (1863–1931) was one of America's most noted philosophers. Succeeding generations of scholars have lauded and evaluated Mead's contributions to the development of pragmatic ways of thinking; his theories regarding the development of the human mind, the self, and society; and his seminal ideas with respect to symbols in human communication. We turn to a different facet of Mead's thought, one that will help us to explore the foundations of myth. Specifically, we look at Mead's "philosophy of the present."

Can we ever really know the past? This is the problem Mead posed. He answered that we cannot. Why? Because "a past never was in the form it appears as a past; its reality is in its interpretation of the present."[15] People, argued Mead, are prisoners of time in the sense that their reality is always only a *present* reality—what they perceive in the here and now. "Reality exists in a present," he said, and "the present of course implies a past and a future," but "to these both we deny existence."[16] This is not to say that people don't *imagine* or think that they recall a past and *imagine* or project a future. They most certainly do. But they do so not *in* that past or *in* that future but only in the present.

Thus argued, any vision of the past is every bit as hypothetical as any image of the future. Neither is exhibited to us from other than the perspective of the present, *wherein we live.* But, one might retort, granted that we can't really know the future until it happens, surely we can know the past, for it has already happened. We have records, documents, accounts, names, and dates—the stuff of history! Yes, said Mead, we may have all that information about things that have happened earlier. But when do we make sense of it, interpret it, give meaning to it? Not in some unrecoverable past, but in the present. Our past, therefore, our "what was," is not what really happened but a present interpretation, a reconstruction of what might have been. At best, it is but one possibility of what might have gone before. For Mead, then, there simply is no real past back "there" that is irrevocable. Since interpretations and meanings in the present are subject to change, no scroll unrolls an unalterable past.

What Mead is also saying is that knowing is a constructive—indeed, reconstructive—activity: that through our present interpretations, we construct the meanings of the past and the future. These constructions represent what we know, or, more accurately, in any given present, they re-present what we know. Mead goes on to argue that such constructions derive from people interacting with another. In short, our constructions of the realities of the past and the future are social constructions undertaken in the present. These re-presentations are neither static nor fixed but are continuously emerging from ongoing social processes. What we know is not a collection of knowns, but an activity of knowing.

If Mead is correct, then as humans living in the present, we re-present the past and pre-present the future. When those re-presentations take dramatic form, we have myths. All events, wrote the distinguished literary critic Kenneth Burke, occur as dramas and can be depicted in dramatic form.[17] At least this is so of all human events, because what distinguishes humans is that they are symbol-creating, -using, and -misusing animals. Symbols are the essentials of drama. Burke devised a pentad of the five key elements symbolized in any drama: the act, the agent(s) commiting the act, the agency(ies) used to commit the act, the scene—time, place, and setting—wherein the act occurs, and the purposes or motives behind the act. For Burke, there was a logic to the interplay of these five dramatic elements. Precisely that dramatic logic, or form, constitutes the vital character of myth, both for Burke and for us.

Here, then, with due recognition of the contributions by Mead and Burke, is our definition (myth?) of myth:

> *A credible, dramatic, socially constructed re-presentation of perceived realities that people accept as permanent, fixed knowledge of reality while forgetting (if they were ever aware of it) its tentative, imaginative, created, and perhaps fictional qualities.*

This is obviously the broadest kind of definition, but it does have certain advantages for our purposes. Myth is not confined to a fantastic tale of the immortals long ago; it can include current myths held about the world right now. Myth is not reduced to being merely a story; it is not simply a fairy tale or an allegorical narrative. Nor is it a child's or primitive's world-view. And it avoids the pitfall of reducing myth solely to false belief. The definition offered here was the advantage of including myths at a variety of levels and in different contexts. It stresses that myth is something thought to be real and believable; that it adds dramatic color and force to an otherwise inchoate reality; that it re-presents what we take to be real, and thus serves important psychological and social functions for us; and that it gives us a world out there that we can cope with and understand.

Myth and Science Among the Moderns

Ponder other key implications of this definition. First, we assert that myths are *credible*. Every myth is not a truth: Some may even be deliberate falsifications of what they purport to represent, others simply tales that distort more than illuminate. The myth of the pre-Civil War black as "the happy darky"—lazy, shiftless, easygoing, and childlike—was a stereotype deliberately used for a century after the conflict in order to justify second-class citizenship for an entire people. The legendary antebellum South of plantations, magnolias, cavaliers, and auburn-haired maidens, so well depicted in the opening scenes of the ever popular film *Gone With the Wind,* may have been a less deliberate, but no less distorted, nostalgic representation. Emphasizing the credible character of myths, however, guards against the too easy tendency to assume that *all* myths are false; moreover, it assists us in our basic task in this book—that is, to identify the salient myths and their makers in American politics rather than to describe what really happened or happens, which is made unlikely from the perspective of any given present. Saying that myths are credible, then, stresses our interest in identifying what people believe to be true, whether that belief be true, false, a little of both, or simply not demonstrable as either. Walter Lippmann summarized these points thus: "For the distinguishing mark of myth is that truth and error, fact and fable, report and fantasy are all on the same plane of credibility. . . . What a myth never contains is the critical power to separate its truth from its error."[18]

Second, myths are *socially constructed, created realities.* There are two intertwined notions here. One is that what is real consists of the pictures of the world that people invent and accept; there are as many realities about something as are created. But, and this is the second notion, myths are shared realities, pictures constructed through social intercourse. Granted that myths are often created by specific individuals, in specific times and places. The mythmaker offers a picture of a past or present state of affairs and projects it to other times—past, present, future. Alex Haley, for instance, in his best-selling *Roots,* created a virtual myth of paradise by depicting the life and times of the black in his native Africa, a paradise that was lost when the slave trade inhumanly ripped people away from their heritage. But the tale of that narrative was shared by millions who read the book and/or watched the enthralling 1977 television mini-series based upon it. Therein occurred the collective construction of a credible reality, the making of a myth.

Third, a myth is a *dramatic whole,* an account containing, implicitly or explicitly, the five elements of Burke's dramatic pentad and generally told complete with a beginning, a middle, and an end. [19] As a result, a myth conveys the impression of a complete entity in which everything fits comfortably with everything else. By associating things with one another, parts of the story that alone might appear imprecise and incredulous assume the apearance of authenticity. Apocryphal tales, such as that Betsy Ross sewed the first American flag at the request of George Washington, that the Liberty Bell cracked at the stress of proclaiming American independence (no record exists that the bell chimed at all during the period, but there *is* evidence that it cracked in 1835 while tolling for Chief Justice John Marshall's funeral), and that independence came on July 4, 1776 (the *Declaration* was adopted on July 2 and announced on July 8, but the date of the signing is questionable), are much more plausible when blended into a single myth of the Revolution than when related in isolation.

Fourth, myths are *taken-for-granted realities.* That is, once people believe in a myth, their skeptical sense vanishes, they accept it as fact, and—most importantly—the invented reality becomes reality itself, the only reality. Put differently, in creating myths, we invent realities, forget that they are inventions, and then experience our creations as something out there that is—for the life of the myth—the one, fixed, permanent reality of things.[20] This contributes to a fifth implication, that myths are *pragmatic:* "A myth is told," notes Tudor, "not for the sake of amusement, but in order to promote some practical purpose."[21] If myths were popularly accepted simply as folk tales, they would be little more than entertainment. But when accepted *as reality,* they can be employed by all manner of persons—demagogues, pitchmen, con artists, hucksters, soothsayers—to serve selfish ends and by all manner of other people purporting more reputable, altruistic ends.

Flowing from our definition and its attendant implications is one other point: that *mythical and scientific thinking are related but distinct activities.* They are related in that, for one thing, they are both modes of knowing—that is, ways of representing, describing, explaining, and interpreting observed phenomena. They are, as Frazer asserted in *The Golden Bough,* natural, human efforts to understand the world. Moreover, even though it produced vexation for Cassirer to face it, mythical and scientific thought rest side by side in modern civilizations.

But the two modes of knowing differ in critical respects. As we have reiterated, and as Tudor summarizes so well, "A myth, I suggest, is an interpretation of what the mythmaker (rightly or wrongly) takes to be hard fact. It is a device men adopt in order to come to grips with reality; and we can tell that a given account is myth, not by the amount of truth it contains, but by the fact that it is *believed* to be true and, above all, by the dramatic form into which it is cast."[22] In myth, the mode of *knowing* is supplanted by the belief that something is forever *known*. By contrast, in scientific thought, knowledge is not fixed but tentative; the search for understanding is not closed but forever open; constructions are not taken as real but are subject to experimentation and novel, truth-defying reconstructions. Moreover, the realities created by scientific thought about some phenomena are plural, each being recognized as but one of *possible* multiple interpretations of the event. In myth, there is but one interpretation, one reality of what happened. Finally, although the scientific enterprise can certainly be described in dramatic terms, scientific accounts are seldom cast in dramatic form with a beginning, a middle, and an end and with acts, scenes, agents, agencies, and purposes.

As activities, then, mythical and scientific thought are related, but different. Bear in mind, however, that there is a mythical dimension to scientific thought. That possibility has been suggested by many philosophers of science, most notably in America by Thomas Kuhn in his provocative *The Structure of Scientific Revolutions.*[23] Kuhn notes the tendency for science to become "normal," to engage in the perfunctory verification of dominant theoretical outlooks in any historical period. During such a period, there is a reigning "paradigm," a general agreement among scientists on theories, problem areas, methods, and techniques of inquiry and analysis. The paradigm is the common, shared set of beliefs of the scientific community. Are paradigms myths? If scientists close the door to alternative, novel, competing possibilities, the two may indeed be synonymous, at least to the degree that each becomes the *"reality" they think they know.* We think that may happen with some frequency in the social sciences directed at understanding American politics, a point we explore fully in Chapter 7. For now, however, we merely raise the possibility to caution against making the myth–science distinction too facile. Indeed, one of America's foremost social scientists, Talcott Parsons, has written that the "'facts' of science are myths. . . . We exclude—and what we exclude haunts us as the walls we set up. We include—and what we include limps, wounded by amputations. And, most importantly, we must live with all this, we must live with our wounded and our ghosts. There can be no Bultmann of science, pleading that we 'de-mythologize': *analytical thought itself is mythologization.*"[24]

If Everybody Has to Believe in Something, Why Myths in a Scientific Age?

Myths are accepted uncritically by people because they perform several important, interrelated services. Four general uses of myth are especially noteworthy.

Myths aid comprehension. Whether in primitive societies, such as those depicted by anthropologists, or in highly civilized ones, neither mythical nor scientific thought pervades the whole of a people's consciousness. We undertake our everyday tasks, taking for granted that one day will not differ much from another. Habits, routines, pastimes—these offer continuity to our daily lives. But suppose that something happens, say, we become seriously ill, or we are victims of some natural disaster. The occurrence may tax our powers to deal with it. We are shocked out of our everyday consciousness to a new awareness, frequently to an awareness of discrepancies between what we think we ought to do, what we can do, and what we actually do. We suffer unwelcome contradictions; an incoherence stalks our lives. Here enters myth. Myths provide easily grasped, emotionally satisfying ways of reducing the disorder of things. Chaos and absurdity yield as every untoward act and event becomes comprehensible.[25]

In his award-winning *Who's Afraid of Virginia Woolf,* playwright Edward Albee relates the tale of George and Martha, a married couple whose public and private lives are in sharp contradiction. In public, George is a sedate professor of history at the local college; Martha is a professor's wife and the daughter of the college president. But public appearances are contradicted by what goes on behind the closed doors of the marriage between George and Martha —a quarrelsome, bickering union of all-night shouting, drinking, tantrums, and threats. How is such a marriage held together? George and

Martha manage it by creating a myth, the myth of a nonexistent son: the "little bugger" who, depending upon the teller, is "away," "out" at the moment, grown up and "off to college," but who is never physically present. The play's crisis occurs when George, partly as a means of punishing Martha, reveals that the boy was "killed" in an auto accident. But even then it is not clear that the myth is dispelled, for as grieving "parents" they can still resolve contradictions in their lives by bemoaning the loss of the imaginary child.[26]

In a related fashion, we have myths to reduce political contradictions. How, for example, can we comprehend that the affluent, industrialized American society contains widespread poverty, unemployment, and crime? Political scientist Murray Edelman says that we do it through myths, actually through two opposing myths: (1) One myth asserts that those who suffer from such problems are victims of their own defects and responsible for their own plight; hence, there is no societal solution, for the problems are personal, not social, problems. (2) The other myth says that the sufferers are victimized by the affluent elites who profit from depriving others and, who, in order to resolve the contradiction, simply reform a basically exploitative social structure.[27]

But why create myths at all? Why not just live with our contradictions? Perhaps the answer lies in what philosopher William James called the "will to believe," the inability of people to be comfortable with "blooming, buzzing confusion" and a marked reluctance to live the life of the skeptic. If one reflects on the limits and the tenuous nature of what we know about the world, the effect can be like peering over the edge into an ultimate abyss. But it does not have to be so scary, only a little humbling. It leads to a Socratic admission of how little we actually know and of how much we have to rely on myth in order to cope. And it demonstrates how it is impossible for us to hold up every statement, thought, and image to scientific scrutiny. There is simply too much world and not enough time. It is more comfortable, easier, and useful to live with our myths. Also, myth helps us to retain our sanity by giving our world structure and value and by helping us to avoid the skepticism that would make us look into that terrifying abyss of nothingness, of *nada y pues nada y nada y pues nada.*[28]

Myths forge common bonds. Through the communication of collective myths, we create and reinforce a sense of community, of being in the same boat together. American, English, Scottish, French, Polish, German, Russian, or whatever: Each nationality is defined not merely by a common territory, language, and ancestry but by what anthropologist Joseph Campbell has called the "public dreams" unique to and shared by the people of a culture—dramatic visions of the past, present, and future that serve the dual purpose of uniting a people while setting them apart from others.[29] Think of what the myth of the Promised Land has meant to Israel.

Jacques Ellul argues that entire civilizations—a collection of separate national cultures—can be and are bound together through transcendent myths. Modern western civilization, he says, is sustained by the myths of work, progress, and happiness. The myth of work is that it is redeeming and necessary, a myth appearing in forms varying from the view that "idleness is the source of all vices" to the Marxist lauding of the virtues of the proletariat. Through work, inevitable progress emerges and people ensure continued improvement in their wealth and well-being. The payoff is happiness, a state where sacrifice and suffering are no longer necessary. For Ellul, bourgeois and communist alike are goaded by this trinity of myths that provides a common set of aspirations underpinning the capitalist–communist cleavage throughout the world.[30]

Myths offer identities. Myths are social and collective in character, but from the viewpoint of each of us who holds them, they are what Joseph Campbell designates as self-induced beliefs. As we adopt myths, we not only make the world more comprehensible and share our created realities with others, but each of us creates a unique identity. Or, to think of it another way, we identify the role each of us plays in the drama that is the continuing myth. A Yankee fan identifies with the legend and lore of America's favorite pastime and the very special role—as far as the fan is concerned—of a particular club and its followers. Labeling and thinking of oneself as "voter," by the same token, yields a role in the mythology that surrounds elections—that is, that elections make a crucial difference in what governments do, that through participation we make our voices heard, that officials are made responsible and responsive to our will, and so on. In short, through myths, we take on deeply meaningful identities that satisfy a lingering desire to "be somebody."

Writing in *The Hero with a Thousand Faces,* Joseph Campbell notes that the individual in his life's passage "is necessarily only a fraction and distortion of the total image" of a person. One is, says Campbell, "limited either as a male or as a female" at any given period of one's life as "child, youth, mature adult, or ancient"; and each of us is "specialized as craftsman, tradesman, servant, or thief, priest, leader, wife, nun, or harlot." A person cannot be all, notes Campbell. And again we share in the "body of the society as a whole," and therein the "totality" and the "fullness" of being a person is obtainable. Myths help to provide a sense of self, wholeness, and importance that cold, scientific, technological thought simply cannot supply.[31]

Myths help us get our way. Living as we do in a world where most of us want things but have limited resources to fulfill all of our desires, we often pursue our goals by trying to convince other people of their desirability, thus enlisting allies, assistance, and support. Persuading others to our cause involves what Kenneth Burke calls identification, an activity that involves myth and mythmaking. For Burke, identification means being "substantially one"—that is, when persons identify with one another they develop common sensations, concepts, images, ideas, and attitudes.[32] Myths offer effective tools for establishing such identification. A speaker invoking a myth activates within his listeners feelings of kinship, emotional yearnings, dreamlike aspirations, and unexpressed longings. The stronger the identification, the greater the persuasive appeal, which may almost reach a state of hypnotic communion between a leader and his faithful followers. Such was the alleged persuasive appeal of Adolf Hitler, who never ceased to marshal a host of myths in his oratorical flights.

As a basis for persuasion, myth makes an emotive rather than a scientific use of language. I.A. Richards draws the distinction: In the scientific usage of language, a statement is used to refer to something demonstrably true or false; emotive usage is on behalf of the effects of words on emotions, feelings, anxieties, fears, aspirations, and hopes. Scientific usage results in specific references; emotive usage produces vague, but often deep-seated, attitudes.[33]

In sum, because myths help people to comprehend the incomprehensible, commune with their fellows, and achieve self-esteem, they are especially useful as rhetorical devices that achieve what scientific thought cannot—an appeal to the "psycho" as well as "logical" roots of human existence. This appeal is particularly apparent when we observe the part myths play in political dramas.[34]

YES, VIRGINIA, THERE ARE UNICORNS IN THE POLITICAL GARDEN

The task set at the beginning of this chapter of defining myth, discussing its characteristics, and speculating upon why people cling to myths is now completed. But we have said relatively little yet about political myths—their character, types, and origins. The remainder of this book is about that topic, but a few preliminary remarks are in order before looking in detail at political myths and their makers.

What Scholars Have Said About Political Myths

Political scientists have recognized that myth is important to the operation of political orders, and there have been sporadic attempts to develop the concept of myth for use in political inquiry. For instance, Robert MacIver begins his classic, *The Web of Government,* with the centrality of myth, or "the value-impregnated beliefs and notions that men hold, that they live by or live for. . . ." MacIver made as broad a claim for the importance of myth as we:

> Every society is held together by a myth system, a complex of dominating thought-forms that determines and sustains all its activities. . . . Every civilization, every period, every nation, has its characteristic myth-complex. . . . The myth mediates between man and nature. From the shelter of his myth he perceives and experiences his world. Inside his myth he is at home in his world.[35]

A more sustained treatment appears in Henry Tudor's *Political Myth.* After a survey of some of the more familiar historical myths —the Roman Foundation myth, national revolutionary myths (the myth of the Norman Yoke in England), the myth of the Aryan race, the myth of the Proletarian Revolution—he concludes by restricting myth to a tale that "tells the story of a political society"; a myth is "always a story, a narrative of events in dramatic form."[36] Unfortunately this limits the concept of myth to only one type, what we will call "master myths." Myth, we contend, is dramatic in form, but it is not always a narrative of events nor a story. Contemporary myths about the presidency (e.g., whether the office and its holder are strong or weak) or about political heroism do not necessarily involve a large-scale "story of a political society" but are, rather, a dramatic image specific to a political present and only tangentially related to the large-scale myths of the historical-political order.

Other recent works by social scientists have touched on the nature of political myth. Harold Lasswell and Abraham Kaplan define it as "the pattern of the basic political symbols current in a society . . . the political perspectives most firmly accepted. . . ."[37] George Woodcock describes political myth as "a projection into the past or, more often, the future of a mirage based on the desires of a section of the people, which is used to induce them to follow some political group or embrace some program under the illusion that they will attain what they have seen in the mirage.[38] Political myth, says Murray Edelman, is "an unquestioned belief held in common by a large group of people that gives events and actions a particular meaning."[39] Other definitions have stressed many of the same elements: Myth is a symbolic image of politics; major myths survive and function by being held by many people; they are often projections into the past or future, but in any case, they give meaning to the present; their reality is in the eye of the beholder.

Introducing the Unicorn to Politics

What scholars have said about political myth fits our view of myths as credible, dramatic representations of phenomena. What makes myths political is the subject matter. If religious myths deal with gods and their worship or cultural myths with the origins and hopes of a people, then political myths are about politics—the use of government by people to achieve order through the accommodation of social disputes. As with any myth, political myths are believed true because they help people to make sense of an unknowable and remote past, an imposing and often contradictory present, and a yet-to-arrive future. Political myths derive and are told from the standpoint of the present; hence, as the circumstances in which people find themselves change, people reconstruct their myths about politics. Finally, as already noted, political myths have their uses, the principal one being that political leaders use myths to rally popular support.

Students of politics find it useful to distinguish myth from two related notions, ideology and utopia. Without splitting hairs, it suffices to say that ideologies, in contrast with myths, are generally more specific in reference to historical events, are cast in the form of logic rather than drama, purport to explain historical change rather than *the* past or *the* future, and, according to Mark Roelofs, are sets of ideas by which people actually organize for political action: "Ideology gives patterns for political action, . . . is the thought pattern of persons whose work must be done day by day," whereas "myth gives meaning to national existence and endeavor, . . . is the ancient memory and the generational hope of the whole people, its 'civil religion.'"[40] Utopias, in further contrast, are visions of a more perfect world to come. If myths deal solely with the future, they are not strictly myths, but utopias.[41] As we shall see, however, myths often incorporate utopian visions in a dramatic account of past, present, and future.

Differing Types of Mythical Beasts in Politics

It will help in the discussion that follows to recognize that there are differing types of political myths. We consider four broad categories:

> *Master myths* are broad, overarching myths that constitute the collective consciousness of an entire society. As in the case of Ellul's myths of work, progress, and happiness, some master myths transcend nations, economies, governments, and societies. In this book, however, we are concerned only with the master myths that feed the collective consciousness that is America as a state of mind. Three sets of such master myths are relevant: the *foundation* myth that tells the story of our nation's origins, its struggle for independence, and the framing of the Constitution; *sustaining myths,* which are myths enhancing the

maintenance of political relationships (such as those between church and state); and *eschatological myths* that project the nation's destiny on the basis of our past and present.

Myths of "Us and Them" are myths that set specific social collectivities apart from others in the nation. They may be about *institutions* (the myth of presidential power), *groups* (the "party of war" and "party of peace" myths about Democrats and Republicans or the myths of "haves" and "have nots"), or *movements* (such as the myths of populism or of progressivism).

Heroic myths surround the legendary figures of American politics, especially those included in the American pantheon housing Washington, Jefferson, and Lincoln, but they also pertain to villains (Richard Nixon) and fools (Billy Carter).

Pseudo-myths are myths in the making. They are short-term myths formulated about contemporary politics and marketed to serve a variety of political ends. The presidential election of 1968 gave us the myth of "The New Nixon"; that of 1976 the myth of "The Outsider"; and a year of the Carter presidency brought the myth implied in the question, "Can Carter cope?" All were myths in the making that may or may not enter national political folklore in later generations.[42]

LOOKING FORWARD
The Centrality of Myth in American Politics

In the remainder of this book, we consider a host of American political myths and the people who make them. In the rest of Part One, we shall do two things: Chapter 2 examines reigning myths about America's political past, and Chapter 3 considers selected contemporary myths in American politics. In Part Two, we focus on who the mythmakers of America are and how they do it. In Chapter 4, our concern is with politicians and the people who promote them into public figures. Chapter 5 deals with the media of popular entertainment and how popular culture contributes to political mythmaking. Chapter 6 looks at public affairs reporting—by journalists and pollsters—as a key area of mythmaking. Chapter 7 examines another set of actors, the social scientists who purport to explain rather than create political realities; much of what they do also turns out to be mythmaking. Our concluding chapter is an effort to look ahead to the possible mythology of America to come. We hold no illusions that Americans will take kindly to having many of their most sacred beliefs about politics labeled mythical. Nor will many identified as mythmakers willingly admit to that appellation. Yet we feel that the argument is worth making. Our purpose respecting political myth is not to reduce every political idea, action, or event to myth but to take due note of where myths most certainly are important in our nation's politics. We both describe and explain, debunk and celebrate, criticize and marvel. And along the way, we may even add to the body of American political mythology. For there are in politics instances, as Paul Watzlawick says about life generally, "where everything is true, and so is its contrary."[43]

REFERENCES

1. James Thurber, "The Unicorn in the Garden," from *Fables for Our Time* (New York: Harper & Row, 1940).

2. See William I. Thomas, *The Unadjusted Girl* (Boston: Little, Brown, 1928).

3. Walter Lippmann, *Public Opinion* (New York: Macmillan, 1960), p. 12.

4. The Kennedy quotation appears in William Safire, *The New Language of Politics* (New York: Collier Books, 1972), p. 410.

5. Patrick Gerster and Nicholas Cords, *Myth in American History* (Encino, Cal.: Glencoe Press, 1977), p. xiii.

6. Ernst Cassirer, *The Philosophy of Symbolic Forms, Vol. II, Mythical Thought* (New Haven: Yale University Press, 1966).

7. Ernst Cassirer, *The Myth of the State* (Garden City, N.Y.: Doubleday, 1955), pp. 1-2.

8. Mircea Eliade, *Myth and Reality* (London: Allen & Unwin, 1964).

9. A portion of the discussion in this section relies upon the excellent summary in Henry Tudor, *Political Myth* (New York: Praeger, 1972), pp. 17-60.

10. Sir James Frazer, *The Golden Bough,* Vol. 1 (New York: Macmillan, 1934), p. 220; see also Joseph Campbell, *Myths to Live by* (New York:

Bantam Books, 1973), especially Chapter 1, "The Impact of Science on Myth," pp. 1–18.

11. See Freud's "The Interpretation of Dreams" in A. A. Brill, ed., *The Basic Writings of Sigmund Freud* (New York: Random House [Modern Library], 1938), pp. 181–549, and Joseph Campbell, ed., *The Portable Jung* (New York: Viking Press, 1971).

12. Bronislaw Malinowski, *Magic, Science and Religion* (New York: Doubleday, 1954),

13. Carl J. Friedrich and Zbigniew K. Brzezinski, *Totalitarian Dictatorship and Autocracy* (New York: Praeger, 1965).

14. Jacques Ellul, *Political Illusion* (New York: Knopf, 1967).

15. George H. Mead, *The Philosophy of the Act* (Chicago: University of Chicago Press, 1938), p. 616.

16. George H. Mead, *The Philosophy of the Present* (Lasalle, Ill.: Open Court Publishing Co., 1959), p. 1.

17. A useful, readable introduction to the views of Kenneth Burke's complex theory is his essay, "Dramatism," in Lee Thayer, ed., *Communication: Concepts and Perspectives* (Washington, D.C.: Spartan Books, 1967), pp. 327–353.

18. Lippmann, *Public Opinion*, p. 123.

19. On the character of myths as dramatic wholes, see A. J. M. Sykes, "Myth in Communication," *Journal of Communication,* 20 (March 1970): 17–31, and Bill Kinser and Neil Kleinman, *The Dream That Was No More a Dream: A Search for Aesthetic Reality in Germany, 1890–1945* (New York: Harper & Row, 1969).

20. On how people invent realities and then assume them not invented, see Paul Watzlawick, *How Real Is Real? Confusion, Disinformation, Communication* (New York: Random House [Vintage Books], 1976).

21. Tudor, *Political Myth*, p. 16.

22. Tudor, *Political Myth*, p. 17.

23. Thomas S. Kuhn, *The Structure of Scientific Revolutions* (Chicago: University of Chicago Press, 1970).

24. Charles Ackerman and Talcott Parsons, "The Concept of 'Social System' as a Theoretical Device," in Gordon J. DiRenzo, ed., *Concepts, Theories and Explanation in the Behavioral Sciences* (New York: Random House, 1966), pp. 25–26.

25. The function of myth in resolving perceived contradictions is discussed at length in Claude Levi-Strauss, *Structural Anthropology* (New York: Basic Books, 1968).

26. For an intriguing discussion of the Albee play, see Paul Watzlawick et al., *Pragmatics of Human Communication* (New York: Norton, 1967), Chapter 5.

27. Murray Edelman, "Language, Myths and Rhetoric," *Society* (July/ August 1975): 14–21.

28. The phrase is from Ernest Hemingway's story, "A Clean, Well-Lighted Place," in *The Short Stories of Ernest Hemingway* (New York: Scribner, 1938), p. 383.

29. Joseph Campbell, "The Historical Development of Mythology," in Henry A. Murray, ed., *Myth and Mythmaking* (Boston: Beacon Press, 1960), pp. 19–45.

30. Jacques Ellul, "Modern Myths," *Diogenes,* 23 (Fall 1958): 23–40.

31. Joseph Campbell, *The Hero with a Thousand Faces* (New York: New American Library [Meridian Books], 1956), pp. 382–383; see also Jerome S. Bruner, "Myth and Identity," in Henry A. Murray, ed., *Myth and Mythmaking* (Boston: Beacon Press, 1960), pp. 276–287.

32. Kenneth Burke, *A Rhetoric of Motives* (New York: Prentice-Hall, 1953), p. 21.

33. I. A. Richards, *Principles of Literary Criticism* (London: Routledge & Kegan Paul, 1963).

34. On the nature of "psycho-logic," see George N. Gordon, *The Languages of Communications* (New York: Hastings House, 1969), pp. 11–12.

35. R. M. MacIver, *The Web of Government* (New York: Free Press, 1965), p. 4.

36. Tudor, *Political Myth,* p. 137.

37. Harold D. Lasswell and Abraham Kaplan, *Power and Society* (New Haven: Yale University Press, 1950), p. 116.

38. George Woodcock, "The Nature of Political Myth," in Richard Carlton Snyder and H. Hubert Wilson, eds., *Roots of Political Behavior* (New York: American Book Company, 1949), p. 527.

39. Murray Edelman, *Politics as Symbolic Action* (Chicago: Markham Publishing Co., 1971), p. 6.

40. H. Mark Roelofs, *Ideology and Myth in American Politics* (Boston: Little, Brown, 1976), p. 4; see also Ben Halpern, " 'Myth' and 'Ideology' in Modern Usage," *History and Theory,* 1 (1961): 129–149.

41. Willard A. Mullins, "On the Concept of Ideology in Political Science," *American Political Science Review,* 66 (June 1972): 498–510.

42. There are, of course, other ways to classify myths. See, for examples, Tudor, *Political Myth;* Carl Joachim Friedrich, *Man and His Government* (New York: McGraw-Hill, 1963), Chapter 5; and Kenneth Burke, *Attitudes Toward History* (Los Altos, Cal.: Hermes Publications, 1975), Chapter 2.

43. Watzlawick, *How Real Is Real?,* p. 67.

CHAPTER 2

George, Sit Down, You're Rocking The Boat

Myths Of America's Political Past

Few Americans have failed to see it, whether reproduced in a civics textbook or hanging in the local court house, post office, or some other public building: "Washington Crossing the Delaware," an 1851 painting by Emanuel Leutze, a German-American painter. Working in his studio in Dusseldorf, Leutze depicted a momentous event in the American Revolutionary War. On Christmas Day, 1776, 2,400 American troops set out to surprise a British force, made up chiefly of Hessian mercenaries, by crossing the Delaware to engage the enemy above Trenton, New Jersey. The weather was foul, and the river covered with floating ice. Many of the American troops failed, or simply refused, to cross. Undaunted George Washington took a small command, crossed the Delaware in the darkness of the following morning, surprised the Hessians, and achieved victory in what many a history text has labeled the "turning-point of the Revolution."[1]

Turning point or not, the daring exploit added luster to the growing heroic stature of George Washington. It was this legendary Washington that Leutze captured in his famous and popular painting. But like so much surrounding the figure and the event it seeks to portray, the painting does more to build a myth combining what might have occurred with what clearly did not than to picture what really happened. To be sure, Washington did cross the Delaware and did win an important victory, helping to prop up flagging American morale. But Leutze's conception of the event—which is the most popular available—borders on the ludicrous. We see Washington standing sternly, but precariously, in the prow of an overmanned rowboat, so that the slightest shift in the General's weight would capsize the small craft. Standing beside him is a brave warrior holding an American flag that at the time of the crossing had not even been designed, a flag not adopted by Congress until nearly six months later. Finally, the ice-covered river painted by Leutze was the German Rhine, not the Delaware.

Perhaps such fictions are harmless, even if they are fastened in the minds of many Americans as uncontestable fact. In any event, similar fictions abound in the mythology of America's political past, so much so that it is often impossible to sort the political myths that have credence from those having no substance whatsoever. In this chapter, we illustrate the nature of this difficulty by discussing two varieties of what we referred to in Chapter 1 as master myths, those broad, overarching myths that penetrate the collective consciousness of America's past. Specifically, we shall look at America's *foundation myth,* of which legends surrounding heroic figures such as George Washington are but a small part.

PATRIOTS, REALISTS, OR TECHNICIANS?
Three Versions of America's Foundation Myth

Chapter 1 argued that one of the reasons people believe in myths is that, from the standpoint of time, they literally can't go home again (Thomas Wolfe's phrase). Both past and future are knowable only in the reigning present. This is certainly the case of America's political past, for it, too, we know only in the present. Scholars probing the origins and character of America's founding as an independent nation have looked back on the period of the American Revolution, the Articles of Confederation, the making of the Constitution, and the early years of the republic from a variety of vantage points. However, three have been particulary important, what we might think of as three different "presents" in which America's political past has been exhibited and interpreted. As a result, Americans are blessed or cursed with three overlapping versions of their foundation myth.

The Patriotic Version:
Giants Walked the Earth

The first present that served as a perspective for viewing America's past developed in the nineteenth century. Then, people took pride in viewing the birth of the American nation as an heroic venture carried out by altruistic patriots praised as near demigods. The acts in the founding drama were simple and straightforward. They constitute the essentials of history curricula in both primary and secondary schools: The American Revolution was the response of brave men to oppressive tyranny; a successful war of independence yielded in the early 1780s to a period of economic and political crisis that, in turn, was vanquished by "the miracle of Philadelphia," an "Olympian gathering of wise and virtuous men who stood splendidly above all faction, ignored petty self-interest, and concerned themselves only with the freedom and well-being of their fellow countrymen"[2] in formulating the Constitution of the United States; finally, men of vision—Washington, Hamilton, Adams, and later Jefferson and Madison—stepped forth to render the new republic a continuing miracle, the world's most perfect self-governing nation.

The sources of the patriotic version of the foundation myth lie in the character of nineteenth-century America. It was an insecure place. There was no unifying tradition to bind together Americans, many of whom had only recently arrived on these shores. Americans were threatened by all manner of menaces both foreseen and unforeseen—external threats from foreign powers, internal strife over the nature of the union, slavery, industrialization, and countless other questions. In this milieu of potential disunion, it was comforting to look back on the period of the founding as a Golden Age and to believe the hand of God at work in selecting a chosen people to become independent, to design a sacred governing document, and to provide demigods to ameliorate the difficulties of the early years of self-government. After the Civil War, veneration for the founding fathers increased. They became the progenitors of the union proved indissoluble, of an economic system paving the way for unfettered capitalism, and—ultimately—of the conditions for producing the richest and most powerful nation in the world. If there were any doubts about what had happened at the founding, it would be for a new century to reveal them.

The Realist Version: Debunking the Founding Fathers

The twentieth century produced a different era from which to view the past, and as a result, scholars witnessed a different past. The Industrial Revolution left its mark on post-Civil War America, and not every aspect of it was positive. In fact, there were unsavory side effects—exploitation of laborers, the rise of smoke-laden cities, robber barons reaping vast profits from monopolies over productive resources, and so on. Political observers, both journalists and historians, argued that vested interest, not altruism, was the motivating force underlying economic and political realities. "Muckraking," the early twentiety-century version of investigative reporting, exposed the "shadowy powers that manipulated things and made them run the way they did."[3] Vested interests conspiring to run the country were everywhere.

As suspicions of vested interest and conspiracy became popular in the twentieth century, it was not long before the same ideas were applied to thinking about the past, especially to revising views of what had happened at America's founding in the eighteenth century. The modern, educated, and informed version of the founding fathers was to view them not as altruistic, disinterested patriots bent upon expanding popular rule, but as self-serving, hard-fisted conservatives protecting special interests at the expense of the rabble and riffraff.

Typical of the early twentieth-century revisionist view of the founding fathers was the noted historian Charles A. Beard's 1913 volume, *An Economic Interpretation of the Constitution of the United States.*[4] For Beard, the motivation for a new constitution in the 1780s was not patriotism or a commitment to popular government, but selfish economic interest. The Federalist authors and supporters of the Constitution held financial securities and could profit from a strengthened national government. Protection of personal property was paramount in their scheme. Anti-Federalists, by contrast, were a mass of agrarian debtors pressuring state legislators to confiscate property, ignore debts, and inflate the economy. Hence, for Beard, the Constitution represented a victory of conservative over radical vested interests.

To be sure, like any scholarly thesis that receives widespread notice, Beard's interpretation was attacked from a variety of viewpoints as too severe, reductionist, and narrow, as well as being overly selective in the use of supportive evidence. Interestingly enough, however, Beard's detractors were much more interested in demonstrating that he had incorrectly or too narrowly defined the vested interests involved in the struggle over the Constitution than in denying that vested interests were the motivating force of the conflict. A noted defense of the Articles of Confederation, for instance, denied that the Confederation lacked energy to deal with economic crises (thus taking issue with Beard) but said that the demise of the Confederation was due to a dedicated band of nationalists desiring to replace a government of local majorities with one of centralized authority. Nationalism, not economics, was the linchpin of vested interest.[5] Yet another critique of Beard argued that the struggle over ratification of the Constitution hinged not on economic interests but on whether each state believed it could not go it alone as an independent nation. Those that could not, such as Georgia, in need of military protection from the Indians, supported the Constitution; those that envisioned themselves as independent entities, such as New York, were much harder to win to ratification.[6] Thus, vested state interests replaced personal economic interests as the underlying reality of the foundation myth.

The Technician's Version: The Founding Fathers as Scientists and Engineers

We live in a technological age. Whether out of admiration or fear, there is evidence from nationwide surveys that scientists, engineers, and technologists command respect, certainly more so than do people in politics, business, organized labor, and other endeavors.[7] It is not surprising, then, that the contemporary vantage point for knowing America's political past is a technological one and that the founding fathers emerge as technical experts applying eighteenth-century science to human problems—that is, that they were the forerunners of contemporary social engineers.

The technician's version of the foundation myth defines politics as a purely technical, nonideological enterprise. Politics is a process of engineering acceptable and workable solutions to social disputes. "Acceptable" and "workable" imply agreements disputing parties can live with, not necessarily solutions that end conflicts in perfect ways or in perpetuity. Taking this view, what were the technical ways the founding fathers used to create a new independent nation? A few examples provide the flavor of this version of the foundation myth.

A highly reputable contemporary political scientist argues persuasively that the designers of the American governmental arrangement believed that truth is best discovered through the systematic investigation of experience. Using their experience as a basis for action rather than relying on predefined principles or ideological strait jackets, the founding fathers applied their findings to the design of political institutions. One key was the conviction that all such institutions were experimental, to be revised as future systematic investigation of experience dictated.[8] The founding of the Confederation— and later, its supplanting by the Constitution—was not a matter of altruistic patriotism, economic determinism, or ideological struggles over some abstract "best" form of government but the application of an eighteenth-century empirical political science to an engineering problem. Hence, the Constitutional Convention of 1787 wrought no "miracle of Philadelphia" by inspired demigods, nor was it a conspiracy to thwart popular rule. Rather, it was a caucus of politicians, of skilled applied scientists, devoted to an acceptable and workable solution to the problems of building a government with sufficient energy and effectiveness to act.[9]

But what of the origins of the American nation? Surely patriotism, economics, and ideology all played a part in provoking the American Revolution. To be sure, all may indeed have been possible stimulants. But contemporary scholarship focuses less on those factors than, again, on the scientific knowledge and skills possessed by the founders. For example, the received wisdom, that is, the myth, surrounding the drafting of the *Declaration of Independence* has been that Thomas Jefferson applied the principles, theories, and even words of the English theorist, John Locke. The *Declaration* as a document of Lockean principles has been accepted theory in hundreds of American history and government textbooks for decades. Not so, says the scholarship of our technological age. In a painstaking and insightful study of Thomas Jefferson's *Declaration of Independence* (entitled *Inventing America),* Garry Wills has argued that the *Declaration* owes much more to the scientific thinking current in the era of the Enlightenment than to John Locke. Indeed, on many points, Wills finds the original *Declaration* inconsistent with Lockean views—on the nature of rights, the social contract, property rights, and the right of revolution. In fact, Wills even questions that Jefferson owned or had read the basic Lockean treatise on which the *Declaration* was allegedly based.[10]

In offering these two examples of the technical version of the foundation myth, that is, those of the Constitution and *Declaration of Independence,* we do not intend to say that we now know what really happened. Rather, we wish to underscore the point that because people living in a present cannot know the past as those living then did, we build myths about that unknowable past. Those myths are colored by the perceived realities of the present in which we live, perceptions that we project backwards in time. That is why the myth of America's foundation has three faces. Let us now consider the facets of that myth expressed in those countenances.

FROM REVOLUTION TO REPUBLIC:
Building the Foundation Myth

There are four acts to the unfolding drama of the American foundation myth, each with subplots that enrich the legend of the founding fathers.

Act One: The American Revolution

As anyone who recalls the American bicentennial in 1976 knows, the story of the American Revolution has strong patriotic overtones. These are particularly apparent in the myths surrounding the origins of the break with the British Empire and the conduct of the Revolutionary War. Among the former, the following stand out:

☐ *The myth of patriotism* attributes the war for independence to the dedication of altruistic leaders to the cause of liberty. Two phrases symbolize the essential plot. The first appears in the *Declaration:* "... When a long train of abuses and usurpations pursuing invariably the same object, evinces a design to reduce them under absolute despotism, it is their right, it is their duty to throw off such government. ..." From what historians can verify, however, the "long train of abuses and usurpations" were more rhetorical fiction than despotic threat. The British Parliament enacted little legislation applicable to the colonies for long periods and, for the most part, colonial legislatures had a free hand in local situations. The second phrase is Patrick Henry's "Give me Liberty or give me Death!" In the patriotic melodrama, Henry's ringing speech did much to "cause" the Revolution. Scholarship suggests, however, that the phrase may not even have been spoken by Henry. There was no written record made in Richmond in 1775. It was four decades until it appeared in print in a biography canonizing Henry. At that, it was pieced together from reminiscences of those claiming to have heard it forty years earlier! Yet the phrase lingers to sustain the patriotic myth in civics books even now.[11]

☐ *The economic oppression myth*, closely related to the patriotic legend, bases the origins of the Revolution on the maltreatment of the colonists at the hands of the English capitalists and Parliament, a maltreatment so onerous as to violate the colonists' natural rights of property. The instrument of oppression was the allegedly heavy tax burden imposed upon the colonists by the mother country. Indications are, however, that the burden was scarcely disabling and that among imperial tax systems in the world at that time, the English system—especially compared to the French and Spanish—was the least oppressive of all. If anything, prior to 1763, the American colonies prospered from a position in the British Empire that at one and the same time was privileged and involved "salutary neglect." Taxes were light, and the British navy protected colonial sea lanes, thus promoting profitable trade. It was not until the British decided to tax the colonies in order to pay for military protection in the era of the financially draining French and Indian Wars that taxation became an issue. Even then, taxes were not oppressive and only paid for one-third of England's total cost of protecting the colonies. But colonial slogans, such as "taxation without representation" (a phrase that was actually English, not American, in origin), aided and abetted the myth that economic oppression produced the American Revolution.

☐ *The representation myth* blends well with the patriotic/economic despotism myths to explain the causes of the Revolution. It argues that the failure to represent the colonies in the deliberations of Parliament was a direct cause of the movement for independence. Had they been represented, so goes the myth, they would have been legally bound to obey English law. Hence, "no taxation without representation." The myth overlooks the possibility that the colonists wanted representation no more than taxation. For instance, limited suffrage *within* the colonies made taxation without representation commonplace. Moreover, within England there were districts not represented in Parliament, yet subject to parliamentary law. And no less a legendary figure than Benjamin Franklin opposed parliamentary representation as late as 1765. What the colonists seemed to say was that in the absence of parliamentary representation, the only link to the empire was through the British monarch. As long as no loyalty to parliamentary law was required for lack of representation and the King made no demands, the colonists could have their cake and eat it too—free to legislate within their own territories and linked to a federal empire via the King. Parliamentary representation was not their cup of tea, despite claims to the contrary.

Taken together, these three myths form an elaborate, albeit questionable, justification for revolution. Myths surrounding the conduct of the war add to the patriotic emphasis on self-sacrifice, dedication to liberty, discarding the yoke of oppression, and pursuit of self-government. Charming though these myths are, some are hard to believe. The famous midnight ride of Paul Revere is a case in point. Perhaps he rode, but certainly not as mythically portrayed by Henry Wadsworth Longfellow, "who put the resolute rider on the wrong side of the river and had him thunder into Concord, which he failed to reach.[12] Or, consider the widely held belief that the proclaiming of independence, through the *Declaration of Independence,* marked the beginning of the Revolution. If so, how is it that the "shot heard round the world" took place fifteen months before the *Declaration*? Not to be overlooked is the myth of Valley Forge, a tale that epitomizes the spirit of self-sacrifice displayed by revolutionary patriots. Legend has it that George Washington encamped his forces at Valley Forge in the winter of 1777–1778, some twenty miles from Philadelphia. Legend goes on to say that the winter was harsh, food was scarce, death was rampant, and dedicated soldiers left bloody footprints in the snow because they had no boots. That conditions were difficult, there is little doubt, but as to how difficult, historians question. Certainly, the soldiers were not the price demanded by the Great Spirit, to whom Washington supposedly knelt and prayed in the snow. In fact, conditions were bad because of congressional bickering and bureaucratic bungling in the commissary department: There were few supplies, meager rations, and no boots. Nor did Washington kneel to pray, even in church, but remained standing, probably asking the Great Spirit not for release from the weather, but, like many a general, for freedom from quibbling politicians.

Act Two: The Critical Period

Any heroic drama, such as the American foundation myth, demands that its leading characters be tested to prove that they indeed possess the requisite qualities marking them as heroes. The American Revolution provided one such test for the founding fathers. But their capacity to cope with and surmount what in American folklore has come to be known as "the critical period" is what converted them from mere mortals to Olympian figures. The critical period covered the years of the new nation's first constitutional government under the Articles of Confederation from 1781 to 1789. This confederated government, designated a "league of friendship," minimized the powers exercised by central authorities through the Continental Congress, retaining for the states all but the few powers specifically granted the Confederation.

If the American foundation myth is accepted without qualification, then the Articles of Confederation were sadly inadequate. The critical period, we are told, was one of social decay, economic stagnation, and political chaos, chiefly because of fundamental "weaknesses" in the Articles. As anyone drilled in high-school civics or a college level introduction to American government knows, these alleged weaknesses can be ticked off with ritualistic monotony: The Articles made no provision for an independent executive and only provided for a one-house legislature; each state had a single vote with a two-thirds majority required to pass legislation; the power to tax and to regulate commerce between the states and foreign nations was reserved to each state government; no independent judiciary was provided for; and unanimous consent was required for amendment of the Articles. The myth of the critical period was that these weaknesses of the Articles provoked a crisis of disunity, disarray, and disorder. It required unselfish patriots to step forward to save the new nation from impending anarchy, chaos, and destruction. How much of that myth is credible in light of our present perspective on those years, and how much is refutable?

One must grant that the postwar years were anything but easy for the new nation. There were cycles of depression and inflation, threats from foreign powers, and debates over national versus state control of government. Yet, consider what the principal tasks of *any* government would have been during the period: (1) to conduct a war and achieve a peace; (2) to demobilize following that war; (3) to cope with sudden economic change, dislocation, and expansion stemming from the conflict; and (4) to carry on the "Spirit of '76." Judged by these tasks, the period, "rather than [being] an unfortunate interlude in the nation's past . . . was *critical* to the continued growth of American democracy."[13]

First, we must keep in mind that the Confederation did in fact win the Revolutionary War and sign a favorable peace treaty. This alone was no small accomplishment, especially considering that the war itself was never all that popular. Perhaps as many as one-third of the colonists, that is, the Loyalists, opposed the war effort from the beginning.

Second, the Confederation coped reasonably well with a major facet of demobilization, that is, dealing with war debts. A multitude of accounts were reduced to simple forms, and the states assumed the portions of those debts owed to its citizens.

Third, the economic record of the Confederation was not the

dismal failure that the myth makes it out to be. Contrary to legend, most of the ports of the world were open, not closed, to American shipping, even in the absence of formal treaties. The alleged trade wars between states were exaggerated. Reciprocity and equal treatment among the states was the rule in trade and tariff legislation, not trade barriers. And the period was one of economic growth: American merchants owned more ships than during the Revolution and carried a greater share of American produce than before; the export of agricultural products doubled; and cities grew rapidly, with building booms and labor shortages being more common than unemployment.

Finally, the Confederation preserved the revolutionary spirit. The practice of democracy in the states without intervention from a central government was a precise goal that the Revolutionary patriots had sought. Within those states, final power rested in the legislature, with the executive and judicial branches being subservient to the more popular body. Instead of being moribund, the single-house Continental Congress passed significant pieces of legislation, particularly the Northwest Ordinance establishing procedures for developing the western lands. Moreover, Congress was in the process of evolving a national executive that might have assumed the character of a parliamentary cabinet model. And, lastly, Congress "laid foundations for the administration of a central government which were to be expanded but not essentially altered in functions for generations to come."[14]

Despite these achievements, contemporary textbooks in American government sustain this portion of the foundation myth, with rare qualification. The following quotations from leading texts demonstrate that in evaluating the critical period, the perspective of the present has changed little since the close of the last century:

1896: "The fortunes of the country seemed at a lower ebb than even during the war with England."[15]

1948: "The new government faced many difficulties with which it was unable to cope and the period which it was in operation has been designated the 'Critical Period in American history.'"[16]

1948: "Whatever the theoretical deficiencies of the Articles of Confederation, there was no doubt about the failure of the Confederation government in practice."[17]

1969: "The Confederation . . . did not work very well and lasted only a short time. Thinking men all over the United States began to feel something had to be done."[18]

1977: "The most significant fact about the government created under the Articles was its weakness"[19]

Refutable or not, the myth of the critical period remains credible, at least to authors of American government texts. That credibility introduces the next act in the drama of the foundation myth.

Act Three: The Constitutional Convention

The patriotic theme dominates the first two acts of the drama of the American foundation. That theme is paramount in the third as well, but it is often upstaged in contemporary times by images of the founding fathers as realists or technicians rather than as patriots. The patriotic version, familiar as it is to any reader who has survived a course in civics, requires only brief recapitulation. Weaknesses inherent in the Articles of Confederation, uprisings and rebellions, demands for national action: All combined to provoke the convening of a meeting of fifty-five of the states' most notable figures (including George Washington, James Madison, Benjamin Franklin, Alexander Hamilton, and Gouverneur Morris) in Philadelphia in May 1787 to revise and improve the Articles. Instead, in but four months, they brought forth a bold new plan, one brief in content, intricate in design, and unique in the world.

This is not to say that the task of saving the nation was accomplished without difficulty. Indeed, the delegates fell to debating, arguing, and even bickering. Conflicts were so strident that Benjamin Franklin called for prayer to invoke the aid of the Almighty. Henceforth, goes legend, the hand of God moved in the convention.

The arguments, however, were not over petty matters. These statesmanlike debates were over matters of *principle*. Chief among them, to quote a civics text that perpetuated the patriotic version of the foundation myth to generations of Americans, was the question, "Should there be a government in which the states would exercise most power, in which the central government should be subordinate to the states; or should there be a strong central government, with the states subordinate?"[20] The Virginia Plan proposed a strong central government with states represented in a single-house legislature in proportion to population; the New Jersey Plan proposed more power for the states and equal state representation. Since representation proportionate to population favored large states, whereas equal representation favored small states, the two plans entered the lexicon of the foundation myth as the Large State Plan and the Small State Plan respectively.

Being patriots devoted to principle rather than to the interests of large or small states per se, the founders, as reasonable men, placed the best interests of the nation first. The statesmen thereby struck a bargain, "The Great Compromise." They agreed to a two-house Congress—the lower, the House of Representatives, representing states in proportion to population and the upper, the Senate, representing states equally. Powers to be exercised by Congress were enumerated in the Constitution, and states retained important powers. Thus a *federal* form of government, an ingenious solution to the vexing problem of central versus state authority, came into existence.

But that was not the limit of the founders' genius. To prevent Congress from running amuck, a separate executive—the president—had authority to check congressional excesses through a veto of legislation. Likewise, there was a check on the president, for the Senate had power to confirm or reject presidential appointments and treaties. A separate judicial system served as a body for appealing both presidential and congressional excesses. But it had some responsibility to both branches in light of the fact that the Constitution provides that the president appoint and the Senate confirm judicial nominations, most importantly to the Supreme Court. Thus two other principles joined federalism as hallmarks of the founders' ingenuity—*separation of powers* and *checks and balances.*

There were other problems before the convention, including the troublesome issue of the slave trade, the status of slaves themselves, how to select the chief executive, provisions for regulating domestic and foreign commerce, and so on. But the framers faced up to each, debated the underlying principles, and arrived at reasoned solutions. Then, having completed their work on September 17, 1787 (regarded as Constitution Day, yet strangely enough not a national holiday, despite our national reverence of the document), the framers donned the mantle of Federalists to combat the opposing Anti-Federalists and win ratification in a series of state conventions.

These, then, are the main outlines of the patriotic version of how the Constitution came into being. Despite challenges from two sides, it remains the predominant version and retains widespread popular credibility. Its first challenge came from the realist school, which argued that princip*al*, not princip*le*, motivated the framers that is, they were but pocketbook patriots serving economic self-interests. In order to protect those interests, they conspired to scuttle the democracy derived from the Revolution and replace it with an oligarchical arrangement.

The mythbreaking efforts of the realist school had two effects. First, to those who found the realist version palatable, one credible hypothesized past soon became *the* past. A new myth had been born. No longer was it the hand of God moving in the convention, or even the debates of nationalists versus states' righters. Now it was the dialectic of economic determinism holding forth. Second, stimulated by the new mythology, the realist version was challenged. Scholars noted that, among other things, the framers' wealth was tied not to securities—which would have profited from the new governing arrangement—but to land. Moreover, of the delegates to the convention holding large securities, seven deserted the proceedings and did not sign the document. Finally, with respect to the Constitution being a sellout of the democratic principles of the Revolution, consider the following:

1. Seven of the *Declaration*'s signers were at the Constitutional Convention.

2. Thirty of the forty-three living signers of the *Declaration* supported the Constitution.

3. The ratifying procedures for the Constitution were more democratic than those used to adopt the Articles of Confederation.

4. Delegates to the Constitutional Convention were younger, *less* affluent, and *less* powerful in their states than those fomenting the Revolution.

5. George Washington, legend of the Revolution, presided over the Constituional Convention.

6. The "Father of the Constitution," James Madison, was the friend, disciple, and confidant of the "Author of the Declaration," Thomas Jefferson, and—most importantly—his closest political ally.[21]

In sum, the realist version of the framing of the Constitution is, like the patriotic one, a credible but not testable possibility of what might have happened. So also is the third version, that of the framers as technicians. It differs from the patriotic version in proposing that the framers were not concerned with matters of principle but that they differed over matters of structure and tactics. It differs from the realist version in arguing that the framers were not antidemocratic and conservative, but democratic and liberal. Seen from this perspective, the Constitutional Convention was a gathering of democratic politicians committed to improving governmental forms and mobilizing public approval for their actions.[22] Although the delegates represented differing local interests, they were politicians willing to compromise parochial interests on behalf of a unifying nationalistic principle. They had *more in common as politicians* (that is, a willingness to compromise in order to achieve agreed-upon ends despite differing means) than whatever differences divided them as representatives of local constituencies. As skilled politicians, they employed understandable political techniques: They capitalized on the popularity of George Washington by having him preside over the convention; they recruited leading figures from the Revolutionary era to the cause; they employed the unifying symbols of American nationalism; and they maintained secrecy for their deliberations so as to pose a single plan for public approval.

Again, as in the case of the patriotic and realist versions, there are features of this interpretation that render it believable. For one, the differences in the Virginia and New Jersey plans were not so great as the patriotic telling of the tale suggests. What the New Jersey Plan proposed was a suitable alternative to the Virginia Plan, suitable in the sense of being more palatable to the folks back home. Its proponents did not oppose strong national government in principle—support for that notion was widespread at the conclave—they only opposed a strong national government serving only large state interests. In fact, the origins of the Supremacy Clause of the Constitution ("This Constitution, and the laws of the United States which shall be made in pursuance thereof; and all treaties made, or which shall be made, under the authority of the United States, shall be the supreme law of the land") lie in the New Jersey Plan.

Or, consider again the "Great Compromise." It resulted not as an effort to bring warring factions within the convention together but as a ploy to provide an acceptable plan to all local constituents, regardless of their interests. Once that compromise was reached, there were added efforts to strengthen the central government's powers, not to diminish them. In sum, structure and tactics were matters for bargaining and compromise; they were not the overriding unifying principle of the convention—namely, that a strong national government was essential.

Technicians the framers might well have been. The level of their skill, however, should not be taken for granted. Provision for the selection of the president is a case in point. Selection by the electoral college was not proposed as an antidemocratic device but as a means of making indirect selection acceptable to popular views. Selection by the House of Representatives was probably preferable to most delegates. But they knew that it would not sell to the home folks. As a result, they devised a scheme whereby the majority of electoral votes would elect the president. They apparently assumed that after Washington's incumbency (taken for granted by most delegates), no candidate would get a majority of electoral votes and that the decision would then be made by the House of Representatives, each state casting but one vote. What they did not foresee was the likelihood of two candidates from the same political party receiving the same number of votes, both for president and vice president, and thereby raising the specter of the House not being able to reach a decision. That, however, is precisely what happened in 1800 when both Thomas Jefferson and Aaron Burr—running for president and vice president respectively on the same party ticket—received the same number of electoral votes. Only through a prolonged dispute and eventual compromise did the House select Jefferson as president. The flaw in the constitutional selection formula overlooked by the eighteenth-century technical masters had to be corrected with the passage of the Twelfth Amendment, one of twenty-six amendments passed to make the perfect document of the Constitution even more perfect.

By and large, the myths of economic realism and of political know-how have not supplanted the view that the framers of the Constitution were patriots and statesmen. That popular image of the framers, so persuasive in the nineteenth century, has not been diminished even today: "This attitude toward the Fathers has actually never died out; it still tends to prevail in American history curricula right up through most of the secondary schools."[23]

Act Four: The Early Republic

The final curtain falls on the dramatic account of the American foundation myth after a brief denouement telling the tale of the early days of the republic. As with the earlier acts, it relates a story of patriots and statesmen serving their country against the onslaught of narrow-minded politicians. We need not recount all of the scenes in the final act; a few will suffice to illustrate the character of the drama.

Take as one the myths surrounding the presidential administration of George Washington, "first in war, first in peace, and first in the hearts of his countrymen." Also, he was the first president of the newly born republic. Mythology paints a picture of a relatively serene, unifying presidency led by a calm, cool president and staffed with a cabinet of visionary statesmen. As with myths generally, this one is neither wholly true nor false. To begin with, the first presidency, working with Congress, achieved notable accomplishments: It established the executive departments, developed the presidential cabinet as an advisory body, established a foreign policy, developed a series of domestic economic programs, and launched the federal judicial system with passage of the Judiciary Act of 1789. Whether all of this could have developed as smoothly without the legendary Washington as president, no one knows. Yet his presence added a legitimacy and luster to the early days of the republic that might have been problematic otherwise. And the new government did have impressive individuals in strategic positions: Alexander Hamilton as secretary of the treasury, Thomas Jefferson as secretary of state, and James Madison as a key congressional figure.

Beneath the surface serenity and statesmanship, however, lay deep cleavages and a struggle to advance competing interests. The French Revolution and the subsequent war between France and England polarized supporters of "frog-eating, man-eating, blood-drinking baboons" (the stereotype of France) and "British bootlicks." The issue divided the Washington cabinet as well, Jefferson supporting France, Hamilton the British. Ultimately, Washington issued his renowned Neutrality Proclamation. But the proclamation, in fact, was not one of neutrality (the word does not appear in the proclamation) but out of noninvolvement and of conduct friendly and impartial toward both powers. The myth of American noninvolvement in foreign struggles was to reappear in another legendary statement, Washington's Farewell Address. That statement was not a delivered address at all, but a piece of campaign propaganda designed to elect John Adams president in 1796. The document was less Washington's than Hamilton's and was a partisan attack on permanent alliances with nations such as France, not a plea for isolationism and strict noninvolvement with other nations.

Nor was the image of the father of the country as calm, cool, and deliberate totally accurate. It was Washington who, upon close, critical questioning by the Senate over his policies, angrily stormed out of the session and thereby terminated the practice of presidents appearing in person before that body for obtaining advice and consent. Likewise, the actions of some of his appointees did not always match the statesman's image attributed to the administration. His secretary of war, Henry Knox, for instance, floated a highly questionable but very sizable speculation in lands. William Duer, Hamilton's secretary, went to jail over speculation in government bonds.

Finally, the early days of the republic were noted not for domestic tranquility, but for outbreaks of turmoil. When angry farmers tarred and feathered federal tax collectors seeking payment of an excise on distilled spirits in 1794, Washington called out militiamen to put down the "insurrection" that entered our political mythology as the Whiskey Rebellion. Such incidents, combined with conflicts over foreign and economic policy, did much to diminish the aura of greatness surrounding the Washington administration and the president himself. So much so that it has been written that "in fact, no president with the exception of Andrew Johnson after the Civil War (and more recently Richard Nixon) left office under more criticism."[24]

A CRACK IN THE FOUNDATION:
The Myth that the System Works, Civil War Era

In the mid-1970s, as the Watergate drama unfolded before their eyes, many Americans wondered if the republic bequeathed by the founding fathers still worked. As judicial trials and congressional investigations ran their course and, ultimately, a president resigned his office in the face of possible impeachment, a catchphrase developed—"Watergate proved the system worked." What that meant was that the republic and its institutions were sufficient to meet the challenge raised by the scandals surrounding the Watergate caper.

More than a century earlier, the republic faced another challenge, and it, too, raised serious questions about the viability of the governing arrangement founded by the framers. Faced with deep cleavages over slavery, the nature of the union, economic questions, and other issues, Americans fought and killed one another in a widespread civil war. That conflict certainly raised questions about the credibility of the foundation myth. For if the myth were true, how could a nation founded through the wisdom of Olympian demigods, a nation governed by the world's most perfect document, fall on such hard times? Were Americans no longer God's chosen people? Termination of the Civil War and preservation of the Union did not remove the nagging questions. In this context, two key myths developed to serve as the cement that repaired the cracks in the foundation: One pertained to the origin of the struggle, the other to America's greatest folk hero since George Washington.

Myths of the Origins of the Civil War

One way to reconcile the fact that the citizens of the world's most perfect union took it upon themselves to slaughter one another is to look upon the Civil War as an aberration, a unique event that arose not from any defects in the constitutional system but as a result of a confluence of unique happenings. So viewed, the war tested the strength of America's Constitution and institutions, a test that sustained the national government. Post-Civil War historians were quick to supply explanations reinforcing the belief that the Civil War tested and sustained the work of the founding fathers but did not derive from it.

One of the earliest of such myths was that of the war of the rebellion. The drama can be simply told: The South, as a slave empire, had never been reconciled to the democratic ways of the Union; the southern states conspired to break the Constitution, illegally seceded, and were thus solely responsible for the conflict. This scenario was the product of northern historians. It was believable to many, not because of the evidence amassed to prove it but because it fit the biases of the war's victors and, as is often the case, to the victors belong not only the spoils but the telling of the tale.

But Southern historians created a counter-myth, that of a war between the states. In this drama, the South is a romantic land of dashing cavaliers, beautiful women, happy blacks, and single-minded dedication to tradition, high moral principles, and the true meaning of the Constitution. Secession and the founding of the Confederate States of America were steps taken to save American institutions and traditions from northern destruction. However, it all turned out to be the South's lost cause, a tragedy along the lines depicted in Margaret Mitchell's *Gone With the Wind,* a drama that went on to become a movie classic.

Both northern and southern myths of the origins of the war were formulated in a present—the immediate postwar period—in which it was tempting for both schools of historians to impose their biases and prejudices on the unknowable past. The early part of this century provided a more dispassionate reading of the past, and historians developed a new myth, that of the inevitable conflict. Essentially, that myth attributes the origins of the struggle not to human motivations, accountability, and actions but to uncontrollable forces. One version points to the South's "peculiar institution"—slavery—as the cause. That institution set in motion forces that neither North nor South could control. A later version of the myth of the inevitable conflict focuses upon economic determinism as its key; that is, it posits a capitalistic industrial Yankee economy pitted against an aristocratic and agricultural South. In either version, "peculiar institution" or "economic determinism," the implication is that *no* constitutional arrangement, not even that of the founding fathers, would have been adequate to prevent the conflict. But, and most importantly, the Constitution did survive the test by providing the framework within which that conflict was resolved, albeit violently.

In the 1930s—in part as an aftermath of World War I and also as a concern over what appeared to be another conflagration about to break out in Europe—there were strong antiwar sentiments. These were reflected in the works of a new generation of Civil War historians and imposed upon the past. The result was the myth of the repressible conflict. It sees the origins of the war in misunderstandings, principally in the fictitious images that people in the North and South held of one another. These, combined with the ineptness of politicians at the time, provided artificial issues that could have and should have been revealed for what they were. The war, in sum, should never have happened. But it did, and, again, the system survived.

What all these myths of the origins of the Civil War have in common is two-fold: First, all have been formulated by historians imposing a vision of the present upon the past:

> In the final analysis, what historians have said about the causes of the Civil War vary widely. They have functioned as myth-makers in that they have too often offered far too many simple explanations of a very complex era. . . . A total reconstruction of past reality is impossible, and it is equally impossible for a historian to divorce himself from his times.[25]

Second, all of these myths attribute the cause of the Civil War to something other than the constitutional arrangement of the founding fathers, that is, to a southern conspiracy, to southern loyalty to cherished values, to uncontrollable forces, to a failure to communicate, to ineptness, and so on. None speak to the possibility that a constitutional arrangement that divides governing powers between a host of competing states, governing levels, and governing branches too often runs the risks of stalemate. Unable to act in the face of intensifying crises—whether the sources are slavery or economics, as in the 1850s, or energy, inflation, and dwindling resources in the 1980s— the system is itself mythical. Fragmented, piecemeal efforts, not coordinated programs, result. Myths of the origins of the Civil War reinforce the myth that the system worked; they do not challenge it.

Lincoln's Historic Quest

Through the legendary figure of Abraham Lincoln, the crack in the American foundation myth wrought by the Civil War is not only sealed, but the very myth itself emerges stronger than ever before. Lincoln, indeed, is in American political mythology not only heir to the Olympian heroic qualities of the founding fathers; he also becomes one of the founders himself.

The mythical images surrounding Abraham Lincoln are numerous. As other writers have noted, there is a lengthy laundry list of Lincolns: Self-Made Man, Rail-Splitter, Great Democrat, Honest Abe, the Great Emancipator, Father Abraham, Savior of the Union.[26] What is not so often appreciated by many believers in the Lincoln mystique is that "the first author of the Lincoln legend and the greatest of the Lincoln dramatists was Lincoln himself."[27] For our purposes, two aspects of the Lincoln legend are especially relevant to linking it to the myth of America's foundation.

The first concerns the relation between the images of Lincoln as the Great Emancipator and as Savior of the Union. By creating a mythology about the former, Lincoln was able to enact the role of the latter. Although the Lincoln legend credits him with a lifelong heroic quest, against stiff odds, to end slavery and free the blacks, when it comes to slavery, historians view him as "fuzzy on the issues" (much as Jimmy Carter was accused of being on issues in the 1976 presidential campaign). Lincoln was not an abolitionist. He was a politician. In his early years, he was not militant on the slavery issue, expressing that it would die a "natural death" if not allowed to expand and if contained as the South's "peculiar institution":

> I hold it a paramount duty of us in the free States, due to the Union of the States, and perhaps to liberty itself (paradox though it may seem), to let the slavery of the other states alone; while on the other hand, I hold it to be equally clear that we should never knowingly lend ourselves, directly or indirectly, to prevent that slavery from dying a natural death—to find new places for it to live in, when it can no longer exist in the old.[28]

Thus spoke Lincoln in 1845. Nine years later, for the first time in his life, he spoke out against slavery as a "monstrous injustice." But even then he saw no means of eliminating the institution in "any satisfactory way." Said he, "What next? Free them, and make them politically and socially our equals. *My own feelings will not admit of this,* and if mine would, we well know that those of the great mass of whites will not."[29]

As a politician, Lincoln faced a problem. Large numbers of potential voters thought slavery morally wrong. But even a larger portion of the public—indeed, overlapping with members of the first group—did not want political and social equality for blacks. Lincoln's formula was to agree that slavery was morally wrong but to let it die a natural death in the South while preventing its spread in other territories. He did not make his argument against its spread on moral grounds but on economic merits. If slavery were to spread, the value of free white labor would diminish. In a speech that literally played in Peoria (he gave it there), he spoke of how the new territories of the Midwest should be treated. "We want them for homes of free white people," he said. "This they cannot be to any considerable extent if slavery shall be planted within them."

It was this containment, not abolitionist, position that helped Lincoln to the presidency. Once there, his focus was not on ending slavery but upon preserving the Union: "My paramount object in this struggle is to save the Union, and it is *not* to save or destroy slavery."[30] When he did issue the Emancipation Proclamation, it was not to free slaves—in fact, it freed not one, since it applied only to those behind Confederate lines and was thus unenforceable at the time of its issue in 1862—but to placate abolitionists critical of the war effort, to win foreign opinion to the Union cause, and to hold off possible foreign intervention on the side of the South. In short, Lincoln became Great Emancipator in order to be Savior of the Union, a point quite consistent with the pattern of his career as a politician but inconsistent with legend.

By saving the Union, Lincoln preserved the American foundation. Through his eloquence, he reinforced the mythology that surrounds that foundation. The Gettysburg Address is a case in point. Legend has it that Lincoln, dedicating a national cemetery in Pennsylvania in 1863, spoke in a hushed, hesitant fashion from notes scrawled on the back of an envelope during a train ride from Washington, D.C. Legend also has it that the address was universally panned, both for Lincoln's plodding style and its content. In fact, the speech was written in Washington, with minor changes made after reaching Gettysburg. Moreover, although partisan critics denounced the address, others praised the literary qualities immediately, thus debunking the folk tale that it was long after 1863 that the address received notoriety.

But laying myths about the address aside, it is the content, the verbal imagery, that invokes the greatness of the founding fathers and ties the Civil War drama to that of the American foundation. Recall those words? "Fourscore and seven years ago" is a gentle reminder of 1776. The phrase, "Our fathers brought forth on this continent a new nation, conceived in liberty and dedicated to the proposition that all men are created equal" is a master stroke of praising the creativity of the founding fathers, of noting that *our* foundation was *our* doing and not something imposed on this *new* nation from abroad. Moreover, it hearkens back to the ringing phrase of the *Declaration* regarding the equality of men. "Now we are engaged in a great civil war, testing whether that nation, or any nation so conceived and so dedicated can long endure" achieves the required linkage. In short, the Civil War becomes the testing ground of the American foundation. The achievements of the founding fathers were not in error, implies Lincoln, but are only being tested. Will they measure up? Lincoln assures that they will for "we here highly resolve that these dead shall not have died in vain." In fact, the foundation will be the stronger for it, since "this nation, under God, shall have a new birth of freedom; and that government of the people, by the people, for the people, shall not perish from the earth." And with these closing words, Lincoln sustains the American foundation myth.

AMERICA'S PAST: Reusable or Pop-Top, No Deposit, No Return, Throwaways?

In one of the countless talk show interviews that he appeared on after the highly successful television adaptation of his novel *Roots* in 1977, author Alex Haley was asked if his depiction of the life of African communities prior to the slave trade was exaggerated. Had black Africa been all that idyllic—virtually a paradise? No, Haley admitted, it had not. But, he went on to say, every people need an Eden and he was supplying one for blacks.

Haley was not the first storyteller to assist a people in need of common roots, tradition, culture, and history in creating a "usable past."[31] The American foundation myth; the legends surrounding this nation's sin, suffering, sacrifice, and salvation during the Civil War; and the mythology of an expanding popular democracy are all parts of the contrived memory that constitutes this country's usable past. The notion of usable past derives from two assumptions. One we have already introduced, that is, the idea that we can know the past only in the present and, hence, never really know it at all. The past, necessarily reflecting projections from our present and our imagined future, is thus always a contrivance. The second assumption is that nation-building is considerably easier if people share a common territory, religion, government, language, history, and traditions. If they do not, then the illusion of common bonds must be fostered by creating and imposing on the early years of nationhood a believable, shared experience, even at the expense of exaggeration, romanticizing, and fantasizing. In short, mythmaking creates a usable past.

Such was the American case. Diversity was the trademark of the early years. Regionalism and parochialism prevailed. Separation of church and state and religious freedom bred religious diversity. State governments held sway, even after the new and untested Constitution had been ratified. And many immigrants spoke their native language rather than English. Finally, being such a new nation, the United States scarcely possessed a common history or tradition. To many, the phrase "my country" meant their state, not the union of states.

Into this swirling diversity stepped the mythmakers—not merely early historians but poets, balladeers, novelists, and storytellers as well. George Washington's first biographer, Mason Locke Weems, contributed considerably to the creation of a usable past by fashioning the Washington legend. It was Weems (sometimes called the Father of the Father of His Country) who, in 1806, in the fifth edition of his biography of Washington, spun the tale of Washington and the cherry tree with the quotation known ever after to generations of Americans: "I cannot tell a lie, Pa; you know I can't tell a lie. I did cut it with my hatchet." There were seventy-six more editions of Weem's book, which ended publication in 1927. They all related the tale, a fiction still alive and well today.

Weems was not alone in adding luster to America's past, telling stirring tales of noble deeds, and creating heroic figures. The roll of what one historian has called the "Founding Fathers of American literary nationalism"[32] is extensive—Washington Irving, Walt Whitman, Nathaniel Hawthorne, James Fenimore Cooper, Oliver Wendell Holmes, Ralph Waldo Emerson, and on and on to contemporary authors and artists, such as Herman Wouk, Pete Seeger, Walt Disney, Milton Caniff, or Charles Schultz. To them we owe remembrance of Miles Standish, Rip Van Winkle, Daniel Boone, Davey Crockett, Uncle Tom, Huck Finn, Mickey Mouse, Charlie Brown, and others—all as much a part of America's usable past as Washington, Jefferson, Lincoln, and so on.

> What resulted from all of this was a history both splendid and romantic. The American past would be built of a mixture of fact and fantasy; the story of the nation would emerge as a tightly woven blend of history and myth. It was a past that was in many ways factually false yet psychologically true for a nation which very much wanted a usable past in which to anchor its destiny.[33]

By the mid-1840s, that destiny was emerging, the destiny of God's chosen people with missionary zeal to spread the ideals of freedom, republicanism, and democracy to everyone everywhere. Thus was born the myth of manifest destiny. In the name of making liberty and freedom manifest to all, Americans settled a continent, engaged in numerous wars, and assumed world leadership in making the world safe for democracy in this century. Even today America lectures foreign powers on the sanctity of human rights. The usable past, in short, gets reborn in the present.

However, in getting reborn, that usable past sometimes changes. New myths substitute for older versions. Thus the realist version of the foundation myth replaces the patriotic drama in the minds of many, or the technological version replaces both. In light of an ever-changing present, the usable past of yesteryear appears not so usable today. The search for a usable past, in short, is unending. Thereby, mythmaking is unending as well.

The point is best summed up in a Jules Feiffer cartoon, circa 1970. It depicts a construction worker, the stereotypical "hardhat," facing the reader and saying that when he went to school he learned that George Washington never told a lie, that slaves were happy on the plantation, that the men who settled the West were giants, and that we won every war because God was on our side. Now his kid goes to school and learns that George Washington was a slave owner, that slaves hated slavery, that the pioneers of the frontier committed genocide, and that the wars we won were victories of United States imperialism. Dolefully, he remarks, "No wonder my kid's not an American. They're teaching him some other country's history." Or perhaps this present's past?

REFERENCES

1. Wayne Andrews, ed., *Concise Dictionary of American History* (New York: Scribner, 1962), pp. 289–290.

2. Stanley Elkins and Eric McKitrick, "The Founding Fathers: Young Men of the Revolution," in Nicholas Cords and Patrick Gerster, eds., *Myth and the American Experience,* Volume 1, (New York: Glencoe Press, 1973), p. 112.

3. Elkins and McKitrick, "The Founding Fathers," p. 116.

4. Charles A. Beard, *An Economic Interpretation of the Constitution of the United States* (New York: Macmillan, 1913).

5. Merrill Jensen, *The New Nation* (New York: Knopf, 1950), *passim.*

6. Forrest McDonald, *We The People* (Chicago: University of Chicago Press, 1958), *passim.*

7. *The Harris Survey,* September 25, 1978, news release.

8. Austin Ranney, "'The Divine Science': Political Engineering in American Culture," *American Political Science Review,* 70 (March 1976): 139–148.

9. John P. Roche, "The Founding Fathers: A Reform Caucus in Action," *American Political Science Review,* 55 (December 1961): 799–816.

10. Garry Wills, *Inventing America* (New York: Doubleday, 1978).

11. For an excellent account of the myth surrounding Henry's "speech" as well as other myths of the American Revolution, see Nicholas Cords and Patrick Gerster, *Myth in American History* (New York: Glencoe Press, 1977), Chapter 2.

12. Thomas Bailey, "The Mythmakers of American History," *Journal of American History,* 55 (June 1968): 6.

13. Cords and Gerster, *Myth in American History,* p. 48.

14. Jensen, *The New Nation,* pp. 347–348.

15. James Bryce, *The American Commonwealth* (New York: Macmillan, 1896), p. 8.

16. Fremont P. Wirth, *The Development of America* (Boston: American Book Company, 1948), p. 181.

17. Alfred H. Kelly and Winfred A. Harbison, *The American Constitution* (New York: Norton, 1948), p. 108.

18. Floyd G. Cullop, *the Constitution of the United States* (New York: New American Library [Signet Books], 1969), p. 16.

19. Milton C. Cummings, Jr. and David Wise, *Democracy Under Pressure* (New York: Harcourt Brace Jovanovich, 1977), p. 40.

20. Wirth, *The Development of America,* p. 196.

21. Wills, *Inventing America,* pp. 352–343.

22. Roche, "The Founding Fathers: A Reform Caucus in Action," *passim.*

23. Elkins and McKitrick, "The Founding Fathers: Young Men of the Revolution," p. 112.

24. Cords and Gerster, *Myths in American History,* p. 65.

25. Cords and Gerster, *Myth in American History,* p. 146; details regarding myths of the Civil War can be found in pp. 142–147.

26. Cords and Gerster, *Myth in American History,* p. 152.

27. Richard Hofstadter, *The American Political Tradition* (New York: Vintage Books, 1954), p. 94.

28. Quoted in Hofstadter, *The American Political Tradition,* p. 109.

29. Quoted in Hofstadter, *The American Political Tradition,* p. 111.

30. Quoted in Cords and Gerster, *Myth in American History,* p. 156.

31. Henry Steele Commager, "The Search for a Usable Past," in Cords and Gerster, eds., *Myth and the American Experience,* pp. 136–151.

32. Commager, "The Search for a Usable Past," p. 150.

33. Cords and Gerster, *Myth in American History,* p. 63.

CHAPTER **3**

How Firm
A Foundation?
Contemporary
Political Myths

The previous chapter traced the historical background of the major American political myth of the foundation. This myth emerged for specific reasons in the past, but it has had remarkable survival power and continuity over time. American politics cultivates and uses the heritage of political myth that it draws from the past. Past myths are thereby the prologue to present myths. In this chapter, we distinguish between the continuity of *long-standing* myths, exhibited in the present, and *topical* myths, those derived and created in the political present. In the former instance, we look at the current version of the foundation myth, the sustaining myth of civil religion, and selected institutional myths. As for the latter, we discuss myths of an ideological nature, myths about the current state of politics, myths about political figures of importance, and myths of political change. Finally, we will specuiate about what we call the "mythic gap."

LONG-STANDING MYTHS,
Or Re-Presenting the Usable Past in the Here and Now

The term "contemporary" poses a problem not only of defining what a present, or contemporary period, is but also what the relationship of that present is to earlier presents. This includes the relationship of present myths to those held over from past periods. The continuity of political cultures suggests that myths from an earlier time, broadly and deeply held, reappear—new wine in old bottles—in a transformed or revived state. Political cultures thus involve *long-standing* myths that go through historical convolutions to be revitalized and restored to prominence in a new form from time to time. The present restatement or reaffirmation of an old myth then strikes an old political nerve, but in a new, contemporary form, often as a contemporary restatement of what we have called a master myth, an overarching cultural myth of ancient origin. The constant restatement of myth is a political present's way of using the past by placing present actions and actors in the historical legacy of earlier myths. In this respect, American politics is a series of revitalization movements in which a current political coalition attempts to revitalize old myths for present purposes.

Why Presidential Addresses
Yield a Feeling of *Déjà Vu*

This phenomenon can be illustrated by the various slogans employed by recent presidential administrations that use the term "new" but which place that newness—new initiatives, new programs, and so on—within the historical flow of mythic continuity extending back to the foundation. What we do now thus appears sanctioned by and is the logical outcome of the intent of the founders. The needs of the moment thereby draw vitality from mythic re-enactment. Hence, the New Deal, the New Frontier, the New Federalism, and other such programs that every presidential administration feels compelled to offer hearken back to the long-standing foundation myth.

Jimmy Carter's "New Foundation," the theme of his 1979 State of the Union address, is yet another transformation of the foundation myth. ("How Firm a Foundation" is a favorite Baptist hymn with which born-again Christian Carter is undoubtedly familiar.) The New Foundation lacked the programmatic agenda of, say, Lyndon Johnson's Great Society. It did not have the "new spirit" theme of Carter's inaugural address, which sounded like a call for all America to be "born again," reminiscent of Woodrow Wilson's New Freedom. Yet Carter placed his New Foundation in the grand tradition of Democratic epigrams of the past: He evoked Wilson's New Freedom, the New Deal of Franklin D. Roosevelt, and the New Frontier of John F. Kennedy. He spoke of issues that must be faced if America's mythic heritage is to be fulfilled: "The challenge to us is to build a new and firmer foundation for the future—for a sound economy, for a more effective government, for political trust, and for a stable peace." The speech concluded by direct reference to the original foundation myth:

> To establish these values, two centuries ago a bold generation of Americans risked their property, position and life itself.
>
> We are their heirs. And they are sending us a message across the centuries. The words they made so vivid are now growing faintly indistinct, because they are not heard often enough. They are words like justice, equality, unity, sacrifice, liberty, faith, and love.
>
> These words remind us that the duty of our generation of Americans is to renew our nation's faith—not focused just against foreign threats, but against selfishness, cynicism and apathy. . . .
>
> Tonight, I ask you to join me in building that new foundation—a better foundation—for our country and our world.[1]

In such fashion, Carter invokes long-standing veneration for the foundation myth to "renew" our faith in and commitment to ancient truths that are growing "faintly indistinct." So our "duty" in "building" is really nothing new; rather, it is a continued construction of the original edifice, built on a rock rather than on shifting sand. Such rhetoric is typical of presidential addresses, balancing a tension between confidence in our ability to meet the challenges of the present with the peril that we will not live up to our heritage. That there is a recurrent rhetorical style associated with major presidential addresses indicates a compulsion to return to the foundation myth for legitimating purposes in a changing present. Perhaps, however, Carter's awareness of shaky foundations was on the mark: His speech met with widespread cynicism and apathy.

Civil Religion: Faith of Our Fathers, Holy Faith, We Will Be True to Thee Till Death

Carter's speech is but one of the latest examples of the long-standing foundation myth. Why does such a myth stand or reappear again and again? The reasons are complex, but basically the myth fulfills a deep collective need for *legitimacy,* giving the present significant meaning by linking it with a mythical past. In the unfolding political drama, recurrent crusades and challenges simply make the present the latest act of the play. It is an almost universal impulse for political cultures to make government something more than a mundane administrative matter, "sanctifying" it by placing it within a mystical sociopolitical "sacred canopy."[2] This kind of mythifying sounds almost religious. Indeed, it is.

The desire for legitimation provokes a political order to turn to the institutions that are the guardians of transcendent values for sanctification. Usually, this means religious institutions. Religious myths. serve as referents for political rhetoric and ritual in order to provide a symbolic base for legitimation. In other words, clothing the state in religious garments and investing government with the rich robes of godliness yields popular acceptance. This political use of religious myth amounts to a "civil religion."[3]

Allegedly, the United States is a modern, secular, religiously plural society. Its mythic founding document, the Constitution, explicitly separates church and state, forbidding an "establishment of religion" and permitting the "free exercise" of practically any belief. The United States is not a medieval kingdom with an established church and is not a theocracy, such as an Islamic republic. Yet from its very beginnings, long before the Revolution, there was a belief in the blessed nature of the country. The New England Puritans, in particular, believed themselves to be building a "city on a hill" based on their special covenant with God. And the American revolutionaries, who were religiously diverse (some were even Deists), felt compelled to invoke the Almighty for their cause. Jefferson concludes the *Declaration of Independence* by "appealing to the Supreme Judge of the world for the rectitude of our intentions" and affirming "a firm reliance on the protection of Divine Providence." At the Constitutional Convention, Benjamin Franklin proposed and the delegates agreed that they begin each day with prayers "imploring the assistance of Heaven, and its blessings on our deliberations. . . ." The tradition has persisted in practically every public occasion. Inaugural speeches, for example, typically carry some reference to the ascendancy of God and invoke His blessing. In such speeches, various helpful images of God are conjured up: God the Inscrutable Potentate, God the Witnessing Author, God the Wise and Just, God the Genial Philanthropist, even God the Object of Affection.[4] A president, indeed, is expected to be a kind of large-scale village shaman who leads the people through rituals that reaffirm the myth of the country's special relationship with the Deity.

Civil religion is a sustaining myth for a political culture because it links transcendent values to the nation. America's manifest destiny (recall Chapter 2) can be justified as having divine sanction. Each new leader and program seeks placement in the American heritage by invoking not only the symbols of that heritage but also the transempirical foundation that informs it. Each political time legitimates itself by linkage to an ancient and extant covenant, by externally invoking a sacred source, by "putting themselves in harmony with the fundamental order of the universe."[5] Civic piety, then, is not only a ritual obeisance but has its political uses as a source of sanctification. This is especially true in periods of political threat. In war, for instance, as heavyweight boxing champion Joe Louis reminded us in World War II, "We're on God's side." Threatening enemies are outside the realm of sanctification, labeled "heathen Japs" or "Godless communists." We should not think the Islamic conception of a holy war odd; after all, Western Christian nations sanctify their wars (even against enemy Christian countries) by invoking the aid of the Almighty. World War II, our last "holy war," was conceived as a "crusade in Europe," and every battle was the subject of prayer. A chaplain even said a prayer on Tinian in the early morning hours of August 6, 1945, before takeoff for the crew of a B-29 called the *Enola Gay,* which then dropped an atomic bomb on Hiroshima. General Patton once asked a chaplain for a weather prayer, asking God to lift the fog around Bastogne so that the allies could make air strikes against the Germans.

This is not to say that there are not conflicts and even competing traditions in a political culture over the nature of the mythic covenant. Candidates in elections, for instance, often disagree over the meaning of our blessed status. They emphasize the two major dimensions of the American Dream, as it has been called, either identifying our blessing as materialistic or moralistic. In the Nixon–McGovern race in 1972, for example, Nixon emphasized that our blessing was manifest in the God-given cornucopia of material wealth that we enjoy; McGovern emphasized the moralistic duty to realize God-given rights for all.[6] The conflict is not often so clear. Many politicians strike a rhetorical balance, emphasizing both our material and moral blessings and stressing that, although God-given, they are the result of human efforts, too. Civic piety places us under God, but it does not usually tell us to eschew hard work and moral duty.

It is even possible to talk of different civil religions that revolve around different myths held in a particular region or class within a society. Michael Novak identifies four American civil religions. The first is the *high civil religion of the Northeast,* a liberal and responsible myth held in the "good families" who have a right and duty to lead— the Roosevelts, the Kennedys, the Rockefellers. The myth derives from both Puritan and Anglican sources, giving it both a reformist and an aristocratic flavor. It is a "high" civil religion in the sense that it supports civil liberties and democratic goals more ardently than the other traditions. The second civil religion is the *evangelical and fundamentalist tradition of the South and Midwest,* a populist and even sometimes cynical and vindictive strain. Central to this tradition is the myth of the "little man versus the big boys." Huey Long, George Wallace, and others were part of this political strain. This civil religion overlaps with the third distinct type that Novak identifies, the *purifier's civil religion.* This is a tradition "of those whose vision of American politics is primarily moral and whose felt mission is to purify the American soul, to return the nation to the high ideals of its origins."[7] The purifiers carry the myth of their own moral superiority and believe in that superiority. William Jennings Bryan, Woodrow Wilson, George McGovern, and Jimmy Carter belong to this tradition. The final civil religion is a middle one, one that believes in the myth of small-town and rural virtue but also possesses the shrewdness of the small-town hustler. Basically, it relies on the myth of intrinsic bourgeois goodness and is at home with businessmen. This tradition includes Eisenhower, Truman, and Ford. All in all, these four competing civil religions offer alternative myths to which emerging leaders can appeal.

Because there are different traditions, and because there are restraints on the extent to which political religion can affect government, civil religion in America has been muted. Myths of the State and its religious roots are celebrated, but beyond rhetorical obeisance, traditionally, they have been limited. However, with the recent rise of a fundamentalist Right (both Protestant and Catholic) that is militantly activist and superpatriotic, we may see an attempt to impose a new myth that will attempt to realize directly religious values through political reforms of a reactionary nature. Given the right circumstances, this new myth could mobilize many diverse peoples and groups together in a fanatical "tribal religion in demonic form" that would merge Christianity and America together in a new and politically aggressive covenant.[8]

INSTITUTIONAL MYTHS
Sacred Offices, Sacrificial Office-holders?

Long-standing political institutions survive because of the mythical legitimacy accorded them, but aspects of the myth change. The legitimacy accorded the institution may remain high, even though public perception of the current performance of the members of an institution may decline. The resiliency of an institution, then, may stem from a deeper myth than the popular myths of its current operation; the presidency, for instance, may survive contemporary evaluations of presidents. But our images of an institution do change, and what one era believes about and expects out of an institution varies from another.

Once and Future Presidents

The contemporary presidency is without doubt the most spectacular example of this phenomenon. Historically, Americans have vacillated in their mythical conceptions of the office. After a major scandal, they become disillusioned, but their faith is restored with the election of a new and exciting figure. Sometimes we want strong presidents, at others, weak presidents. When events overwhelm occupants of the office, as it did for the Watergate-beset Nixon, we turn abruptly to the myth of the weak presidency. When the power of the office seems overwhelming, then we are cheered or alarmed by the strong presidency.

Presidents walk in the mythical shoes of giants and live in a mansion that is a mythic museum strewn with the holy relics of the giants and their ladies. One can see the Lincoln bedroom, the room of the "martyred Christ of Democracy's passion play," to use Clinton Rossiter's phrase.[9] But in fact, the office has been occupied mostly by men of less than gigantic stature—Buchanan, Arthur, Coolidge, and so on. Further, there have been long periods when the myth of presidential power has been discredited, since the real power in American politics resided in other institutions—Congress or the Supreme Court.

Not only do ordinary people vacillate in what they want out of the presidency, so, apparently, do intellectuals. In the late nineteenth century, Lord Bryce wrote a famous chapter entitled "Why Great Men Are Not Chosen President" in order to explain that the great majority of presidents are undistinguished and that the office is weak. In 1940, another Englishman, Harold Laski, argued that although the weak presidents are a problem, crises have been solved by strong presidents equal to the task; or, in his words, ". . . The hour has brought forth the man."[10] Up until Franklin Roosevelt, liberals thought the office too weak; after Roosevelt, conservatives thought it too strong. The cult of the presidency kept urging additional powers for the president, and liberals in Congress resisted conservative efforts to curtail, for example, war-making powers and treaty-making powers. But with the Johnson and Nixon presidencies, the liberals became scared of the imperial presidency, especially with the national security powers they fantasized that Nixon was exercising; yet many conservatives defended the strong, even defiant, presidency as the way to ensure law and order and aggressive anticommunism. By the late 1970s, the situation seemed reversed again, with liberals calling for a renewed powerful (and of course liberal) presidency and conservatives chipping away at presidential initiatives.

It is plausible that the difficulties faced by the United States in the late 1970s were the result more of historical developments than of the loss of the presidential magic wand after Watergate. But many Americans invest so much mythological currency in the presidency that they imagine the office and the occupant to possess heroic qualities far beyond those of ordinary mortals. Others have such a negative view of the office and its occupants that they can't believe that presidents have any positive qualities. Both views are myths: the former the more traditional myth of the benevolent and powerful presidency, the latter the post-Watergate myth of the malevolent or diminished presidency.

Not only are myths about the office mercurial, so also are myths about the individual presidents. It is astonishing that, except for Eisenhower and Kennedy, every president since Roosevelt has left office with his popularity in public opinion polls collapsed. Truman, Johnson, Nixon, Ford, and Carter lost heavily in the polls as their administrations progressed. (Eisenhower and Kennedy had their problems too: Eisenhower's popularity plummeted to 40 percent approval during the recession of 1958, and Kennedy's fell from a high 83 percent approval after his worst decision, the Bay of Pigs, to 57 percent just before his death, after a summer of civil rights activity.) Upon assuming office, presidents are usually accorded high popularity, especially in the case of Truman and Johnson (87 percent and 80 percent, respectively), who succeeded presidents who died in office. This suggests that people, as Richard Nixon said in one of his taped conversations, "still want to believe."

The myth of the president suffers, however, when the occupant does something, or when something happens, that the public thinks should have been handled differently. Sometimes presidential popularity rises after a failure (such as the Bay of Pigs) or a dramatic little success (such as the rescue of the S.S. *Mayaguez*) but goes down after a controversial victory (for example, Senate ratification of the Panama Canal Treaty) or even an event over which presidents have no control (for example, the fall of China or Iran). These wild shifts and unpredictable positive and negative reactions probably reflect the paradoxical myths that characterize popular expectations about the presidency.[11] Presidents are, in a sense, damned if they do and damned if they don't: If they are restrained in foreign policy, for example, they are scored for being too conciliatory and not "standing up to the Russians" or some such; if they are aggressive, they are scored for dangerous adventurism and "gunboat diplomacy." As Cronin notes, a president is in a dilemma where "he is asked to use power continuously, even though by doing so he will usually lose popular support and prestige."[12]

Indeed, presidents we eventually regard as great are often not so perceived in their day. Lincoln, of course, was very unpopular during much of the Civil War, and Jefferson and Truman left office in great public disfavor. But historians, who appear to enjoy "Top Ten" mythifying as much as political scientists (see Chapter 7), recurrently vote to rank the presidential giants. These rankings may be accurate, but it is almost always in retrospect (as in the case of Lincoln) that a president takes on those mythic qualities that he was not seen by his contemporaries to possess. A reputation for greatness emerges only after popular perceptions as well as historians' perceptions change through the perspective of temporal distance. Truman, for instance, left office damned for "corruption, Korea, and communism" with one of the lowest public opinion ratings ever; but later, in nostalgic remembrance and in the light of some subsequent presidents (not to mention adroit self-promotion by the aged ex-president), Truman became a mythic figure so venerated that an actor, James Whitmore, made a successful national tour in a one-man show about Harry Truman. (Truman now ranks eighth in historians' estimations.[13]) Also, in the heat of political turmoil, presidents are often scapegoats, convenient culprits for our troubles. But in time, the negative assessment can be transformed into a positive judgment. If it is true that many of us believe in the myth of the presidency, perhaps presidents really acquire a mythic mantle only when they are safely retired or dead. Revisionism, then, is not only a mythifying habit of historians but one of the popular mind as well.

Perhaps what sustains the myth of redemption through presidential action, despite a host of disconfirming messages, is a popular need to believe that a president can somehow save the country through miracles. Despite Lincoln's confession that he did not control events but rather that events controlled him, we still want to believe that presidents do control events. It is like the archaic faith in the magic of kings, who were thought to call upon supernatural powers to bend reality to their will. Also, as in tribal societies, there is the impulse to blame the president if times are hard and frustrations mount. If inflation spirals or declines, it is the result of his policies. If Iranians revolt against the Shah, he should have anticipated and controlled the situation. In the presence of domestic or international problems, presidents become convenient mythic scapegoats, identifiable targets for blame. We reassure ourselves with the myth that "if _____ were president, he would have done X, or he would not have let Y happen." Presidents are objects of mass transference. At times, the desire is for heroic presidential action, but at others, the president is the object of mass displeasure.

Myths of Contemporary Presidential Figures

There are myths about important political personages other than presidential figures, but the news media and the public spend most time talking about those people who are, or could be, president. There are relatively few political figures perceived to be presidential timber and running for the office. They attempt to create and perpetuate myths about themselves, popular myths develop around them, and the news media make personal and interpretive myths involving them.

Both potential and actual presidents have a state in the propagation of positive myths about themselves. Presidential press offices try to shape popular perceptions by portrayals of the president; for example, he *always* works hard, even on vacation (the working vacation). Similarly, presidential aspirants communicate qualities that are part of the mythic role model for the office. The presidential hopeful must appear decisive, vigorous, and experienced. If there are negative aspects to the image, they must be overcome. The Nixon team in 1968 heralded the "New Nixon"—more mature, less combative, a voice of moderation and peace. The Nixon myth was accepted by enough people in that campaign to alter his image and make him a viable candidate. As an alternative, if a candidate's public image is ambiguous enough, people can read into it whatever they desire.[14] Jimmy Carter was such an unknown quality in 1976 that people could mythify that he was what they desired in the next president.

Popular mythmaking about presidential figures may occur independently of either the candidate's publicity efforts or the press, although both are major sources of popular myth (see Chapters 4 and 6). Popular myths usually derive from a combination of all three. But popular mythmaking alone is important. There were, for example, popular fantasies about the 1970 incident at Chappaquiddick in which Edward M. Kennedy drove a car off a bridge and a young woman was drowned. The incident has receded in popular consciousness for the moment, but it is likely to resurface if Kennedy were to become a presidential candidate. There are a variety of tales about Chappaquiddick in popular gossip—true or false, sincere or vicious: that Kennedy was drunk, that Mary Jo Kopechne was pregnant, that they were on their way for a nude moonlight swim, and so on. Such gossip is not unusual when it involves major public figures, but it clearly has political effects. Such myths haunt presidential figures, and they often find it difficult to put mass rumors about them to rest. Certainly Kennedy, as a presidential candidate, would find the inevitable revival of such tales disturbing, since by implication they would raise again the old questions about his stability and integrity.

Since we deal with the press as mythmaker elsewhere (Chapter

6), we need not belabor the role the press plays in presidential myth-making. We do note here that the news media make at least two kinds of myths about presidential figures: (1) myths about them personally, and (2) myths about what they mean or augur, that is, interpretive myths. The former is simple enough: The press engages in presidential mythmaking by communicating a president's and/or aspirant's personal habits and political style to the public. If he or she is pictured as larger than life but also possessing human qualities, as many presidential candidates are, the media paint a verbal and picture portrait consonant with widespread presidential myths. Photo journalists are fond of picturing presidents in moments of heroic intensity or ponderous brooding: Kennedy's outlined form leaning over an oval office table; Ford exulting over *Mayaguez*; Carter alone at the Camp David talks or at the Mideast peace settlement, seeking inspiration.

Perhaps more important are interpretive pieces on presidential figures. These appear in Sunday supplements to newspapers, "Segment Three" reports on evening news programs, and in the slick periodicals, such as *New Times*. The election of Carter inspired much mythmaking about the rise of the New South and the shift of power in the country to the southern rim. James Dickey, the Southern poet who gave an inaugural poem at Carter's inaugural, saw Carter as a mythical hero from the South representative of its virtues—its earthiness, its gentleness, its ability to endure. "The South is the future," he intoned, and a southern president augured the spread not only of that region's power but also of its virtues.[15]

But as the Carter administration proceeded, the press (and the public) had difficulty evaluating Carter (see Chapter 6 for a detailed account). He occupied a kind of "fuzzy middle" and identified with neither regional values nor bold, innovative programs. This inspired a host of Carter images: Carter the amateur, the inept, the unappreciated, the weak, the man for the times, the strange, the historically unlucky. Perhaps all this was simply a product of Carter's deliberate decision to retain maneuverability. In any case, one thing seems clear: part of the ambiguity in the perception of Carter was that he lacked mythic definition; that is, he lacked some accomplishment that excited people and gave his presidency a definite symbol as mythic referent. The energy bill, the administrative reform bill, even the China recognition caused rancor and confusion for many and certainly did not inspire excitement. Perhaps every president needs some key event, some identifiable achievement that will provide mythic definition, the anchoring entry in his biographic sketch in *The World Book* encyclopedia. The Kennedy myth was made by the Cuban missile crisis, the Johnson myths by the flurry of Great Society legislation and then by Vietnam, and the Nixon myth by Watergate. Carter, it seems, still needs to make a myth. For a moment, it appeared that the Camp David accords on the Middle East were promising, but the seemingly endless bickering and stalling of the follow-up task spoiled the dramatic first blush of the accords, and Carter's precipitous rise in the polls slowly evaporated. As yet, the press has not been able to puts its finger on a Carter deed that has enjoyed widespread approbation or condemnation.

Carter's potential rival in the press, Senator Edward Kennedy, has a readymade myth definition, the myth of Camelot. The Camelot myth is the powerful and romantic political myth in contemporary America. The original Camelot, of course, is the mythical kingdom of King Arthur, where the good king and his Round Table of noble knights commit themselves to the fight for justice. They fail, but their ideals and their heyday are honored; indeed, they may be merely resting in a cave in Avalon, from whence the "once and future king" will someday return, and the Golden Age will be restored. A few nights after John F. Kennedy was assassinated in 1963, the bereaved Mrs. Kennedy gave an interview to Theodore H. White, which was later published in *Life* magazine. Mrs. Kennedy recounted how at night the President liked to hear the last song from the musical, *Camelot,* and especially Arthur's last line: "Don't let it be forgot/that once there was a spot/for one brief shining moment/that was known as Camelot." Mrs. Kennedy told of how Jack, as a sick child, liked to read of the Knights of the Round Table and how "for Jack history was full of shining heroes."[16] Camelot became the metaphor of the "brief, shining moment" of the Kennedy presidency. In the shock and pathos of the assassination and funeral, the realities of the poor legislative record; the Bay of Pigs; and the decline in the polls, with the civil rights impasse in Congress and the increased agitation in the South faded: What formed was a romantic myth of the gallant knight cruelly slain and his lady fair left to pine. Nearly two decades after 1963, the Camelot myth retains considerable salience.

In the years following JFK's death, Kennedy apologists disassociated themselves from policies, especially Vietnam, that Kennedy had been instrumental in perpetuating. Articles frequently asked, "What would JFK have done?" with old Kennedy hands maintaining that he would, of course, not have made the mistakes of his successors. An interesting popular piece in 1977 by Jack Anderson talks again with "those who knew him best" and finds that they "believe the world would have been brighter." Unfortunately, ". . . more than a President was killed in Dallas; a promise for the future died with him." There would have been no Vietnam, no Watergate; J. Edgar Hoover would have been fired; Kennedy aide Ted Sorenson claimed there would have been "a different atmosphere": no black unrest, alienation of the young, or loss of idealism.[17] So the "if only JFK had lived" myth became part of the contemporary American political folklore, fed by political turmoil and social problems that made people nostalgic for a happier and more hopeful time. Such mythmaking perpetuates more than the Camelot myth; it also perpetuates the myth that, given the right president, heroic action will save the day. The "if Kennedy had lived" myth was to be complemented later by the murder of Robert Kennedy when he ran for president. And the long flirtation of Senator Edward Kennedy with the office keeps it alive.

Even now, there is an inexhaustible interest in the glamorous Kennedys. Joan Kennedy, estranged wife of Ted Kennedy, "came out of the closet" about her alcoholic, psychiatric, and marital problems in celebrated fashion. There is endless speculation about "Will Ted run?" Kennedy believers abound among pundits and columnists. In 1978, Jimmy Breslin wrote a remarkable column comparing the dull Carter with the "powerful, exciting voice" of Edward Kennedy, concluding that ". . . tomorrow morning people get up and the day waits and the prices are too high for them and the income is too low and there is a steady undercurrent of being troubled and there is one voice that goes against what everybody else is saying, and at the same time it becomes the only voice that reminds us that perhaps we can be happy."[18] Even though Jacqueline Kennedy sorrowfully concluded, in the original White interview, "There'll never be another Camelot again," the myth and the romantic hope behind it die hard. It seems clear that the emotional investment journalists like White and Breslin have in the Camelot myth ensures its continuation, and indeed the press and public fascination with the myth might play a role in the re-emergence of Kennedy as a presidential contender. Kennedy's lead in public opinion polls over Carter and any other major presidential figure remains substantial. Significantly, his lead transcends ideology, class, region, age, and other factors.[19] This gives us a clue that his appeal is less programmatic than mythical. Perhaps there is, in the depths of despair of the late 1970s, a desire for the reincarnation of Camelot. After all, Arthur was supposed to return from exile in Avalon someday to restore the Golden Age.

Kennedy's contemporary mythic inheritance and Carter's mythic ambiguity pale beside the puzzlement surrounding California Governor Edmund "Jerry" Brown. If Carter is the representative of the New South myth and Kennedy of the Camelot myth, then Brown is the representative of the California myth. This myth takes many forms in contemporary America, but it boils down to the belief that California is the wave of the future, the augur of trends, the setter of styles. California is the future, the center of a postindustrial American civilization, what Brown has called a "Pacific culture." California is now what the rest of the country is or will soon be, and it is destined to be the center of power and adventure in the future. Some interpretive journalists make much of the "California Dream" in a cultural sense and declare that the election of Jerry Brown as president would symbolize the political surrender of the rest of the country to California values and style. The myth is that because California influences much of America's taste, style, and communications, the rest of the country will adopt not only its culture, but also its politics. Skeptics doubt whether many other areas of the country are like California culture, except in the most superficial ways. Similarly, other states have very different political cultures and habits than California: It seems unlikely that Indiana and New Hampshire politics will more and more resemble California politics. Moreover, California politics and culture have a negative reputation that might inhibit the spread of "Californianess" and of strong national support for Brown. California has a reputation for the bizarre: cults, hippies, Hollywood, and Marin County, not to mention such political extremes as the radical right groups of Orange County. Brown's national candidacy might reveal how much many people participate in the negative California myth, for example, that Brown is strange, opportunistic, full of hype, trendy, unpredictable. For good or ill, presidential figure Jerry Brown lies within the mythic field of California, and it remains to be seen whether this scenery will help or hinder his apparent ambitions.

It should be noted that myths about presidential figures change over time. Perceptions of politicians alter, given transformations in the public persona of a political figure. A long-standing public figure can undergo several transformations in the course of a career. A classic recent example of this was Senator Hubert Humphrey. Humphrey was a major Senate figure and potential presidential candidate from the late 1950s through 1976. But the public face of Humphrey underwent several changes. There was HHH, the Liberal Dynamo of the 1950s Senate; Humphrey, the Amateurish Candidate of 1960; Vice President Humphrey, the Liberal Connection of 1964; Humphrey, the Establishment Candidate of 1968 ("Bump the Hump," chanted the antiwar activists); the "Last Hurrah" Humphrey of 1972, running futilely against McGovern; and the Foolish Humphrey of 1976, toying with the idea of one last run at it. Finally, there was the terminally ill Humphrey of 1977, who became Hubert the Beloved Elder Statesman, the Happy Warrior tragically denied the presidency in bygone days. Younger politicians of national stature should reflect that a long public career will undoubtedly contribute to shifting public and press myths over time. Given the vagaries of a national public career, one's ability to control myths about oneself is probably limited and is often the joker in the deck of presidential accession and success, and of final apotheosis.

Congress: The Citadel and Claghorn

Congress is an institution about which Americans have never made up their minds. The greatest deliberative body in the world, some say: The citadel of freedom in which "profiles in courage" emerge. A second traditional image is more negative: Congress is corrupt, remote, inefficient, reactionary. "There is no permanent criminal class in America," said Mark Twain, "save Congress." The popular image of Congress includes the mythical Senator Claghorn, an alcoholic blowhard who, although geriatric, leads a libertine and corrupt existence in an institution that moves at a glacial pace. Popular conceptions of the contemporary Congress are not high. Pollster Louis Harris reported to a congressional committee in 1976 that Congress ranked low in perceived ethics. Of ten groups scaled, only corporation executives and labor leaders ranked lower. Briefly in 1974, when the House Judiciary Committee considered the impeachment of President Nixon, the Congress got a higher public job rating than the presidency. But by 1978, in another Harris poll, those expressing "a great deal of confidence" in the Congress fell to 10 percent of the public, an all-time low, and the executive branch had fallen to 14 percent, in neither case something to brag about. Yet, amazingly, in the same poll, when people were asked to rate the job *their* own congressman was doing in contrast to Congress as a whole, they rated their representative 49 to 43 percent positive! The logical contradiction between the two positions might well relate to the negative myths about Congress as an institution. An individual congressman, on the other hand, is palpable and is perhaps perceived as hard-working, honest, and effective, especially if he serves constitutents' demands; but at a mythic level, shadowy processes and sinister figures operate. Although *our* congressman is not a part of it, Congress as a whole is suspect, a variation of the "us and them" myth (see Chapter 1). As an institution, then, Congress fares poorly in public esteem, although individual members fare much better.

The notion that Congress does not work very well, that it has let its power erode to the executive branch, and that it is populated by reactionary do-nothings is challengeable. Most congressmen, argue their defenders, are sincere and diligent public servants. They have their problems, the defense goes, but they are not very different from people in other organizations—corporations, universities, even churches. Corporate executives, for instance, probably have as many womanizing and alcohol problems as congressmen. The perquisites of power, such as expense accounts, are a fact of business as well as legislative life. Congressmen are probably no more unethical as a professional class than, say, accountants, and it is likely that they are more efficient than many boards of directors and, certainly, nonpolitical legislative bodies. They are, as a whole, probably more well informed on public matters than the mass of people in the country, and they may well make more rational decisions than most. As to their power eroding to the executive branch, one would have great difficulty convincing recent presidents of that. For good or ill, Congress gutted Carter's domestic programs, hamstrung Nixon's foreign policy (and nearly impeached him), and became the elite center of opposition to Johnson's Vietnam policy. Condemnation of Congress as an institution is based on ignorance, since many people have little idea as to how the institution works and cannot even name their own congressmen (in the Harris poll mentioned above, it was found that just half of those polled could name their representative and that only 42 percent knew which political party the legislator belonged to). However, there is just enough truth to negative myths about Congress to keep them alive. The press and the public thrive on stories of moral turpitude about a member of Congress, which reinforces their "bad man" myths about congressmen. Spectacular stories about the escapades of a Wilbur Mills or a Wayne Hays feed the image of congressional lechery and alcoholic endeavor. Similarly, "Koreagate" and other affairs involving money perpetuate perceptions of crookedness. Construction of palatial congressional office buildings strikes many as a throwback to imperial Roman luxury. News items often reinforce the popular image of Congress: "Those people up there" are doing terrible things at our expense. If the popular myth is partially accurate, it should be pointed out that congressmen are *local* elites, recruited from parochial areas. The corrupt acts so widely condemned may be accepted fare among local fellows back home. It is likely, however, that the corruption myth performs something of a similar popular function as the presidential myth described above.

Our problems can be displaced onto the popular political object "Congress" by mythifying it as a citadel of waste and frivolity. The slow pace of legislation, the persistence of unresolved problems, and the complexities of the legislative process can all be reduced and explained through the corruption myth.

Congressmen attempt, of course, to allay popular myths, and indeed congressmen often succeed in preserving positive popular conceptions of themselves by disassociating themselves, even by running against, the institution in which they serve. By keeping the mess in Congress at a mythical level, they save their careers. Voters can vote for them while experiencing no conflict with their myth of the institution. Congressmen thus try to build independent myths about themselves: that they deliver for the district, that they fight against evils on Capitol Hill on their constituents' behalf, that they are powerful figures in the councils of government. Congressmen nominally sponsor many bills to prove to their constituents that they are active. When they speak to groups in their district, they often drop lines such as "When I spoke to the President in the Oval Office the other day. . . ." Well-publicized errands for constituents build a local myth about the quality of the legislator's service and concern.

Thus politicians in Congress can turn out a good myth of their own for political purposes. Myths in embryonic form can be exploited (although not necessarily cynically) in order to publicize the congressmen and/or the issue. Through the political magic of a congressional shaman, many an issue can be conjured up. Take the ever-vigilant congressional official who identifies evil and exposes it with alarm. A famous use of myth for political gain was the outcry over communism after World War II, especially by Senator Joe McCarthy. The Communist issue was partially created by opportunists, but it did evoke very real fears that many people entertained about Soviet expansion. Communism was given a domestic existence by congressional publicity. It then became an insidious "cancer" eating away at our social vitals. Communism became a congressional obsession with many people, both in Congress and out, for several years.

Such popular myths become politically important through the good offices of someone in the House or Senate who can bring the myth to reality by exposing it in a public forum. In response to some lurid or titillating public event, congressmen can then hold alarmist investigative hearings to promote the event into a mythical threat about to engulf the nation. The Communist scare of the 1950s aroused fantasies about the Chinese Communists swarming ashore at San Diego and indeed entered popular culture in many overt and covert forms (see Chapter 5). There have been many such investigations, catching the imagination of press and public with varying success. Organized crime—the myth of the Mafia—has had its inning, but after *The Godfather,* it seems to have been played out. Members of Congress and the Ford administration mounted a nationwide inoculation program based on the myth of an imminent swine flu epidemic.

Recently, the menace of religious cults has become a favorite subject of congressional inquiry. Senator Robert Dole held informal hearings on the matter, and jeremiads and horror stories flowed from witnesses. One witness claimed that 20 million Americans belong to alien and dehumanizing cults. Spectacular insanities (such as the Jonestown massacre) and the omnipresence of Moonies and Hare Khrisna on city street corners fed the myth of the spread of cultism. Congressional exploitation of the cult myth taps a very real mass fear: Cults symbolize the consequences of the abandonment of old values, the presence of false gods and prophets, and the disturbing infusion of the bizarre in American life, all of which may affect our children. Like domestic communism in the 1950s, cultism in the 1970s seems an insidious threat that may affect us personally and, like communism, may turn our children into robots manipulated by an alien ideology and a foreign master. But again like the Communist myth (and indeed the organized crime myth), the cult menace provides an identifiable and defeatable phenomenon. Like Alger Hiss and Al Capone before them, Jim Jones and Reverend Moon serve as mythic figures personifying threat in the wake of rapid change, more easily identifiable—and more entertaining—than amorphous and complex threats, such as global corporations and nuclear proliferation. Congress often supplies the forum for such titillating myths, which reinforce our fears and fantasies. Our myths about Congress may not be as unreal as the myths congressmen make about us.

The Supreme Court: Mythmaking in Black Robes

The Supreme Court of the United States is a unique judicial institution, and there have been many myths about it in both the past and the present. Indeed, whatever power it has derives in considerable measure from its mythic status as guardian of the Constitution. The Court's legitimacy stems from its Olympian separation from the humdrum of ordinary politics. Therein lies the mystique of learned jurists interpreting a sacred document and enunciating eternal principles of law and justice. This myth extends to large sections of both the mass and elite public.[20] This is not to say that specific decisions, or even specific Courts, do not bring about negative reactions, and even negative myths. But in the long run, even as the Court is embroiled in controversial political issues—racial integration, criminal procedure, and school prayer—the myth of the guardian Court survives specific issues.

The myth of the guardian Court is all the more astounding when one reflects that it constantly reinterprets the Constitution, a venerated document virtually chiseled in stone for many Americans. The Court gives new meaning to the Constitution out of respect for "the felt necessity of the times," applying the document to novel circumstances. Even when the Court overrules a past interpretation, it frequently argues that it has now discovered what the original intent of the Constitution was all along! Such action sustains the Court as a mythic institution and the Constitution as a mythic document.

Through legal fictions, the Court does not make political decisions, only mythic ones.

The power of the myth of the Supreme Court lies in its institutional reputation; indeed, whatever power it has to shape public policy also stems from this. The Supreme Court has survived various attempts by the Congress and the president to curb its activities and indeed has survived widespread public refusal to comply with its edicts. Long after it decreed in 1954 that public schools be desegregated "with all deliberate speed," they are still segregated. School prayer is still practiced. For all the talk about judicial activism, federal court powers of enforcement and indeed willingness to intervene in controversial issues are still restricted. The Supreme Court is reluctant to overturn congressional or executive acts. For example, it would never rule on the constitutionality of the Vietnam War. It is true that it agreed to hear and rule on the extent of executive privilege in the Watergate crisis, culminating in *Nixon v. United States* (1974). But one can argue that this was a case that sorely tested the myth of the Court itself. Nixon's claim that the presidency had qualities placing it beyond legal jurisdiction was in defiance of the central myth of the Court as final arbiter of the supreme law of the land. Nixon's political and legal position was a threat to the very myth that sustained the Court. Court justices may have sensed that whereas it can let school districts quietly defy desegregation orders, it could not survive a defiant president who claimed to be above the law. The contemporary respect accorded the Court was such that, unlike Andrew Jackson, Nixon reluctantly acceded to the ruling.

Even though a topical myth—such as believing that lenient criminal procedure decisions increase crime rates—may weaken public support for the Court, the long-standing guardian Court myth still has considerable depth. Whenever there is some great public controversy, there is a strong impulse to take it to the Supreme Court. The myth that courts are more impartial and fair than other, more "political" institutions, feeds this impulse. Supreme Court justices are above politics, freed from the constraints associated with Congress and the president. But judicial decisions are no less political than other institutions; judges read public opinion polls and election returns like anyone else and are sensitive to what's happening in their political environment. Not only is the Supreme Court reluctant to rule against the political tides of the moment, but it is adept at side-stepping or equivocating important decisions that arouse great conflict and passion. Solomon-like, it will often structure decisions so that everybody thinks he or she gets a piece of the action. The *Bakke v. Regents* case over affirmative action in medical school admissions gave all sides the impression that they had gained something by the decision. In such fashion, the Supreme Court survives as a powerful force in politics. Oddly, the Court is both empowered and constrained by its own myth: Whatever power it has to affect things stems from the long-standing myth of the wisdom and umpire status of the Court; but if it attempts to extend its power into areas that are too controversial or to run against the political grain, the Court endangers its mythic base. This illustrates both the power and the fragility of myth, and demonstrates why institutions walk an historical tightrope between maintaining the long-standing myth of the institution and responding to the vagaries of the moment.

POLITICAL MYTHS IN IDEOLOGICAL GARB

Political ideologies are a third set of myths of long standing adapted to the contingencies of the present. An ideology consists of interrelated images and ideas yielding people a mythic map of the political world, orienting their political images and responses to the past, present, and future. Throughout American history there have been ideologies variously labeled liberal, conservative, radical, and so on. They all have a tradition and a past, a set of more or less enduring ideas and goals, and a way of looking at the political world. Their interpretation in the present and their political programs for the future are usually linked to long-standing myths from the past. Liberals, for example, link their aims with the myth of civil religion (for example, the push for black equality sanctified by America's divine mission) as well as the myth of institutions (for example, the strong liberal presidency is a voice for progress against parochial and reactionary forces in Congress and the states). Contemporary political ideologies possess a mythic component not only by their linkage to symbols drawn from the past, but also because they have linked to the future. Ideologues believe themselves the wave of the future: Given time, the public will either return to or realize the wisdom of their perspective and program.

It is significant that advocates of all major ideological positions in America appear to share a myth of majority support for their aims. They believe that out there is an incipient, hidden majority that will someday rise and do what should be done. Liberals have long entertained the notion of a liberal majority in the country, conservatives of a conservative one. Both the ardent followers of liberal George McGovern in 1972 and those of conservative Barry Goldwater in 1964 believed in the existence of a hidden majority that would magically appear on election day and sweep their man to power. Radicals of both the right and left make the same claim. Activists of the far right fantasize about great potential support among a correctly informed mass, and far left leaders believe in the potential of mass consciousness and the advent of a large revolutionary force. In all cases, there is an impulse to validate narrow beliefs by claiming that they are shared, or could be shared, by the mass public. All schools of thought thus believe in a kind of democratic myth: that their views are valid because they are shared by an imagined majority.

Every ideological camp sees the contemporary world from a mythic viewpoint. Although the issues of a moment are topical, ideologies interpret the present in terms of the myth they bring to the issue. The recognition of the People's Republic of China can be viewed through an ideological pair of glasses: The liberals see it as a long overdue recognition of reality, the conservatives as a sellout to a communist power, the radicals (of both right and left) as a way in which powerful elites are extending influence. These are ideo-mythic responses, reactions to a present issue or choice deriving from mythic principles of a given perspective. The liberals, for example, explain the recognition of China as flowing from the growing maturity of America's relationship with communist countries and justify it in terms of opening doors and thereby lessening hostility.

Thus political actors who are closely identified with one part of the ideological spectrum respond to a current event by using myth as a cue. Many political events and processes evoke oftentimes predictable mythic responses. During the developing shortage of gasoline and other fuels in the 1970s, for example, conservatives like Ronald Reagan argued that de-regulating the fuel industry and thereby creating the incentive for profit and investment would help to solve the energy crisis; but liberals like Senator Henry Jackson argued for more regulation and mandatory price controls. The conservatives brought with them to this debate their myth of free enterprise, that the wisdom of the marketplace, the unseen hand of supply and demand, produces positive results. The liberals brought the myth of government action, the wisdom of administration problem solving, the seen hand of governmental regulation, to produce the desired effect. Conservatives see big business, such as the oil companies, as trustworthy and the source of solutions; liberals see such companies as untrustworthy and the source of problems. The liberal–conservative dialectic on this and other matters often proceeds on mythic assumptions. John Maynard Keynes once remarked that when you hear a contemporary politician talking about economics, he is likely to espouse the ideas of some long-dead academic scribbler. The myths of both dead (Adam Smith, Keynes) and living (John Kenneth Galbraith, Walter Heller, Milton Friedman) economists become myths for politicians.

Economic myths are a classic example of the application of a long-standing ideological myth to current circumstances. The panaceas of conservative Republicans and liberal Democrats for current economic ills reflect old myths that they apply to a present. Economic myths derive from a past deemed to serve as a model for the present. Conservative Republicans conjure up the myth of the business boom of the 1920s, liberal Democrats the myth of the success of the government programs of the New Deal and thereafter. The rhetoric of economic debate revolves around a scenario that imposes an ideal model (sound economic principle) upon a current reality. Good outcomes (prosperity) are the expected result. But rigid commitment to economic principle among a president's advisors can lead to disaster, both economic and political, if the president cannot rise above ideology. In politics, there is often a tension between principle and an instinct for political survival. Note that presidents who have overruled their economic advisors and stimulated the economy before an election have been victorious. In 1971, for instance, Nixon eschewed the sound economic advice of his Council of Economic Advisors, initiated wage and price controls and expanded the economy, and was re-elected in 1972. In 1976, Ford listened to his advisors, refused to reduce unemployment or expand the economy, and was defeated.[21] Similarly, it is in the interest of presidential administrations to use economic myths to pass the buck, either to justify policies and to shift blame. For example, most presidents have their cake and eat it too by the claim that recessions are a cyclical act of nature but that economic recoveries are a direct result of wise economic policies. Such mythmaking is, of course, used in their political interest.[22]

Both liberal and conservative myths are in the political mainstream; their adherents adjust those myths to the realities of the present and the use of power. Thus Eisenhower and Nixon adjusted conservative rhetoric to the necessities and limits of presidential office. Carter talks a populist line as a candidate and accepts higher interest rates and holds down wages as president. If a political interest, on the other hand, has no real political clout, there is less necessity for compromising or rationalizing myths. Political fringe groups are usually powerless, outside of the mainstream, so their myths go undisturbed. Indeed, they often prefer it that way. As groups, they hold the fantasy that they *really* know what's going on and that others are poor dupes taken in or misinformed. Since such groups oftentimes talk about politics only with each other, they reinforce what they believe within the group and elaborate their world-view into a consistent perspective with breathtaking scope. The right-wing John Birch Society, for example, developed an impressive world conspiracy theory that is the centerpiece of their ideology. The alleged conspiracy is ancient and vast, and it transcends national interest, ideology (communists, socialists and capitalists belong), and personal rivalries. Conspirators include the most recent presidents, world figures, and the heads of large banks and corporations. They meet yearly to coordinate policy. John Birchers say that large-scale events (the revolution in Iran, the recognition of China) derive from secret motives of the conspiracy.[23]

Similarly, the American left entertains a conspiracy myth. It is interesting how much of their conspiracy resembles the right's. For example, both right and left conspiracy theories identify the Council on Foreign Relations as the central institution of the conspiracy.[24] In one well-known left conspiracy theory, the United States is undergoing a struggle between two elite coalitions competing for power, the Eastern Establishment Yankees and the Sunbelt-New South Cowboys. Assassinations, Watergate, Vietnam, and many other political events are, to holders of this view, understood as conspiracy activities.[25] The appeal of conspiracy myths stems in part from a sense of powerlessness and remoteness from the centers of power among estranged political interests. The world of politics takes on a coherence and dramatic structure in ideology that it is unlikely to possess in truth. Conspiracy myths are fun: One can play with them forever, cultivate a feeling of being privy to an awesome network, and reinforce the notion that something vast and sinister is afoot in the world.

TOPICAL MYTHS
What's Real Is What's New

Long-standing myths drawn from the civil religion of the United States, the major institutions of the political order, and political ideologies persisting over time are relevant to the political present but have a measure of continuity with the past. The meaning of the relationship of the State to God, the perception and power of the presidency, the forensic articulation of conservatism: All undergo marginal change in the present, but they have historical links to past conceptions. In addition to the long-standing myths, however, there are topical myths that are *de novo* in the present, with only incidental linkage to a past. A present political situation produces myths among both elites and masses. These new myths are the currency of political discourse of the moment. Ideas and images develop and spread out among the politically interested, becoming the myths of that period. Most eventually recede from consciousness and lose the salience they once possessed, often to the extent that future generations wonder how anybody could have believed them and puzzle over what all the fuss was about.

Let us illustrate what we have in mind. The Watergate era was a political present now quickly receding from public consciousness. But in 1972–1974, Watergate conjured up a new language of political myths. Indeed, much of the whole Watergate story involved the interplay of, and the attempt to define, myth. The original White House myth about the Watergate break-in—that is, that it was a petty third-rate burglary— became less and less plausible as the story unfolded. A counter-myth developed that the break-in was the tip of the iceberg, part of a whole fabric of conscious policies designed to undermine the Constitution and create a National Security State. During the Senate Committee hearings chaired by Sam Ervin in 1973, the press began to ask: "Does the trail lead right into the Oval Office?" The Saturday Night Massacre (Nixon's firing of officials charged with investigating the whole affair) made the unthinkable—impeachment—thinkable. Senator Barry Goldwater refused to believe the president culpable unless "a smoking pistol" was found. Questions emerged about Nixon's mental health. Presidential tapes revealed a world of rugged conversations. A debate proceeded over the extent of presidential power. With Nixon's resignation, there was much handwringing over the crisis in confidence. Some even took it to mean that the system works.

The world of Watergate developed in a political present, a world of events and processes that were the topic of that time. The myths about Watergate occupied us during "that point in time." They were the topic of focus, of interest, of talk, of the press. Vietnam and SALT and the Mideast were there, but on the fringes of our minds. Political reality was the Watergate story. It was salient, hot, at the center. We participated in, believed and disbelieved, the various myths that swirled around the controversy. But now that time is past, and the topical myths of that period recede from view. We no longer sense the centrality and immediacy of the question of executive privilege nor do we debate the credibility of John Dean's testimony. The concerns of that present had an historical fallout, but what was at stake was transitory. Similarly, looking back at other pasts, the burning issue of the day seems puzzling or quaint, and we wonder what everybody got so excited about. Who can recall the monumental importance of Quemoy and Matsu or of bimetalism?

In any political present, there is contemporary concern with issues, trends, and moods. The situation in that present seems to exhibit a definite meaning in the here and now. But these aspects of a present are mythical as a property of that present and do not transcend it. Furthermore, the importance ascribed to an issue, trend, or mood is often wrong, a creature of that present's exaggerated imagination. Issues come and go, and the world continues on without their resolution. The issues of the late 1970s, such as a constitutionally mandated balanced budget, were as often as not pseudo-issues, bogus threats and alarms that agitated few people. The proposal to call a constitutional convention to seek an amendment for a balanced budget, for instance, appealed to a deeply help popular myth and was offered as a quick panacea for economic ills. But one doubts that the issue will still be raging in 1985 or that such an innovation would solve as many economic problems as it would create.

Similarly, people living in a political present attempt to identify trends, that is, what the present augurs for the future. Much of journalism concerns itself with such soothsaying (see Chapter 6). But again this is mythmaking. Since the future has not yet occurred, it cannot be predicted; but it can be imagined. Alarm over or anticipation of the future is exciting grist for the mill of the political present, since much of what is at issue involves prediction as to what will happen if we do or do not do something now—for example, if we do not increase defense spending, the Soviet menace will grow. The trend myth is twofold: It typically asserts that we can predict the future and that doing X now will affect the future. In the late 1970s, there was much trend analysis that predicted gloom and doom, drift and decline, penultimate change. Futurism became a major new knowledge industry, largely predicting either Armageddon or a new Dark Age. We were urged to prepare for shortages, social upheaval, nuclear war, and so on. But there is no guarantee that such cataclysms will happen, although one does get the sense that many futurists will be disappointed if they don't. It would seem that such trendmaking is just that: a myth that emerges in a present as a perspective on the future but is only incidentally related to it. The myth tells us more about the present than the future.

A final form of topical mythmaking is mood reading. By this we mean the habit (cultivated by journalists, politicians, survey researchers, etc.) of making generalizations about the collective ideas and feelings of the public. As Walter Lippmann pointed out long ago, the public is a phantom, a reified entity that is the product of the minds of mythmakers.[26] Attributing a mood to such a fictional grouping gives an inchoate mass of people the character of a person, and a mercurial one at that. Even professional pollsters cannot resist the urge to impute a collective will and power to public opinion, as if it were a singular force to be reckoned with. Many journalists do impressionistic mood-of-the-country stories that envision some massive and important shift in the mind of that sleeping giant, the public. "Is

America turning Right?" asks a cover story in *Newsweek*. Pundits see a conservative tide or a rightward drift in the late 1970s. Mood reading, we contend, is largely mythmaking, attributing a structure to a public mind that does not exist. The so-called rightward turn seen by the mood readers was a classic example. The conservative tide myth inspired handwringing and analysis and was believed in by many politicians. The success of Proposition 13 in California, the anti-Equal Rights Amendment movement, anti-abortion activism, and the huge fundraising for conservative politicians and fundamentalist churches proved to many that America was in the grip of the Yahoos. But this mood also occurred in an era in which Edward Kennedy topped presidential preference polls; great majorities in polls favored legal abortions, ERA, and other such liberal measures as gun control; and the Democrats controlled the Congress and most statehouses.

PAST MEETS PRESENT

It has been our argument in this chapter that in any contemporary era, one sees long-standing myths extant in perhaps a new form in the present. Further, topical myths about political issues, trends, or moods emerge from that present but are largely specific to that time. Long-standing myths are strains in American political culture that help to shape expectations in a present. Topical myths help to give the present its unique content. The two types of myths are, of course, related. New conservative myths helped to create the myth of the conservative tide. An institutional myth can itself become a topic at issue, such as the imperial presidency myth. Long-standing myths are often in the back of our minds and undergo modification in relation to the shifting tides of successive political presents. Topical myths come to the front of our minds in a present, but they are subsequently forgotten. It should give us pause to consider that much of what we believe now to be real and true and important about politics is mythical, even more so when we consider that our long-term myths will undergo change and that new topical myths will come and go throughout our lives.

REFERENCES

1. Jimmy Carter, quoted in *The New York Times,* January 24, 1979, p. A13.

2. See Peter L. Berger, *The Sacred Canopy* (Garden City, N.Y.: Doubleday, 1969).

3. See, variously, Robert Bellah, "Civil Religion in America," *Daedalus* (Winter 1967): 1-21; Martin Marty, *A Nation of Behavers* (Chicago: University of Chicago Press, 1976); Michael Novak, *Choosing Our King* (New York: Macmillan, 1974); Sidney E. Mead, *The Nation with the Soul of a Church* (New York: Harper & Row, 1975).

4. Roderick P. Hart, *The Political Pulpit* (West Lafayette, Ind.: Purdue University Press, 1977), pp. 70-72.

5. Berger, *The Sacred Canopy,* p. 33.

6. Walter R. Fisher, "Reaffirmation and Subversion of the American Dream," *The Quarterly Journal of Speech,* 59, no. 2 (April 1973): 160-167.

7. Michael Novak, "In Praise of Cynicism (or) When the Saints Go Marching Out," Poynter Center essay, Indiana University, 1975.

8. Hart, *The Political Pulpit,* pp. 64-65.

9. Clinton Rossiter, quoted in Thomas E. Cronin, *The State of the Presidency* (Boston: Little, Brown, 1975), p. 28.

10. Harold J. Laski, *The American Presidency* (New York: Grosset & Dunlap, 1940), p. 52; James Bryce, *The American Commonwealth* (Chicago: Charles H. Seigel & Co., 1891), pp. 73-80.

11. Cronin, *The State of the Presidency,* pp. 6-10.

12. Cronin, *The State of the Presidency,* p. 9.

13. Henry Steele Commager, "Our Greatest Presidents," *Parade,* May 8, 1977, p. 16.

14. Steven R. Brown and John D. Ellithorp, "Emotional Experiences in Political Groups: The Case of the McCarthy Phenomenon," *American Political Science Review,* 64, no. 2 (June 1970): 349-366.

15. Diana Loercher, "Georgia Poet Who Cast Carter as a Mythical Hero," *Christian Science Monitor,* October 5, 1977, p. 23.

16. See Theodore H. White, *In Search of History: A Personal Adventure* (New York: Harper & Row, 1979), pp. 517-525.

17. Jack Anderson, "John F. Kennedy: Would the World Be Different If Lee Harvey Oswald Had Missed?" *Parade,* November 20, 1977, pp. 8-11.

18. Jimmy Breslin, "Kennedy Charm Puts Carter on Defensive," *Chicago Tribune,* December 23, 1978, Section 8, p. 20.

19. *Louis Harris Survey,* September 1978, press release.

20. Gregory Casey, "The Supreme Court and Myth," *Law and Society Review,* 8 (1974): 385–419.

21. See Edward R. Tufte, *Political Control of the Economy* (Princeton, N.J.: Princeton University Press, 1978).

22. John Kenneth Galbraith, "Let Us Now Praise (Faintly) Famous Economists," *Esquire* (May 1977), 70–71, 158.

23. See, for example, Gary Allen, *None Dare Call It Conspiracy* (Seal Beach, Cal.: Concord Press, 1971); G. William Domhoff, *The Higher Circles* (New York: Vintage Books, 1971).

24. See references cited in note 23.

25. Carol Oglesby, *The Yankees and the Cowboy War* (Berkeley, Cal.: Berkeley Publishers, 1977).

26. Walter Lippmann, *The Phantom Public* (New York: Macmillan, 1925).

PART **II**

MYTHMAKER, MYTHMAKER, MAKE ME A MYTH
MYTH CREATION IN AMERICAN POLITICS

CHAPTER 4

Have I Got
A Deal For You!
Politicians
And Their Flacks

A former aide to Governor Jerry Brown of California tells the following story: One day during the 1974 gubernatorial campaign, he watched Brown review a "law and order" TV commercial he had just filmed. As the ad unfolded, Brown would repeatedly chop the air with his hand and say, "Buzz word . . . buzz word . . . buzz word. . . ." Brown was mightily pleased with himself and what he "said" in the ad. "In fact," he reportedly crowed, "I haven't committed myself to do anything at all." A buzz word, the author goes on to say, is a word or phrase that conjures up associations that are not directly stated but, rather, are implied by the speaker, evoking a positive response to the speaker without his saying anything explicit. "Swift, sure and just" criminal procedure was one such buzz word: "Swift" implied quick punishment, "sure" implied no trivial technicalities, and "just" reassured civil libertarians. The phrase had something for everyone, but the something was symbolic and not tangible.[1]

People make myths about politics for a variety of purposes, even sometimes quite unwittingly. In many cases, the creators of popular culture, news communicators, and political scientists make myths, but they do not necessarily intend to do so. However, the first and perhaps most important source of political myth—politicians and their "flacks" —most assuredly do intend to make myths, even though some of them might ardently deny it. Even though a good bit of political mythmaking by politicians and their flacks is explicitly manipulative, as often as not they do not think of it as mythmaking and certainly not as wrong. In many cases, the politician may be caught up in his own private political myth and may accept as necessary the use of persuasive communications for political purposes. Indeed, the media experts he hires may be equally imbued with his myth and be sincere in what they do. But a sincere man, as Peter Berger has noted, is "the one who believes in his own propaganda."[2] In other cases, of course, politicians and their flacks create myths quite cynically.

"Flack" is a popular, usually derogatory, term for professionals in modern societies who use their organizational and technological skills to sell whatever there is to be sold—organizations, people, images, programs, policies, politicians. Skill at using mass media for selling a political object has spilled over into American politics to the extent that politicians assiduously study the "flack arts" and put them into practice. Jerry Brown is simply one in a long line of political actors who studied and mastered such communications skills. Whether practiced by politicians or their hirelings, one of the great modern sources of political mythmaking is in the proliferation of political persuasion.

THE PROTOTYPICAL FLACK
Josef Goebbels

The prototype of the flack in modern politics was Dr. Joseph Goebbels, the master of communication who helped to create the Third Reich in Germany in the 1920s and 1930s. Goebbels pioneered modern techniques of propaganda, promotion, and publicity. He made Nazi newspapers in Berlin into popular scandal sheets that poked fun at Jewish officials. His articles and speeches pounded on the theme that the Nazi Party and Adolf Hitler were the hope and destiny of Germany. He exploited the popular myth of the stab in the back, that Germany had lost World War I through betrayal by sinister forces at home. He developed stunning campaign advertising, especially posters. He was clever at promotional activities, even at luring non-Nazis to meetings by publicizing provocative themes. He staged publicity stunts, such as marching through communist areas of Berlin to provoke violence and then casting injured Nazi stormtroopers as freedom fighters and martyrs. He was adroit at squeezing publicity out of trivial events, but he also had a gift for political pageantry, developing a set of Nazi rituals and choreographing the Nazi Nuremberg rallies.

Most importantly, Goebbels was instrumental in the creating of the *Führer* myth. He sold an unknown, emotional Austrian, Adolf Hitler, as the "god of the awakening Germany." He introduced the greeting, "Heil Hitler!" and the medieval title of *Führer*, to which all party members swore personal loyalty. He marketed the *Führer* as the embodiment of the Will of the Nation, a personage of mythical background whose mission was to realize the German destiny. Rarely seen in public, Hitler was photographed only in full regalia addressing a mass meeting, hosting foreign leaders, or at his mountain retreat with children or dogs. The *Führerkult* reached the point of almost Christ-like adoration. Pictures showed the Hitler of the early days addressing an eager audience of disciples with the caption: "In the beginning was the word." Women in childbirth would scream Hitler's name or title as an analgesic reflex.[3]

Why mention all this? Because the career of Dr. Goebbels illustrates so many things about the power and possibilities of flackdom in politics. Goebbels was both caught up in the Hitler myth and cynically helped to further it for the German nation. He saw what he did as both manipulative and necessary. And the "little doctor," as Goebbels was called, pioneered many of the techniques of political selling we see now in American politics: political advertising, publicity and promotion, and public relations. Flacks today operate much in the tradition of Dr. Goebbels. Their skills, like his, are in the art of political mythmaking through the adroit use of the mass media. Goebbels simply demonstrates the extent to which a flack can make political myths.

THE PERSUASION INDUSTRY

Flacks may be thought of as "new men" or "new engineers" whose ascendancy has been one outcome of the advent of "technomedia" society. "Foxes rather than lions," Andrew Hacker predicted in 1957, ". . . they can meet the imperatives of a time which calls for the sophisticated manipulation of men's attitudes and sensibilities. . . . Values are judged not by their place in the prescriptive scheme of things, but by their current utility. For the new men it would be suicide to regard individuals as ends in themselves: they must always be viewed as resources to be managed.''[4] (Note that the ranks of the ''new men'' are not chauvinistic; they include many bright and ambitious ''new women,'' of which the character Diana Christianson, played by Faye Dunaway in the movie *Network*, is a parody.)

In many ways, of course, the skills we associate with modern flacks are old hat to politicians and political pros. Andrew Jackson was no less an ''image'' candidate than contemporary politicians, building the myth of Old Hickory. Party managers, such as Mark Hanna, were adept at creating mythologies about politicians (McKinley) and political situations (if Bryan were elected President, the country would go to ruin). Politics has always involved persuading people that something is or is not the case, and communicating that is a highly prized skill.

But in the last several decades in advanced technological societies, a persuasion industry has emerged. This industry involes a set of organizations and jobs that are directed at selling just about everything. Advertisers, TV programmers, public relations firms, publicity agents, promoters of various things: All are engaged in the communication of myth. Modern flacks use their sophisticated technical skills in the propagation of some largely mythical message. Their pitch is to associate what they want to sell with some value or desire on the part of an audience. More subtle than P.T. Barnum, they nevertheless belong in the tradition of finding and appealing to suckers.

Modern flacks are thus propagandists. As the student of modern propaganda, Jacques Ellul, points out, they are scientific in their approach. They use the findings of modern psychology and other behavioral sciences; they are trained in the methods of propaganda useful in a particular field (e.g., advertising and marketing) and belong to professional associations; they work for organizations whose purpose is to propagate messages for effect; and they constantly attempt to refine the methods and impact of their propaganda.[5] They use increasingly precise methods to create and communicate myths.

The major activity of modern flacks is, in the contemporary vernacular, to ''hype.'' Hype is what flacks do: market and sell the myth of some product, person, organization, or whatever. Everything is hyped nowadays: breakfast cereal, rock groups, movie stars, movies, books, religion, universities. The power of hype is central to the flack arts. They must, and do, convince people that there is a difference between aspirin brands; that fashionability can be expressed through dressing a certain way; that movie stars are glamorous; that corporations are benevolent associations comprised of hard-working, ordinary people like you and me; and that driving a particular car makes one distinctive. The proliferation of hype can be seen by the extent to which outrageous self-publicity can create a celebrity: The careers of Muhammad Ali, Evil Knievel, and Alice Cooper are cases in point. Less spectacularly, marketing new products or developing the image of an institution or person is based on the same premise: Carefully constructed communications designed for a perceived audience can affect how people think about the object. Mythmaking is the intent of hype and, if successful, the result.

Primal Themes

Vance Packard, in his book, *The Hidden Persuaders,* pointed out in the late 1950s the degree of sophistication that the flack arts were acquiring. He noted that the requirements of a consumer economy had bred new forces designed to induce further consumption: Depth psychology, motivational research, brand image, and other such terms became the currency of the new marketplace. The new men were increasingly adept at understanding and manipulating deep human needs and desires. "Primal themes" were researched and related to a particular product, institution, or person. Primal themes are deeply held, sometimes unconscious, myths people hold about themselves and the world. For example, Packard identified eight "hidden needs" commonly exploited by advertisers: emotional security, reassurance of worth, ego-gratification, creative outlets, love objects, sense of power, sense of roots, and immortality.[6] This partial list gives an idea of the vanities and fears to which advertising appeals can be linked. The primal theme emphasizes that using a certain product helps one become fashionable, popular, sexually potent, secure, even immortal.

Perhaps the most pervasive primal theme in advertising is the myth of family. Family love and solidarity is a deep-seated emotion and desire in many people. Advertisers repeatedly link the myth of family with a product. We go to a family restaurant; theme parks are family fun; choosy mothers are careful shoppers since "it's for my family." The implication is obvious: The hyped product enhances family life. Consumption is related to a primal myth; by consuming, one's anxieties about family, health, approval, and so forth are allayed. Ads typically present a "fantasy skit" that shows prototypical individuals being "saved" by a product. A woman restores her husband's affection by removing the "ring around the collar," or she wins the approval of significant others by having shiny dishes that are "a nice reflection on you."

Packard, and more recently Wilson Bryan Key, suggest that much of the primal mythology in advertising is subtle, even subliminal. In other words, ads have secret messages that communicate primal themes at an unconscious level. The mere arrangement of objects and persons in visual ads is manipulated to appeal to primal desires. Themes may range from the suggestion of illicit sex being negotiated at a party where a certain brand of liquor is imbibed to hidden images of sexual partners in ice cubes. Key claims that ancient archetypal themes—universal mythical symbols and images—are constantly manipulated by advertisers to appeal to these underlying primal desires.[7] There appears to be no question that there is considerable awareness of and use of primal themes in the expensive and competitive world of advertising. Indeed, even charities use ads constructed by Madison Avenue flacks as threatening and sentimental appeals in order to hype contributions. The National Society for the Prevention of Blindness hired an ad agency that creates horror-movie posters to produce an ad that would appeal to fear: The ad pictures a hand holding an eyeball with the caption: "Kiss Your Eyes Goodbye!"[8]

Pseudo-Reality and Pseudo-Myth

Flacks have been instrumental in the creation of pseudo-realities that people are told they should desire or like. They communicate, through mass media, mythical environments, events, or persons which audiences are supposed to relate to, identify with, enjoy, or act upon. It is a fantasy world that flacks conjure up, one that is linked to the primal desires just mentioned. Advertising, public relations, and publicity flacks have made this into high art. Oil company ads would have us believe that Exxon is a struggling company of just plain folks who are motivated by Salvation Army benevolence and have a high environmental consciousness. Housing developers tell us that we acquire the good life by living in Heritage Acres. Utility companies hire pretty girls to give public information presentations to local groups about the safety and benefits of nuclear power plants. Agents for movie stars stage publicity stunts or encourage fan magazine gossip about the star to aid their client's fame and career. In myriad ways, the mass public is constantly bombarded with myths, realities created for mass consumption.

The proliferation and acceptance of mythical environments, events, and persons in contemporary America is astonishing. We buy not only the pseudo-reality of the world of advertising but also the invented actuality of the game show or talk show on TV. We are accustomed to being entertained by the sit-com peopled by attractive, funny types or by action shows that feature private detectives or bionic women. We are familiar with the marketing of celebrities (rock stars, TV characters, etc.) who often come and go quickly. Perhaps it is a tribute to man's ability to believe in mythical universes; it may also be a tribute to the ability of modern flackdom to bamboozle audiences.

What Is Sold?

Flacks sell many things. Anything that some group with the money wants to sell the public is translated into a marketable commodity by flacks. We have already alluded to many of the things sold, but here we wish to point out how the selling of a variety of things amounts to mythmaking in the process. All of the things we mention here are essentially products, objects for which flacks cold-bloodedly plan proper strategies in order to market them to mass audiences.

Images for sale. Flacks hype images of people. They have the often difficult job of building, maintaining, and sometimes changing the myths that persons want to foster about themselves. Introducing a new movie star, rock singer, or sit-com hero usually involves a publicity agency conducting an extensive campaign to communicate to the public the image that the organization or the personality desires. For instance, when Farrah Fawcett-Majors quite the *Charlie's Angels* TV show, a campaign began almost immediately (and had been planned

for months) to hype her chosen replacement, Cheryl Ladd. Not acci-
dently, Ms. Ladd's picture and information about her began to appear
in *People* magazine, newspapers, and Hollywood gossip magazines
around the time she made her debut on *Charlie's Angels* at the beginning of the fall TV season.

However, it is difficult to maintain the constructed public image
of someone if that person does something that disconfirms the flack
myth. Cher's image was hard to sustain during her marital problems.
Ann-Margret's image changed from that of a sexy and somewhat
floozy young star to that of a more intelligent and mature actress.
Cheryl Ladd, Cher, and Ann-Margret were handled by Hollywood
superflack Richard Grant.[9] Like most image campaigns, this involved
the communication of mythical qualities (in the sense of qualities that
the actresses mentioned may not possess—interests, maturity, even
sexiness).

Flacks also communicate the images of organizations. Corporations, unions, universities, churches, associations, cities: The list is
endless. And it is nothing new. Ivy Lee, a reporter turned flack early
in this century, did publicity work in the 1904 presidential election,
but his first major public relations (PR) account was to build the image of a coal company in 1906. A little later, Henry Ford set up a company News Bureau, since he didn't trust newspapers (especially
Chicago *Tribune* publisher Colonel Robert McCormick, who had called
Ford an "anarchist"). The Ford PR office later became the first "mat
service," sending out stories prepared to put on the presses unchanged
and, of course, favorable to Ford policy. Corporations still invest
enormous time and money in propaganda campaigns. One favorite
pitch that stems from the primal theme tactic is to portray the corporation—which may employ many hundreds of thousands of
people—as a big, happy family. Images of typical employees and
casual, light-hearted management-employee relations portray a
pseudo-reality: that a large modern industrial corporation is a kind of
Walton family that pulls together, loves each other, and gets benefi-
cient things done while whistling a happy tune.

Similarly, cultural institutions once immune to the vulgarities of
selling themselves as products in a marketplace have recently hired
flacks and gone shamelessly after clients. New "media churches" go
after money and converts with a vengeance—vast mailing lists, tele-
thons, slick TV and road show productions, promotional gimmicks,

and so on. The effect is to combine the appeals of that "old-time religion" with modern, cold-blooded propaganda techniques—old myths packaged in new media. Faced with declining numbers of students, American colleges and universities have recently taken to flack arts to hype their enrollments. Many have used, in their mail-out brochures and the like, the primal theme of individuality—the myth that the student will be treated as unique, thus appealing to our modern fears about institutional impersonality and anonymity in the crowd. College flacks appeal to the mythology of contemporary youth without batting an eye. One state university advertised its general education program as "Getting It Together," featuring courses such as "In Pursuit of Awareness" and "Me-ology." A small college put out a psychedelic poster featuring a busty girl wearing a T-shirt strategically captioned "I'm somebody." After hyping the college as a "people place" and a "place where you can be the center of a successful educational experience," the poster invited the prospective student to detach the return postcard, titled "Yes, I'm Somebody Too." The mythical prospect of both individuality and sensuality is a powerful propaganda appeal.

"_____ *Has a Better Idea.*" Flacks hype ideas. On behalf of a particular group or organization, they attempt to convince mass audiences that a certain idea, and the state of affairs or actions stemming from it, should prevail. Idea X sells because of some myth linked to it in a media campaign. This may range from attempts to change ordinary human habits to the reinforcement of master myths. The American Cancer Society hyped the idea of nonsmoking by picturing a fantasy skit involving two cute kids dressed up like their parents while a voice-over said ominously. "Kids love to imitate their parents." Pause. "Do you smoke?" Other groups promote the myths of education, of attending the church of your choice, of freedom of the press. Corporations and business groups in recent years have hired ad agencies to hype their images for the mass public by linking corporate activities to the idea of free enterprise, a master economic myth still held in capitalist America (recall Chapter 3). One recent tactic has been to fund "chairs of free enterprise" in universities, designed to educate students about the operation of the market system. However, such chairs come in for criticism as being veiled propaganda vehicles used by big business to hype a myth, since free enterprise is no longer extant in many market areas (e.g., automobiles, oil, steel, etc.) but serves instead as a convenient slogan for oligopolies or monopolies trying to avoid government intervention.

"Keep truckin'." Flacks also sell the illusion of movement. Many organizations and groups like to convince mass audiences that they are growing, succeeding, changing, or whatever, and they hire flacks to hype, and thus help to create, the force of their movement. The aforementioned media churches constantly conduct extensive campaigns (as in *"Key '73,"* "I Found It!" the recurrent Billy Graham campaigns) that, at least in their media manifestations, communicate the illusion of a great revival, of conversions, and, of course, of contributions. Some observers think that the notion that such campaigns bring about massive increases in the number of believing and practicing Christians is dubious and that the campaigns only reinforce those already prone to believe in and give to such organizations. But the myth of movement is pervasive in their propaganda.

POLITICAL FLACKS AND CONSUMERS

Vance Packard's *The Hidden Persuaders* has a chapter entitled "Politics and the Image Builders," which was one of the first popular accounts of the invasion of politics by flackdom. "Americans," he said, "in their growing absorption with consumption, have even become consumers of politics."[10] By the time Packard wrote in 1957, many social commentators pointed to the growing presence and influence of professional flacks in politics. Actually, the trend had been building for several decades. Whitaker and Baxter had been managing political campaigns in California from the early 1930s. Social scientist Hadley Cantril had advised Franklin D. Roosevelt on public opinion in the early 1940s. Wendell Wilkie was hyped by adroit image-building in the press. Even before television, a man who was to serve as the director of publicity for the Democratic National Committee said of presidential elections:

> The American people will elect as President of the United States in November a nonexistent person—and defeat likewise a mythical identity.
>
> They will vote for and against a picture that has been painted for

them by protagonists and antagonists in a myriad of publications, a picture that must be either a caricature or an idealization.[11]

But with the media revolution of post-World War II, the ability and the opportunity of modern flacks to communicate mythical identities in politics increased. In settings including election campaigns, the White House, and various government agencies, there emerged campaign management firms on retainers; "image committees"; press secretaries; public relations budgets; and an influx of programmers, pollsters, and propagandists. Their successes—and the myths they created about their power—gave them entry into the inner councils of politicians. Some observers, such as political scientists Stanley Kelley, thought that their entry into politics would be beneficial, improving communication between politician and public; others, such as Daniel Boorstin and James Perry, thought that the techniques and cynical attitudes of show-biz and business advertising were destructive of traditional democratic processes.[12] By the 1960s, it was commonplace for major candidates for public office to be handled by campaign management firms, for the White House and major federal establishments (such as the Pentagon) to have large PR staffs, and for political hopefuls to seek advice not from the inner circle of a political party but from the "feasibility studies" of professional consultants.

The advent of the "New Politics" and the access of political flacks to politicians altered the style, the budget, and the experience of many political leaders. Politicians sought photo opportunities, advance men, packaging, aggregate data, PR gimmicks, media exposure, positioning, image management. Richard Nixon, always a bellwether of trends, became a pioneer in this new style. Richard Rovere said of him in the 1950s:

Richard Nixon appears to be a politician with an advertising man's approach to his work. Policies are products to be sold the public—this one today, that one tomorrow, depending on the discounts and the state of the market. He moves from intervention (in Indochina) to anti-intervention with the same ease and lack of anguish with which a copy writer might transfer his loyalties from Camels to Chesterfields.[13]

But Nixon was only symptomatic of a large-scale political trend. Political flackdom is now a billion-dollar industry. People running for national, state, and even local offices increasingly hire professional campaign assistance; flacks pervade the briefing rooms of political executives everywhere; governmental agency heads fret with their flacks over the agency image.

Flacks, politicians, and political commentators talk much about the ethics and long-term effects of the increased sophistication of political selling. Some feel that flackdom in politics translates both the politician and the public into commodities to be produced and consumed, reducing politics to manipulation. More specifically, these critics say, political flackdom makes myths. The candidate's or agency's alleged image is an illusion, a mythical identity with mythical qualities acting in a mythical world. Rather than clarifying political communication with the public, flacks mythologize in order to sell myths about a politician or government or agency to a political audience. Their expertise is *not truth, but credibility*—not how to present the fact of truth, but rather how to present the myth of truth. To these areas and methods of mythmaking we now turn.

FLACKS AND MYTHMAKING IN ELECTORAL CAMPAIGNS

Perhaps the most spectacular area of the growth in political flackdom is the electoral campaign industry. The range (and the cost) of campaign services available is staggering: speechwriting, advertising, computer mail-outs, time buying, polling, fundraising, catering, wardrobe—even complete coordination of every campaign activity. The rationalization of campaign procedures has had many effects, but the one we are concerned with is the use of and creation of myths.

Campaign flacks use myths. It is part of their business to know what myths the voting public hold and to use those myths in the campaign setting. These include primal themes, contemporary myths, myths of us and them, prejudices, and so on. But, as in product advertising, the thrust in elections is to associate the candidate with a mythical theme that will stick.

The most common tactic is to link the candidate with macromyths. The political rhetoric and imagery of candidates typically celebrates the origin and destiny of the political order. The imagery of campaign ads—portrayed in both pictorial and verbal communications—reminds voters of deeply held symbols. Joe McGinniss's backstage look at the 1968 Nixon media campaign found Kevin Phillips writing memo commentary on how to use certain commercials:

> *Great Nation:* This is fine for national use, but viz local emphasis it strikes me as best suited to the South and heartland. They will like the great nation self-help, fields of waving wheat stuff and the general thrust of Protestant ethic imagery. . . . We need a red-hot military music, land of pride and glory special for the South and Border. . . . We need more concern for the countryside, its values and farmers welfare spot, complete with threshing threshers, siloes, Aberdeen Angus herds, et al.[14]

Such imagery, with Nixon's voice-over, reassuring and calm, played upon the deep patriotic feelings many people have about America. Such ads were made systematically and were directed toward regions of the country where campaign organizers thought that linking candidate and macromyth would do the most good.

Since the macromyths of a political culture are complex and even contradictory, presidential candidates often represent different aspects of political mythology in a campaign. The Nixon and McGovern campaigns of 1972 offered two competing rhetorical visions that spoke to aspects of the American Dream. Nixon represented the materialistic myth, whereas McGovern represented the moralistic myth. The materialistic myth is manifest in the American belief in individual effort, work, self-reliance, competition, and the goodness of wealth and success. The moralistic myth is manifest in Christian duty to our fellow man, equality and democracy, reform and morality. (DeTocqueville long ago saw Americans motivated by the incompatible myths of equality and achievement destined to conflict because of the schizophrenia in the American psyche.) McGovern expounded the moral of equality, whereas Nixon extolled the value of individual achievement. McGovern condemned the "special, grasping, greedy interests" who were making the rich richer; Nixon condemned "those who call for a confiscation of wealth." Yet both candidates were haunted by the other aspect of the American Dream: McGovern extolled the work ethic and free enterprise, whereas Nixon, on face value at least, paid respect to egalitarian and compassionate values. Indeed, it may be that when a person votes for a candidate who represents one aspect of the myth, he or she will in effect be nagged by voting against the other aspect that is also part of our political consciousness. As one acute observer noted, "Insofar as one votes for himself in a presidential election, one also votes against himself."[15] In any case, flacks attempt to ascertain what elements of political macromyths their candidates should emphasize.

Myths of "us and them" are also a common theme in campaign propaganda. The most obvious is appeal tp partisanship. Democratic presidential candidates appeal to the ancient loyalties, now somewhat less strong, that sustained the Democratic Party through many an election. Their national conventions, ads, rhetoric, and so on conjure up visions of FDR and the New Deal, Truman, Kennedy, and the whole pantheon of party heroes and attack the villainy of the uncaring and party-of-the-rich Republicans. Jimmy Carter sought to place himself in that Democratic tradition, and he attacked Gerald Ford as the latest manifestation of the Republican villain, Herbert Hoover.

Flacks use primal themes to differentiate us from them by associating positive desires with "our" success, negative fears with "their" triumph. Fears about crime, safety, financial ruin, family values, and the like can be linked to the success of a particular candidate. If the opponent wins, crime will be rife, money inflated, and the authority of the family undermined; if we win, crime will be controlled, money solid, and authority restored. Such fantasies relate deeply held myths close to one's life and inner circle of loved ones with the success of a political candidate remote from that primal scene. Yet such appeals have great success.

Some of the most remarkable political ads ever made linked a deep primal theme with the success of political candidates, for example, ads by Doyle Dane Bernbach, Inc. (DDB) for the Johnson Campaign in 1964. DDB made spot ads reinforcing a campaign myth that Johnson's opponent, Barry Goldwater, was "irresponsible" and that he was a "hipshooter" with nuclear weapons. DDB made subtle ads joining this myth about Goldwater with a primal myth about the health of one's children. The first, called "Daisy Girl," showed a pretty little girl picking daisies in a field, a dream child in her sunny world. As she counted the petals, the scene faded through her eyes to an atomic testing site, and then into a nuclear mushroom cloud. A voice-over (President Johnson) said (without mentioning Goldwater): "These are the stakes: To make a world in which all of God's children can live or go into the darkness. Either we must love each other or we must die." The second, called "Ice-Cream Cone," showed another girl, this time eating an ice-cream cone while a female voice-over said that Strontium 90 fallout could be found in milk and that Senator Goldwater had voted against the Nuclear Test Ban Treaty. The primal fear about the big, bad world hurting children was brought to bear on Goldwater, conjuring up consequences that might stem from his alleged "irresponsibility"[16] In this case, flacks were both using and making myths, employing a primal theme to scare people and at the same time reinforcing a current myth about Goldwater.

Flacks also make candidates into political heroes. Given that there are mythical norms as to the traits that a political hero is supposed to have, it is one job of flacks to communicate that their candidate possesses those qualities. In America, this includes characteristics such as mature, fair, hard-working, active, calm, stable, clean, and practical.[17] Campaign biographies and brochures herald the candidate's qualities and accomplishments. The former might be termed the mythologization of political virtue. The candidate is a "man of the people" (although in fact he is wealthy); he's "his own man" (although he is beholden to his party and to fat cat contributors); he is a "family man" (marital breaks may be patched up for public consumption); he has played other social roles voters can relate to—soldier, farmer, businessman, and so forth. Representatives from congressional and state districts spend considerable campaign effort confirming that they respect and in some sense represent local expectations about them. Flacks focus advertising and press releases on these qualities in order to claim that their candidate lives up to the myths associated with the office.

In 1976, the campaign management firm working on behalf of Gerald Ford stressed his attractive personal qualities as well as the notion that he was a leader of "inner serenity" who, although of presidential stature, had not lost his common touch in the White House. The Carter ads used "vision" themes, developed throughout the primary campaign, interspersed with montages of "Great Nation" landscapes, culminating in a shot of the four presidential faces carved on Mt. Rushmore and followed by a slow close-up of Carter: The subliminal implication was that Carter could be the fifth face.[18] As in most American campaigns, flacks have a dual task: to sell the candidate as personal and presidential (or senatorial or whatever)—as possessing mythical qualities of both areas of life.

Flacks cannot always simply sell the myth of a candidate's personal and political qualities, so they often focus on myths about the candidate's political accomplishments. The candidate will be credited with bringing about a set of desirable states, as if any politician could have the power or magic to create roads, schools, and so on. When a politician is well known—especially an incumbent—it is a common ad strategy to stress accomplishment. In 1966, Nelson Rockefeller was up for re-election as governor of New York. Jack Tinker and Partners were retained to refurbish the Rockefeller image, since his popularity was slipping in the polls, and his re-election was in doubt. Tinker produced a series of ads that never displayed Rockefeller's face or voice. Rather, they simply pointed out all the great things that had happened during Rockefeller's tenure as governor. One featured a fish talking to a reporter about how much cleaner New York's water was after Rockefeller's Pure Waters Program. Another showed a stretch of road, while a voice-over claimed that if you took all the roads that Rockefeller built or fixed, they would stretch to Hawaii and back. Another extolled the number of state college scholarships Rockefeller was responsible for. In fact, there would have been road repairs no matter who was governor, and many other politicians—in the state legislature, for example—were probably as responsible for these things as was Rockefeller. But the campaign ads presented brilliantly the myth of Rockefeller's single-handed power to achieve things. The implication was that Rockefeller was godlike, omnipotent, and capable of mighty acts, and the ad simply depicted accomplishments that were yet another example of his benevolent power.[19]

Flacks spend a great deal of time defining situations for the press and the public in order to sustain the myth of their boss's heroism. In primaries, for example, press secretaries claim victories even though their opponent gets more votes. In 1972, two months before the New Hampshire primary, a Boston *Globe* poll showed Edmund Muskie leading George McGovern as the preference for Democrats by a 65 to

18 percent margin. After the poll release, McGovern flack Frank Mankiewicz announced that if Muskie were to get anything less than 65 percent, it would show that his support was slipping and that McGovern was gaining. As it turned out, Muskie defeated McGovern in New Hampshire by a 46 to 37 percent margin. Mankiewicz's definition of the situation stuck with the press, and the McGovern camp claimed a great "moral victory." Muskie lost while winning, and McGovern won while losing. The myth of what Muskie "had to have" to win was defined by his opponent's flack, and that definition doomed Muskie to eventual defeat. McGovern suddenly had "momentum," press coverage, "support," all built on the myth of his New Hampshire "victory."[20]

The extent to which flacks engage in mythmaking in order to sustain their employer's heroism is astonishing. The flacks of major candidates put out solemn news releases on the personal habits of their Great Man. Much of such trivia seeks to charm the public—that such a giant has little human quirks, just like you and me! In recent years, this has included such tidbits as the fact that Nixon liked ketchup on cottage cheese, that Ford toasted his own English muffins, or that Carter listens to Mozart while he works. But other little facts hyped by flacks relate more directly to selling their candidate's heroism: Carter has an awesome capacity for work; Ford is a man of great inner serenity; Nixon has a grasp of foreign relations and a personal relationship with other Great Men, such as Brezhnev; Johnson dominates any setting he is in; and so on. These personal non-facts are designed to add to the myth of the leader by attributing to him superhuman traits. Similarly, in any context, flacks, with a straight face, assert that their man has another triumph. During the first Ford–Carter debate in 1976, the audio portion of the telecast went off, and there was a long delay. During the pause, Ford flack Ron Nessen emerged and solemnly announced that the debate was a "clear victory for the President"—even though the debate was not even finished!

Finally, campaign flacks drum up a variety of pseudo-myths on behalf of their employers. We distinguish these from the above kinds of mythmaking simply by their immediate and breathtaking cynicism. Flacks may (as we noted at the beginning of the chapter) be caught up in their candidate's heroism, in the goodness of whichever partisan "us" he represents, and in his embodiment and furtherance of some definition of political macromyths. But in the turbulence and anxiety of campaigns, flacks have proven capable of communicating myths about their candidates that are blatantly manipulated in order to produce certain effects. We will mention four familiar ploys: pseudo-qualities, pseudo-associates, pseudo-issues, and pseudo-events.[21]

By *pseudo-qualities,* we mean the manufacture of myths about the personal qualities or professional qualifications of the candidate. This is distinguishable as a form of mythmaking from what we discussed above; in many cases, such as Rockefeller's, there is some truth in the claim made. Here, we have in mind the creation of qualities where none, or only bogus ones, exist. For instance, in 1962, young and inexperienced Edward M. Kennedy ran for a Senate seat from Massachusetts. His campaign brochure showed pictures of him with three foreign figures with the caption, "Familiarity with World Problems." A list of "Kennedy's Community Service" included such earth-shaking achievements as "Judge Advocate of the Polish American Veterans Post of Boston." A study of that campaign concluded that these "are 'contrived' achievements since Kennedy had none of the customary political or professional achievements to his credit as the term is traditionally used."[22] Even so, with the Kennedy name and organization, he won.

Sometimes, of course, one can create a pseudo-quality making a virtue of ignorance or inexperience. One of the more deft efforts in this vein occurred in the challenge of ex-actor Ronald Reagan against incumbent Governor Pat Brown in California in 1966. After the campaign, Reagan's packagers, Spencer-Roberts, frankly admitted that they made an asset of Reagan's total lack of political experience. He was sold as a "citizen politician" running against Brown, the "professional politician." Thus, according to Roberts, ". . . We had an automatic defense. He didn't have to know all the answers. He didn't have to have the experience. A citizen politician is not expected to know all of the answers to all of the issues. It was a foundation point from which, on any issue, he could get as bright as he wanted, but he could always retreat to the fact that he was a citizen politician."[23] Reagan's chief qualification for office, then, was that he was unqualified; Brown's chief disqualification was that he was (in traditional terms, at least) qualified. Brown was a "professional politician," burdened by having to take a stance on issues; Reagan was a "citizen politician," freed by not having to take a stance. The myth that Reagan was different, a citizen politician, was to catapult him into presidential politics. In 1968, he produced a film for Republican presidential primaries entitled "Ronald Reagan: Citizen Governor." The myth of political virginity as a virtue was exploited by other candidates later.

Pseudo-associations refer to using celebrities as explicit or implicit endorsers and, more directly, using them to prove that the candidate has famous friends in areas of life that are important to people. In 1976, Jimmy Carter's campaign ran televised endorsements by racing car driver Cale Yarborough in the South, where both Yarborough and stock car racing is popular. During the same campaign, rock singer Linda Ronstadt and the Eagles played rock concerts to raise money for Jerry Brown. Flacks like their candidates to be seen in the company of such celebrities. Such pseudo-association helps to communicate the myth that a candidate is great because he is known by celebrities, values the same entertainment as his voters (be it Lawrence Welk or the Allman Brothers), or is simply "with it." That the candidate is "with it" can obviously be a myth, and flacks are capable of hiring celebrities for the "rubbing elbows with the glamorous" effect.

A *pseudo-issue* refers to a hyped "controversy" in a campaign, a tempest in a teapot that creates a myth that there is a major difference between candidates. Campaigns often look like the early stages of a boxing match: Both fighters size each other up, look for openings, establish their strategies. Campaigners and their flacks feel around for a slogan, a theme, or an issue that differentiates them from their opponents and strikes a responsive chord among voters. Since oftentimes there is no substantial difference, or pseudo-voters feel such substantial differences are boring, flacks conjure up pseudo-issues, non-differences claimed to constitute a difference. Many campaign controversies whirl around fantasied pseudo-issues that are quickly forgotten after the campaign. Kennedy and Nixon debated the monumental importance of Quemoy and Matsu in 1960. Richard Nixon had a "secret plan" to end the Vietnam War in 1968: He could *not* reveal it since, for one thing, it would no longer be a secret, and, for another, it might "undermine negotiations." The secret plan was a pseudo-issue (the candidates could not debate it), but it helped to create the myth that a Nixon win would bring about a desirable (for both hawks and doves) conclusion to the war. In many cases, pseudo-issues are created in campaigns in order to attack one's opponent, tagging him with a position he doesn't take. In 1972, Republican ads attacked George

McGovern as wanting to put half the country on welfare. In reality, McGovern's welfare reform proposal didn't differ much from President Nixon's; but the myth stuck, and it helped to bring about McGovern's massive defeat.

Flacks stage *pseudo-events,* mythical environments for candidates. Conventions and rallies are choreographed for maximum possible media effect. The Republicans hired George Murphy, actor, public relations director at M-G-M, and later Senator, to "produce" the renominating convention for Eisenhower in 1956, including directing delegate responses, fanfare, cues, and so on.[24] The art of staging conventions and rallies for prime-time mass audiences has since become increasingly sophisticated. The 1964 Democratic convention and the 1972 Republican convention were both mythical environments, scripted and executed in order to eliminate open conflict, on-camera flubs, boring intervals, and droning speeches. The illusion of lavish and unanimous enthusiasm for the candidate was, in both conventions, suggesting that, the enthusiasm of that mythical world could be extrapolated to the country as a whole.

Similarly, campaign ads frequently use a pseudo-event format. Some flacks believe that television news influences voters more than traditional hard-sell political ads, so they attempt to make ads resemble TV network documentaries and news stories.[25] A typical pseudo-event in campaign advertising will show the candidate, perspiring, tie loosened, coat over shoulder, sleeves rolled up, talking candidly to workers in a factory, with the noise of machines in the background. In most cases, the candidate actually did talk to workers, but the "best parts" are edited into the spot ad; the candidate did not go to the factory to find out what a small group of factory workers thought, but to be filmed in that setting. The candidate is making news, but the environment is mythical.

A variation on the pseudo-event in campaigning is what we call the *pseudo-movement.* Campaign flacks, through a variety of means (advertising, direct mailing, etc.), create the illusion of a vast movement, what Theodore White called "the impression of a force in being."[26] In 1964, a small group of Henry Cabot Lodge supporters, through direct mailings and a TV "documentary," created the impression that there was a groundswell of support for Lodge in New Hampshire. The press had exhausted stories about Goldwater and Rockefeller and began to write about the "rising tide" for Lodge, thereby helping to create the "force in being." Lodge's flacks kept hyping new stories and the myth of movement, and they brought off a write-in victory for Lodge against two well-oiled and -financed campaigns.[27]

In summary, campaign flackdom has become remarkably sophisticated in the exploitation of myths. Many of the messages constructed are directed at people's emotions, tugging at deeply held myths about their country, political values, and prejudices. Flacks also create fantasy worlds for people, allowing potential voters to be transported into the drama presented.[28] Many social critics have thus argued that contemporary campaigns are a massive exercise in human gullibility consisting of voters repeatedly believing the myth that a particular candidate can change things for good or ill if elected. In any case, it is likely that campaign mythmaking will continue.

FLACKS IN AND AROUND GOVERNMENT
Selling Leaders, Policies, and Institutions

Flackdom as a social phenomenon can be traced to the growth in size and complexity of large organizations in the modern world—corporations, professional associations, unions, interest groups, political parties, and, of course, government. A corporation responds to a suit through a spokesman who is likely to be a professional flack. A union hires an ad agency to shore up the image by making and running ads where workers sing that people should "look for the union label." But in most cases, the organization takes formal steps to rationalize its relationships with the outside world by hiring flacks who are expert in the management of communications.

So it is with American government. Most major federal offices and agencies (and many state and local ones as well) have large staffs to perform increasingly complex functions, and one major addition has been a vast increase in budget and staff for flacking. Estimates as to how much government spends on public information and the like runs into the many hundreds of millions of dollars.[29] Similarly, other large organizations take political stances and attempt to further political interests through flack staffs hired for that purpose. Here, we discuss selected ways that government flacks and their counterparts in interested organizations use and make myths to further a political leader, policy, or agency.

Political Leaders and Flacks

In most modern states, major political executives (e.g., presidents, governors, prime ministers, secretaries of government departments, chairmen, and commissioners) are surrounded by a personal staff that includes flacks. Presidents have press secretaries who control communications with the press, pollsters who do sampling and advise their employer on public feelings about him and policies, and aides who extol the president in public. Even in nations where political executives are not elected, leaders appear to worry about their popularity. In all cases, flacks build, sustain, or change the myths that the leaders desire people to hold about them.

The contemporary presidency is the most obvious and spectacular case, but the process of increasing flack influence in the life of the executive is not confined to that office. Major presidential contenders keep a stable of flacks on retainer in case they decide to run. The Kennedy family, for instance, has and does hire a variety of flacks to serve their political interests; for example, William Manchester mythologized the death of President Kennedy.[30] Arthur Schlesinger, Jr., a long-time associate of the Kennedy family, recently published a biography of Robert Kennedy that speaks of the "mystical bond" between RFK and "the Other America"; how Kennedy was the "last liberal politician who could communicate with white working-class America"; and how Kennedy was going (in 1968) to reconstruct the Democratic party and win the presidency with a coalition of the poor, blacks, blue-collar whites, and the "kids."[31] More skeptical observers might argue that all this is mythmaking similar to the semi-official history of Manchester: that much of the white working class was for Wallace; that a coalition such as the one envisioned was still a minority and not likely to control the Democratic Party or presidential elections; and that the Other America was a nonexistent (and romanticized) political force that was in reality likely to be as skeptical of Kennedy as it was of any other politician. In any event, when and if

Senator Edward Kennedy decides to run for president, the talented stable of Kennedy flacks will prove useful. At such a time, we might witness the marketing of a "New Ted," more mature and responsible, a myth similar to the "New Nixon" of 1968.

To illustrate the similarity of executive flackdom pervasive in modern states, one may usefully compare disparate operations and see the common bond of mythologizing in the political executive. Take three well-known executive establishments: the contemporary White House, Stalin's Kremlin, and Hitler's Reichschancellery.[32] Flacks in both the "imperial" (Kennedy, Johnson, Nixon) and "nonimperial" (Carter) White Houses devote much time glorifying the boss, polishing his image, agonizing over public opinion, planning the performances and moves of their employer, and so on. The degree of mythologizing their boss's qualities is astounding. Aide Jack Valenti made a speech in which he said he "slept better at night" because Lyndon Johnson was president. Nixon's surrogates in the 1972 campaign attributed to him every imaginable kind of personal and political virtue. Even during Nixon's last year or so as president, when he spent considerable time rambling about or brooding over Watergate, the official version of his mood and activity was quite different. Presidents are typically portrayed by their flacks as on top of fast-breaking events, in control of every situation, pondering and mastering the great issues of the day—men who bear the most awesome responsibilities with courage and grace.

But even in the nonelective setting of the Kremlin and the Reichschancellery, there was considerable selling of the political executive. Both Stalin and Hitler saw that they could not base their rule totally on fear induced by terror; they also created a propaganda machine to induce admiration and downright adoration. Stalin's flacks portrayed him as contemporary as some presidents: He was resolute and cunning in war, a jovial "Uncle Joe" to the masses he sprang from and instinctively understood, and yet also a sort of remote Old Testament God with magical powers of benevolence and vengeance.[33] Similarly, Hitler's flacks made him into an equally remote god with awesome powers and with human touches, such as entertaining a little girl on her birthday. These cases of political myth-making are more extreme than those surrounding the contemporary presidency, but the process is essentially the same: to portray the current leader as possessing, like Superman, "powers far beyond those of ordinary men" and as indispensable. It is interesting to note how contemporary presidents' portrayals, like Stalin's and Hitler's, emphasize men of reason who stand calm and unshakable against the forces that would bring chaos and ruin. Lyndon Johnson stood firm against the "nervous Nellies" who would undermine American interests in Asia; Nixon was "tough" against anarchistic domestic forces that would destroy the country; and Carter stands for "reason" in energy, budget, and foreign policy against a stubborn and fearful Congress. In all cases, flack mythmaking about the boss serves the purpose (if successful) of augmenting public support and political power.

Political Policies and Flacks

Flacks sell policies in a variety of ways. Competing interest groups attempt to influence policy making by hiring flacks to conduct propaganda campaigns. Policy makers attempt to influence public opinion and other deciding institutions by the same tactic. And of course, interest groups and policy makers form alliances for the same purpose.

The American policy process involves much mythmaking. Partisan groups or policy participants attempt to convince others that some particular policy is good or true: If policy X is adopted or continued then result Y will be or is being realized, and that is good, for reasons A and B. This may all be so much eyewash or wishful thinking, but sometimes it is successful in convincing people. The Nixon administration conducted a large-scale campaign to sell the Vietnamization policy as both good and true: good in that it was a gradual withdrawal from the war and no "bug out," and true in that it was in fact occurring with success with the assurance that the South Vietnamese could "hack it" on their own. Actually, there were several major escalations of the war after the Nixon policy was announced, and the South Vietnamese, in the final analysis, did not hack it on their own. Yet at home in America, the policy did command some support. Oftentimes the official myth appears as what will happen unless policy X is followed. Both the Johnson and Nixon administrations hyped the domino theory, that unless South Vietnam was defended, the rest of Asia would fall to communism like dominos in a row. More recently, both sides of the intense debate about the Panama Canal treaty predicted dire consequences if their course was not followed. Similarly, both proponents and opponents of the Equal Rights Amendment predicted that conflicting sets of consequences would flow from adoption or rejection. Opponents, for instance, conjured up the vision of women being drafted and sent into combat if ERA passed.

There are many mythmaking strategies commonly relied upon in policy struggles. The military lobby (e.g., the Pentagon, the armed service organizations, veteran's groups, congressional allies, etc.) trots out the myth of national security during budget fights over military appropriations. The defense secretary warns of new dangers of Soviet aggression and leaks to the press talk of new weapons systems the Russians are supposedly building; Senators warn of the peril of America becoming second in defense, and so on. Such rhetoric appeals to the deeply held myth that we prevent war and make ourselves secure by arming ourselves with more destructive and complex weaponry. After the appropriations and reassurances are forthcoming, the dire warnings abate.

Another standard ploy is to assert that there exists out there a great groundswell of support or righteous indignation about something that is happening or about to happen. The National Rifle Association creates the illusion of great public opposition to gun control legislation by flooding congressional offices with mail from NRA supporters. Various interest groups claim that public opinion is behind them on a certain matter, appealing to the illusion that there is enormous interest in and support for a policy. They commission polls, quite valid in their sampling procedure, but which load questions about a particular issue—for example, "Do you favor creating a vast new bureaucracy costing billions of dollars in your tax money to administer socialized medicine?"—selected results are presented in testimony before Congress and other forums as evidence of public opposition to socialized medicine.

Flacks and the Selling of Government Agencies

Finally, flacks sell not only leaders and policies, but also government agencies themselves. Government establishments are aware that their budgets and policies often depend on their image, on how much support they are believed to have, and on how effective policy makers think they are. The Federal Bureau of Investigation is a well-known example. Its vastly successful public relations program gained it a positive public image and reputation among policy makers that accrued to the agency's benefit. FBI propaganda successfully sold the myth of a vast communist and criminal conspiracy in the country that was exponentially increasing in power all the time, while at the same time convincing policy makers and the public that the Bureau was never more successful in combating these forces![34] The FBI's reputation, of course, was enhanced by the adroit hyping of the long-time director, J. Edgar Hoover, through publicity stunts (such as having Hoover personally arrest some noted criminal for the benefit of news organizations) and cooperation with the popular media (see Chapter 5). There are many other examples of such agency flacking, such as the Pentagon and the National Aeronautics and Space Administration (NASA), but the process is essentially the same: to convince people, especially policy makers, of things about the agency that may be largely mythical.

THE FUTURE OF FLACK MYTHMAKING IN POLITICS

In this chapter, we linked the emergence of economic and political flackdom with the advance of industrial consumer civilization. Perhaps the most remarkable thing about this historical trend is not the adroit use of myth but the constant creation and re-creation of myths about political objects. Bloom noted that campaign flacks made it feasible "to package, test-market, re-package, and re-market the same man several times over. And when the job is finished, the voters will apparently buy a variety of images, even if self-contradictory."[35] That this should be so in a culture dedicated and addicted to consumption and change should not surprise us. Primal and cultural myths would be an obvious target of these new economic and political forces and skills. But the larger view of what this trend augurs for the future of politics has been fearful to contemplate. Perhaps Ernst Cassirer went to the heart of the matter when he wrote the following:

> Myth has always been described as the result of an unconscious activity and as a free product of imagination. But here we find

myth made according to plan. The new political myths do not grow up freely: they are not wild fruits of an exuberant imagination. They are artificial things fabricated by very skillful and cunning artisans. It has been reserved for the twentieth century, our own great technical age, to develop a new technique of myth. Henceforth myths can be manufactured in the same sense and according to the same methods as any other modern weapon—as machine guns or airplanes. That is a new thing—and a thing of crucial importance. It has changed the whole form of our social life.[36]

How much more the increasing pervasion and sophistication of the flack arts in politics will affect our lives is difficult to know. Orwell's famous vision, *1984*, portrays a world in which flacks hype a heroic, yet nonexistent, political leader (Big Brother), a war that probably is not being fought, increases in productivity and abundance that are actually not occurring, and so forth; yet people buy it. However, in the present, many people don't accept many of the economic and political messages put out by professional flacks. Much of the cynicism and rebellion of the present over politics stems in part from the suspicion that the message, as well as the product hyped, is phony. One sees a popular demand for that which is real, natural, free of hype. Yet, people in the present buy Coca-Cola ("the real thing") and "natural" hair coloring and are attracted to politicians who bill themselves as real and natural. In a political world overrun by the flack arts, discerning the real from the phony is ever more difficult. How do we know that the current version of the politically true, beautiful, or good is not simply another myth, with modern flacks manipulating the shadows on the cave wall?

REFERENCES

1. J. D. Lorenz, "An Insider's View of Jerry Brown," *Esquire* (February 1978): 66; see also his book, *Jerry Brown: The Man on the White Horse* (New York: Houghton Mifflin, 1978).

2. Peter Berger, *Invitation to Sociology* (Garden City, N.Y.: Doubleday, 1963), p. 109.

3. See Richard Grunberger, *The 12-Year Reich* (New York: Holt, Rhinehart and Winston, 1973); Z. A. B. Zeman, *Nazi Propaganda* (New York: Oxford University Press, 1973); Viktor Reimann, *Goebbels* (Garden City, N.Y.: Doubleday, 1976).

4. Andrew Hacker, "Liberal Democracy and Social Control," *American Political Science Review,* 51 (December 1957): 1025.

5. Jacques Ellul, *Propaganda* (New York: Vintage Books, 1973), pp. 4–5.

6. Vance Packard, *The Hidden Persuaders* (New York: Pocket Books, 1958), pp. 61–70.

7. Wilson Bryan Key, *Subliminal Seduction* (New York: New American Library, 1974), pp. 55–61.

8. Ron Rosenbaum, "Tales of the Heartbreak Biz," *Esquire* (July 1974): 67–73, 155–158.

9. Marilynn Preston, "The 'A Star is Hyped' Show, Starring Richard Grant," *Chicago Tribune,* October 15, 1977, pp. 21–22.

10. Packard, *The Hidden Persuaders,* pp. 158–159.

11. Charles Michelson, quoted in V.O. Key, *Politics, Parties, and Pressure Groups* (New York: Crowell, 1964), p. 470.

12. See Daniel Boorstin, *The Image* (New York: Harper & Row, 1964); James M. Perry, *The New Politics* (New York: Clarkson N. Potter, 1968); Stanley Kelley, Jr., *Professional Public Relations and Political Power* (Baltimore: The Johns Hopkins University Press, 1956).

13. Richard Rovere, quoted in Packard, *The Hidden Persuaders,* p. 164.

14. Joe McGinniss, *The Selling of the President 1968* (New York: Pocket Books, 1970), pp. 127–128.

15. Walter R. Fisher, "Reaffirmation and Subversion of the American Dream," *Quarterly Journal of Speech,* 59, no. 2, (April 1973): 163.

16. Melvyn H. Bloom, *Public Relations and Presidential Campaigns* (New York: Crowell, 1973), pp. 163–164.

17. Dan Nimmo and Robert L. Savage, *Candidates and Their Images* (Pacific Palisades, Cal.: Goodyear Publishing Co., 1976), p. 66.

18. Joseph Lelyveld, "Ford to Delay Ads on TV Until After First Debate," *The New York Times,* September 14, 1976, p. 28.

19. Perry, *The New Politics,* pp. 107–137.

20. Michael Wheeler, *Lies, Damn Lies, and Statistics* (New York: Liveright, 1976), pp. 16–18.

21. This is an expansion of Boorstin's notion of the "pseudo-event," from *The Image,* cited above, pp. 7–44.

22. Murray B. Levin, *Kennedy Campaigning* (Boston: Beacon Press, 1966), p. 296.

23. William Roberts, quoted in Perry, *The New Politics,* pp. 29–30.

24. Packard, *The Hidden Persuaders,* pp. 167–168.

25. "Political Advertising: Making it Look Like News," *Congressional Quarterly,* 30 (November 4, 1972): 2900–2903.

26. Theodore H. White, *The Making of the President 1964* (New York: New American Library, 1965), p. 136.

27. Bloom, *Public Relations,* pp. 114–117.

28. Ernest G. Bormann, "Fantasy and Rhetorical Vision: The Rhetorical Criticism of Social Reality," *Quarterly Journal of Speech,* 58 (1972): 396–407.

29. Herbert Schiller, *The Mind Managers* (Boston: Beacon Press, 1973), pp. 47–48.

30. See Edward Jay Epstein, "History as Fiction," in *Between Fact and Fiction* (New York: Vintage Books, 1975), pp. 120–141.

31. Arthur M. Schlesinger, Jr., "Robert Kennedy: The Lost President," *Esquire* (August 15, 1978): 25–52, excerpted from his book, *Robert Kennedy and His Times* (New York: Houghton Mifflin, 1978).

32. The comparison is developed by Russell Baker and Charles Peters, "The Prince and His Courtiers: At the White House, the Kremlin, and the Reichschancellery," in Charles Peters and James Fallows, eds., *Inside the System* (New York: Praeger, 1976), pp. 3–16.

33. Adam B. Ulam, *Stalin* (New York: Viking Press, 1973), pp. 436–437, 476–477; and H. Montgomery Hyde, *Stalin: The History of a Dictator* (New York: Popular Library, 1971), p. 363.

34. Murray Edelman, *The Symbolic Uses of Politics* (Urbana, Ill.: University of Illinois Press, 1967), pp. 69–71.

35. Bloom, *Public Relations,* pp. 256–257.

36. Ernst Cassirer, *The Myth of the State* (New Haven, Ct.: Yale University Press, 1969), p. 282.

CHAPTER **5**

That's Entertainment!
Politics Through Popular Culture

*What does it mean when a nation
turns tragedy into comic books?*

CYCLOPS

Unlike professional flacks, the creators of popular culture—moviemakers, TV producers, comic strip cartoonists, the owners of athletic teams, and so forth—are usually not directly in the business of political mythmaking. Nevertheless, for a variety of reasons, the makers of popular culture help to mold political myths. Popular culture, since it consists in part of artifacts and images created for or by mass audiences, reflects and even shapes popular political myths. The study of popular culture, both of the creators and communicators on the one hand and the consumers of it on the other, tells us much about the political myths current and persistent in a political culture. Thus we believe it worthwhile to point to contexts of political mythmaking in popular culture. The relationship is subtle, multifaceted, and often difficult to pin down, but nevertheless it reveals to us much about our political myths.

An initial example points up the intriguing relationship between popular culture and the political order. A major dimension of American popular culture is sports. Americans are sports fans, and the various professional sports leagues attract huge audiences. The popularity of sports suggests that people not only enjoy watching games but that they find something valuable in play. The value of sports spills over into everyday life. We are all familiar with the sports banquet homilies about sports and life and the lessons sports teaches. But the sports analogy goes much further and affects attitudes and actions concerning politics. Politicians often use sports metaphors to describe political life. Campaigners speak of the game plan. Indeed, politicians invoke the rugged values of football to demonstrate that in politics, "you've got to be tough." This includes, in some quarters, bending or breaking the rules and being meaner than your opponent. Nixon's "Plumbers," after all, used a slogan adopted from Vince Lombardi: "Winning in politics isn't everything, it's the only thing." Although many politicians will not go this far, they still pay considerable deference to sports values and sports in general. Campaigners are careful to extol the virtues of the local team (in Boston, one mentions the Red Sox) and to seek the endorsement and public company of famous athletes. Indeed, some athletes have traded on their sports celebrity and entered politics. If someday former pro football quarterback and House member Jackie Kemp and former pro basketball player and now Senator Bill Bradley were to face each other in a presidential race, we would have a sense of the importance of sports celebrity (and maybe a referendum on which of the two sports is more popular). Even the reporting of politics takes on the flavor of sports reporting. Political stories read like a sports column, defining the players, their strengths and weaknesses, and the nature of the contest; it may not be too farfetched to compare the coverage of a political party convention with that of the Super Bowl. Perhaps it is also not unfair to note the similarity of the coverage of sports playoffs (e.g., the NFL football, NCAA basketball) to presidential primary coverage, as each week the field narrows down to the finals.

Reflection reveals some ways in which sports contributes to political mythmaking. If one sees life as violent, aggressive combat (as in football), one is likely to mythify the political game the same way. If one accepts the cultural norm that only the best athletes should compete and that the rest of us should be spectators, then this may support the political myth that we should be mere spectators watching (and following) the triumphant gladiator. If the mass media report politics as a sporting event, then it is difficult for people to take it any more seriously than other spectator sports. If we believe in the heroism of athletes in their playing days, is it not possible for us to believe that there should be heroic political gladiators too? The mythic fabric of a culture interconnects popular culture and politics in subtle and covert ways.

POPULAR CULTURE AND POLITICAL MYTH

Modern politics occurs in a field of popular culture, and thus there is a fluid, reciprocal relationship between politics and popular fare. In Western societies in particular, politics is a popular culture object. In the modernized world, and increasingly in other parts of the globe, we live in popular societies, that is, societies characterized by the assumption that mass desires and ideas are legitimate and even good, and by organizations—economic, political, and cultural—catering to and attempting to mold those desires and ideas. We live not only in a world of the popularization of culture, but also in one where political culture is popularized. The myths such cultures accordingly have are in part the province of the creators of popular culture objects. The mythemes of the political culture in particular are transformed, enacted, and personified by popular culture. Key mythical events (e.g., Valley Forge) are visualized, condensed to contemporary media, and the actors therein (Washington, the Colonial Army) are fleshed out.

Popular Culture and Mythmaking

Popular culture objects—movies, comics, TV programs, music, and so forth—are both a mirror and a lamp. They reflect many of the popular myths people hold about politics, and they also help to shape, reinforce, and perpetuate those political myths. The objects created in popular culture—whether imposed or selected—are key indicators of the persistence and transformation of social and political myths. They are artifacts of social perception, of the process of creating and communicating symbolic objects among mass publics. And since social perceptions change over time, objects of popular culture change as well. Durable political myths, such as those of the founding fathers and the Revolution (see Chapter 2), persist as popular objects, but their meaning often subtly changes and adapts to contemporary circumstances. In a way, even the debunking of myths serves mythical purpose, interpreting a past in new terms. For example, the restructuring of the Western myth in the late 1960s and 1970s served a new purpose. Movies like *Soldier Blue, Little Big Man, Buffalo Bill and the Indians,* even *Butch Cassidy and the Sundance Kid* inverted themes in the classical Western in order to appeal to a new sensibility: that the old Western myth was a lie, that the cavalry was not heroic, that the Indians and the outlaws were not evil, that many of the heroes of the old myth were frauds. However, simply the fact that such a myth must be attacked indicates not only its importance but also the necessity of new mythmaking. The new myth of the West that replaced the old appeals to a contemporary set of popular perceptions, just the obverse of the classical myth: The Indians were noble and heroic, outlaws were sympathetic rebels, law and order relied upon more than a six-gun, and so forth. Many of these new themes reflected the rejection of conventional mythology among largely youthful moviegoers during recent years, but, equally, they also reflected the impulse to construct a new mythology in place of the old. The American West is a durable mythological setting for the enactment of such social dramas.[1]

Popular culture, then, holds vast opportunities for mythmaking, -breaking, and -remaking. By looking at entertainment artifacts, we can see forms of popular art and consumption that give "symbolic expression to a social group's images of the surrounding social drama of the society" and are "generally enactments of the drama of social relations as it appears in the imagination of the status group that identifies with the cultural forms"[2] Popular culture is not merely an imitation of life but, more important, a symbolization of it: Art acts as a vehicle for the representation of life through credible, dramatic representations of perceived realities created and re-created over time, given the perceptions of a present. Our definition of myth (see Chapter I) is thus easily extended to the forms of popular culture that dramatize social and political myths.

There has been extensive discussion of the effect or functions of popular culture in a society.[3] Here, we emphasize only the role of popular culture in presenting, interpreting, and validating social and political myths. Artifacts of popular culture objectify what may have been latent and unformed in the imaginations of people. A popular movie or TV situation comedy may trigger a mass nerve and thereby appeal to a myth people either believe in or want to believe in. In all cases, the popularity of a popular culture object speaks to the climate of opinion or *ethos* of a present, although certainly major mythical themes persist for long periods. For example, in the wake of the complicated social changes of the 1960s and the economic and spiritual depression of the 1970s, there re-emerged, in new form, an old mytheme:

romantic nostalgia for a pre-modern, rural, pastoral, extended family existence believed immune to the whips and scorns of the threatening present. A television show, *The Waltons,* became popular, in part because it appealed to a nostalgic myth: a tight-knit, loyal family, in a beautiful and rural setting, that coped with another bad time (the Depression) through the old values of love and simple virtues. This was a new version of a traditional myth that had been celebrated for a very long time, the image of democratic virtue in a rustic setting, but the new version spoke to deep feelings peculiar to the present.

Popular culture often *displaces* myth. Myths of long standing acquire new life by mythical transference to a new setting. *Star Trek,* for instance, has been an endlessly popular television serial because it transfers American mythemes deeply rooted in the culture to a new fantastic future world. In periods of mythic denial and confusion, such displacement to a past or future setting reaffirms, in safe form, old myths.[4] *Star Trek* and *The Waltons* project a mythic drama and roles into fantasy worlds that we instinctively identify as satisfying. Popular culture takes old, old stories and renews them, thus acting as an important carrier of social and political myth.

Play, Identity, and Political Myth

Popular culture exists for entertainment purposes and is thereby *play.* Man the player takes many forms, from active participation in sports to passive participation in movies. Although *homo ludens* has been important throughout history, playing probably assumes greater impact on individual thought and action than ever before with the massive pervasion of popular media. Popular culture is a growing source of personal cues and images reaffirming or forming our myths about ourselves and the world. With expanded opportunities for play, and with the apparent importance attached to participating in popular culture by so many people, it is likely that popular culture has functions and effects for people other than simple diversion.

Perhaps the most fundamental effect that popular culture has on contemporary people is on their *identity.* Modern man, the argument goes, searches for identity in a world where old sources of social cues—family, church, school—have broken up or been discredited. With the proliferation of the mass media, popular culture serves as a source of our identity. Popular culture figures, for example, provide mythical hero-types that we can emulate or identify with. Everyone would like to have the understanding and loving parents of the Walton family. Prospective parents may reaffirm or form some of their images and habits of parenthood from popular family shows—*Father Knows Best,* for example, and even more realistic shows such as *Family.* Soap operas are a source of cues for how to deal with everyday crises, and they even provide examples of manners and good conversational lines. Some people learn what to say in social situations from remembered scenes in a popular forum.

At the most basic levels, our identity emerges from play. In childhood, we begin to take on identity by playing with others and by playing others (dressing up like Mommy). We rehearse how we are going to act. We "play society" at parties or other fun gatherings. Even our self develops through playing with "Who am I" questions and postures. Many of the sources of play in popular culture are salient in the formation and changing of identity over time. We identify with popular culture figures as role models. We act like them, consciously or unconsciously. We adopt ideas and postures from popular culture that identify us with a lifestyle. In this sense, modern life imitates art: We draw upon figures, actions, and even plots from popular culture as guides to the milieu we must live in and cope with. Since the objects of popular culture are mythical—both in the sense of "not real" and also as representative of cultural archetypes and stories—America is as much a mythologically instructed community as ancient Greece, even though the sources of myth are different. As Jerome Bruner notes, cultural sources provide "tutorial myths" that shape our lives by communicating "a corpus of images and identities and models that provides the pattern to which growth may aspire—a range of metaphoric identities."[5] For example, popular culture may communicate to masses either norms of conformity or of rebellion and deviance. Metaphoric identities of youthful rebellion are represented in popular culture by the tradition of the Rebel in its many transformations, from Marlon Brando of *The Wild One* to James Dean of *Rebel Without a Cause* to John Travolta of *Saturday Night Fever.* From playing with these heroic role-models, a young person may learn norms of rebellion with which he identifies and which become a part of his identity.

Popular culture thereby is not only a carrier of political myth; it is also a carrier of political identity. Popular culture, to be sure, reaffirms and transforms the macromyths of a community—our myths about the presidency, the Congress, the national mission, and so on. But popular culture is also important in transmitting to individuals ideas and images about one's political identity. The effects of popular culture are not only cosmic but also personal. Individuals gain a sense of their political selves through symbolic presentations in popular culture. In democratic countries, such as the United States, a key component of political identity is the reaffirmation of the myth of mass participation ("Your vote counts") and its validation in voting. On the other hand, if one is a dissident or is alienated from mainstream political norms, a landslide defeat of one's candidate may validate the pointlessness of the mass of voters and the futility of voting. In either case, popular culture objects—a TV show, for instance—provides a play context to reaffirm the political self. A television show like *Grandpa Goes to Washington* (NBC, 1978-1979) affirms that mass wisdom still triumphs in the Olympian citadel of the United States Senate. Grandpa, an ancient and inrascible citizen unexpectedly elected to the Senate, brings common virtue and sense to that cosmopolitan and corrupt institution. By personal and feisty persistence, he reaffirms mass values, saves the taxpayers' money, attacks the perquisites of the Establishment (e.g., a lavish birthday party for the president's daughter is made into a charity affair by his man to man appeal to the president), and so on. Such TV fantasy celebrates the wisdom of mass electorates and democratic man and, implicitly, the identity of the voter. On the other hand, the political identity of someone inclined to be an oppositionist or an outsider may be affirmed by a movie like *The Candidate* (1972). *The Candidate* depicts how cynical campaign flacks transform an idealistic young social worker (Robert Redford) into a manipulative politico; he wins but, in a sense, loses his soul. Such a popular drama helps to reinforce for the political outsider the corrupting aspects of the system and assures that nonparticipation and cynicism are justified.

Thus it is our contention that popular culture is not harmless, neutral, or without political effect. Popular culture is play, yes; but it also creates a world of meanings that communicate aspects of social and political myth. In this kind of play, identity as a social and political being gets confirmed or denied. It is no wonder that we seek out nonthreatening popular culture messages and attend to those that are confirming. For instance, perhaps one of the reasons for the inexhaustible popularity of the TV series, *Star Trek,* is the affirmation it offers of the American manifest destiny in a time of widespread doubt. The myth of American empire and values as a benevolent force is displaced into the future and to the final frontier of space; in each episode, the intervention of Kirk, Spock, and the others in foreign affairs is both successful and wise. In disguised form, *Star Trek* celebrates our past, our current struggles, and our future, thus supporting the identity of those who still wish to believe in the American Dream.[6]

Popular culture is a make-believe world, but it is in make-believe that our selves are formed and altered. There is always something of ourselves in the representative dramas of popular culture—our heroic fantasies, our darkest nightmares, the things we like to believe about ourselves and the world. In both those artifacts we find delighting and those we find threatening are images of ourselves. The play of popular culture enhances myths about ourselves, but it also constructs other more disturbing myths. A movie like *Rocky* reaffirms our myths about the underdog who triumphs by trying hard and by being nice to an ugly duckling girl, something we would like to believe about ourselves. On the other hand, a movie like *Psycho* presents a pop-Freudian myth about the possibility of horrible and swift aggression from those who seem harmless and innocent, undermining our reassurances about our own safety from the people around us.

Popular culture artifacts touching on politics similarly dramatize political myths and reaffirm or disturb our collective political identity. For example, war movies during and immediately after World War II and Korea validated the myth of American heroism and mission in those conflicts. Films like *The Sands of Iwo Jima* and *Battleground* did show fighting and death, but they did not question the morality or wisdom of war, the authorities who sent soldiers into combat, or the anonymous malevolence of, most blatantly, "the Japs." But with the 1960s—and especially with the seemingly endless nightly news fare of carnage in Vietnam—attitudes toward and the popular artistic treatment of war began to change. Movies about Vietnam focused on the insanity, the moral ambiguities, and the suffering of war to the exclusion of heroism and high purpose. Indeed, past wars were reinterpreted in light of this new myth. In the movie and TV series, *M*A*S*H,* the bloody suffering of the wounded, the cynicism of the doctors, the bureaucratic snafus, became the focus. The enduring popularity of Joseph Heller's novel, *Catch 22,* also reflects this new attitude. For those who still adhere to the old myth about war, the new films and shows are upsetting, even unpatriotic; for those who have adopted the new myth, the old films are chauvinistic and oversimplified.

One of the key aspects of identity is one's attitude toward authority—parental, institutional, political. Popular culture is a major form of expression of that identification of authority. According to one's definition of personal identity, we support, deprecate, or are ambivalent toward authority. Popular culture has long celebrated both the wisdom of parental authority and the love-hate, obedience-rebellion attitude of youth toward parents. TV shows like *My Three Sons* dramatize the myth of the wise and compassionate parent. But the myth of youthful rebellion that deprecates or displays ambivalence about authority abounds also, ranging from created rebels, such as Huckleberry Finn and the James Cagney of *Public Enemy,* to folk rebels, such as Billy the Kid and Bonnie and Clyde.

By extension, then, we can tell much about myths of authority in a particular place and time by looking at the depiction of authority in popular culture. For example, the deprecation or support for authority in the movies of a particular era gives us a clue to the mood or climate of opinion that made such movies representative of the era. The movies of the 1930s, for example, ranging from the optimistic Frank Capra films (e.g., *Mr. Smith Goes to Washington*) to the social-class movies (e.g., *Dead End*), presented authority figures as insensitive, evil, oppressive, against the people. This reflects the mood of the Depression and the sense of the failure of authority. But films of World War II support authority: Political leaders and generals do not make mistakes, and their motives are unquestioned. In *Yankee Doodle Dandy,* for instance, George M. Cohan (James Cagney, once "public enemy") is invited to the White House, where he deferentially relates his life story (including writing patriotic songs) to an authority figure who is obviously President Roosevelt. Obviously, popular culture is not a perfect instrument for detecting attitudes toward authority; nevertheless, the patterns of a particular era do resonate in popular objects.

Political myth, then, is one of the symbolic properties of popular culture. Wittingly or not, popular culture affects our perception of ourselves and our relation to political life. If there are lesions or contradictions in our identities, then it is likely that popular culture will treat them. Political myths in tribal society were usually carried and passed on by holy men whose job was explaining old myths to new people in the wake of new events. Now, political myths are carried by popular culture, which explains myths to audiences caught in the onrush of time.

Political Mythmaking and Popular Culture: Relationships

The relationship of popular culture to political mythmaking is often subtle, implicit, and difficult to state in mathematical and causal formulas. But we can suggest some of the ways and offer some evidence, and some speculation, about the connection.

Political myths can be communicated in popular culture in a variety of ways. The lessons or messages of popular culture about politics may be explicit or implicit, manifest or latent, intended or unintended. For example, a popular format may be used for open political propaganda, as in movies during wartime. But often a theme may be interwoven into a popular culture object that, by implication, communicates a political message. Political myths are thus subtly reaffirmed or restated and altered in a Disney movie, a popular song, a TV show, a comic strip, and the like. Susan Sontag points out how many contemporary fantasies about politics are projected into science fiction movies, especially the "camp" B-movies of the Cold War era of the 1950s. In these popular culture objects, fantasies about physical annihilation or multilation by atomic weapons emerge. Fears of foreign invasion are transferred to outer space—Martians rather than earthly Russians and Chinese. Hopes about a united mankind against the common threat, which speak to the desire for national or Western unity, result from the gravity of the threat. Further, such films "may also be described as popular mythology for the contemporary *negative* imagination about the impersonal." Planetary invaders were usually emotionless zombies devoid of morality, desirous of destroying human (i.e., American) values, a common fantasy at the time about the Russians and Chinese: They were ten feet tall, cold and unbelievably cunning, and desirous of undermining our values and reducing us to their slaves. This theme probably speaks to a more inclusive myth, that of depersonalization in modern society. In one of the most famous of such films, *The Invasion of the Body Snatchers* (1956, not to be confused with the 1978 remake), the aliens replace the people of Santa Mira with beings who are physically duplicates but are psychologically alien: devoid of feeling, totally obedient, and servants of the group—a typical description of the myth of totalitarian man. Thus, *in toto,* such films enact, in displaced form, two myths that were much on people's minds in that period: fantasies about collective annihilation and fantasies about individual dehumanization.[7] Now it is unlikely that these commercial entertainments were produced to perpetuate any political message; producers were interested in what sells with audiences. But in the process, producers incorporated themes that expressed political myths current at the time.

Although popular culture has an effect on continuity and change in political myth, the relationship is impossible to state in direct causal ways. There are instances of a popular culture object being the precipitating cause of political action. The film, *Birth of a Nation* (1915), dramatized the myth of black culpability for destroying the southern way of life, apparently contributing to attacks on blacks after its presentation in some American towns. A popular creation can become a focus for political conflict, usually because it presents or attacks some myth held dear by some group. The antiwar movie, *All Quiet on the Western Front,* was picketed by the Nazis when it was released in Germany and was withdrawn from circulation by the Weimar government. Politically controversial popular figures (actors, comedians, radio commentators) often experience hostile receptions when they appear in some public forum. Vanessa Redgrave can expect hostility from Jewish and other groups because of her political activities.

But we are more interested here in the long-term and inclusive effects of popular culture on political perceptions and, thereby, on behavior. To what extent does popular culture make, reinforce, or break political myths for large numbers of people? What effect do nonpolitical and political popular artifacts have on our image of politics? To use an example: In the last few years, there has been a popular daytime soap opera called *Ryan's Hope* on ABC, with a character named Frank Ryan, who recurrently runs for office. The typical kinds of personal problems intervene—his wife's jealousy, an illegitimate pregnancy, and so on. Frank must deal with media moguls, underworld figures, and hostile reporters. After considerable frustration, he finally wins an election. We are not here concerned with the details of Frank Ryan's fictional life but with the larger implications of the depiction of politics. Does such a vehicle perpetuate the myths that politics is corrupt, that one has to deal with powerful and evil figures to succeed, that one's personal life is of central concern to voters? Does Frank Ryan reinforce the myth that good politicians are handsome, stylish, and sexually active? Is our image of politics reinforced or even created by watching such fare?

There is scant evidence to confirm or deny such a connection. Indeed it is the habit of many social scientists to discount the import of popular materials. But we cannot deny the mass attention paid to popular culture and the dramatization of social and political myths in popular formulas. One would expect that many popular culture objects could be deliberately designed to reinforce or at least not to disturb overtly popular political myths, although obviously this is not always the case. But certainly the great bulk of many popular vehicles does not threaten mass images and attitudes. As noted earlier, the vast majority of American war movies made during and after World War II and Korea were supportive of the war effort and of the official mythology of enemy culpability and allied nobility and justice. Even during Vietnam, there were few popular vehicles that directly attacked the official myth, and the major film of the period about the war, *The Green Berets* (one of the most popular films of 1968!), was highly supportive. Later, as we said, films became more critical, but this occurred long after the war was over and after the attitudinal change it had wrought was widespread. One of the most successful movies that implied criticism of the assumptions and conduct of the Vietnam War, *M*A*S*H,* muted it by displacing it to a safer war, the Korean, and relieving it with G.I. comedy.

If the *intent* of a popular culture vehicle is to communicate a political myth, the *effect* may be quite different than what was intended. Indeed, if a popular message is not supportive of widespread beliefs, popular perceptions can be markedly different than intended. The most famous case of this phenomenon occurred with the popular 1970s TV show *All in the Family* and the central character Archie Bunker. Producer Norman Lear and the CBS decision makers saw Archie as a comic figure who would be a funny foil against social prejudice and working-class ignorance. But evidence indicates that large portions of the audience did not see Archie as satire. Many viewers identified with him and his bigoted views![8] Prejudiced viewers used Archie to rationalize their own personal myths about the world. It is not clear how many other such misinterpretations take place, but *All in the Family* demonstrates the capacity of mythholders to retain beliefs in the face of popular dramas designed to communicate an alternative myth.

Unintended effects in popular vehicles have a subtle impact on people's perceptions of the world and thus on their mythology about government. Some studies argue that heavy television viewers have a distorted view of the world: They believe that more violence is occurring that actually is; they overestimate the percentage of private investigators in the population; and, in general, they tend to be influenced in their view of reality by the mass media.[9] This would mean that the mythology they hold about the world is actually created by popular shows. It is unlikely that the creators of *Hawaii Five-O* desired to propagate the mass feeling that psychopaths lurk everywhere or that private eye shows strive to argue that the police are either inept or hamstrung by restrictions in fighting crime. But such a popular conviction may be fostered by such shows, ultimately becoming a widespread perception created by constant re-enactment in popular drama.

Some popular culture objects provide political reassurance or reconfirmation of myths that people want to believe, even though they are not directly created to do so. Social tensions can be defused by the reaffirmation of political and social myths. One study of radio comedy during the Depression of the 1930s (*Amos 'n' Andy, The Rise of the Goldbergs,* etc.) found that such popular shows help to "relieve the social tension" of the period by "depression gags," reaffirming traditional pre-Depression values (e.g., the work ethic), conveying a sense of everybody being in the same situation, and deflating the egos of the pompous (as did Jack Benny, Charlie McCarthy, etc.). The radio comedies were highly supportive of Roosevelt and the New Deal, and people saw no contradiction between the traditional folk commonsense solutions that were the fare of the comedies and the complicated remedies of the New Deal.[10] Thereby the continuity and positive value of political institutions were confirmed.

The confirmation of myth by popular culture frequently occurs when people are involved in a historical movement that brings doubts as to national purpose. Again, such confirmation might not have been the intent of the creators of the object, but it became a symbolic focus for reconfirmation at the time. The television series, *Victory at Sea,* came to be such a symbolic object in the early 1950s. With the confusing stalemate of Korea and the advent of the Cold War, Americans experienced doubt about the national purpose so heroically advanced in World War II. The myths of American rightness in foreign policy—as militant defender of freedom and policeman of the world—were reconfirmed by that TV series. The series, of course, was about World War II, especially the naval operations, but the visual imagery was so heroic, and the narration so dramatic, that for many it seemed to validate what "must never be forgot." Thus the recent past was mythologized into a "drama of commemoration" that had an emotional impact relevant for the uncertainties of a present.[11]

It is to be expected that political leaders will *use* popular culture to further myths about themselves and the institutions they represent. Candidates for office commonly show up at popular events—the World Series, the Super Bowl, or stock car races—to communicate that they are regular guys who enjoy the same mass sports as ordinary folks. Candidate Richard Nixon, running for office in 1968 as a "New Nixon," made a cameo appearance on NBC's *Laugh-in,* saying, "Sock it to *me*?" Politicians work at mastering popular phrases, take up fads, change personal dress and hair style according to fashion—all to demonstrate that they are "with it." Presidents even bestow political legitimacy on popular phenomena, as when the press discovered that President Kennedy was a fan of James Bond novels.

Political deference to popular tastes and values can reach fantastic proportions in democratic, media-pervaded societies like the United States. President Carter felt obliged to drop by when one of America's most mythic figures, Mickey Mouse, visited a White House children's party on the occasion of his fiftieth birthday in 1978. Public deference by politicians to such icons from popular entertainment, sports, or religion is apparently necessary because of the mythic status of such symbolic figures.

The importance attached to popular culture by political actors and institutions extends to attempts to *influence* the message of popular formulas. Political organizations have tried to co-opt popular culture creators in a variety of ways. The Pentagon, for instance, long co-opted movie companies by offering them access to military bases, airplanes, tanks, troops, and technical advice in exchange for a measure of control over the script. In effect, this gave the Pentagon a popular forum to reinforce positive myths about the military. Undoubt-edly the most successful user of popular culture in recent American politics was J. Edgar Hoover and the Federal Bureau of Investigation (recall Chapter 4). As Richard Gid Powers has pointed out, Hoover appropriated the modern action detective motif by encouraging pop-ular fiction and dramas to use G-men as heroes. Public relations gim-micks—the "Ten Most Wanted List," staged and filmed arrests, the museum at headquarters—helped to undergird the FBI myth. A variety of radio shows *(The FBI in Peace and War, I Was a Communist for the FBI)*, movies *(The FBI Story)*, television series *(I Led Three Lives, The FBI)*, comic strips, magazines, and so on all contributed to mythologizing the agency. In the wake of the popular TV series, *The FBI*, starring Efrem Zimbalist, Jr., as Inspector Lou Erskine, Hoover even insisted that agents conform to the "Zimmy image"; reality had to measure up to myth! Hoover understood how a bureaucratic agency could be transformed into mythology through the adroit use of popular culture: The G-man was not just a government official, he became the stuff of myth, an action detective symbolically embodying social virtues and the wrath of the community against malefactors. The myth, as enacted in popular entertainment, served agency pur-poses by symbolically showing the power of the FBI in winning the war against crime and subversion. Although in reality the FBI was not very good at catching big criminals (and Hoover resisted efforts to make the FBI into a national police force), popular culture helped to create in the popular mind the FBI myth that is still deeply ingrained in the American consciousness.[12]

The creation of a political or governmental myth can extend to capitalizing on a mood in the mass public that is reflected in popular culture trends. For example, the turbulent period of Vietnam and Watergate contributed to an ensuing depressed and pessimistic mood among many people about America and its future. The present seemed complicated and threatening, and the forecasts of futurists seemed apocalyptic. Several genres of movies and TV shows reflected the mood wherein dramatic formulas caught the popular feeling. In par-ticular, catastrophe films and movies about Satanic possession typified the sense of gloom, the feeling that the world was coming apart. Tidal waves, towering infernos, earthquakes, comets, endangered airplanes and ships—even the activities of man-eating sharks—confirmed a feel-ing of imminent disaster. Films dramatized the 1970s sense of people at the mercy of uncontrolled forces. It was a drama of Titanic irony: the ironic sense—exemplified in the unsinkable *Titanic* that went down on its maiden voyage—that no matter how safe or powerful one feels, people are buffeted by forces they are not equal to. Americans flocked to movies to see the punishment of the wicked (since bad people were often singled out by the earthquake or fire for destruction) or a more general satisfaction derived from seeing rich and arrogant social groups suffer. Similarly, movies like *The Exorcist* and *The Omen* were popular vehicles confirming the idea that evil is a powerful, even ineradicable force in the world. Like the catastrophe movie, the "Devil" films reflected the sense of man's contemporary helplessness against the power of evil. To repeat, such genres appeal because they provide vehicles of mythic confirmation, acting out some felt belief about the world.

But popular vehicles also act out for us *desired* states of affairs, confirming myths about what we want or, at least, about something good we believe once existed. Norman Rockwell made a lifelong career painting America as many desired it to be or believed it once was. In the 1970s, the popular phenomenon that most exemplified this was undoubtedly the TV show, *The Waltons.* The Walton family was like animated Norman Rockwell paintings, enacting a nostalgic past that never was but that we now would like to think existed and that we wish we could recapture. The core of the mythic appeal of *The Waltons* was not that they lived in a time of rural peace and pastoral simplicity but that they lived through times of troubles (the Depression, World War II) successfully because they had resources the 1970s does not believe it has anymore—family loyalty, character, deeply held values, religious faith, common sense. *The Waltons* captured a mood of a nostalgic, mythical, better time in the past, a sense observed in other popular successes—the movie *American Graffiti,* the TV shows *Happy Days* and *Laverne and Shirley,* and K-tel record collections of World War II songs that revived memories of that "happy time!"

In the wake of this popular mood, the election of 1976 occurred. To the surprise of many, Jimmy Carter, a national political unknown, won the Democratic nomination and Ronald Reagan nearly took the Republican nomination away from President Ford. Why? Obviously there were many factors, but in part their success can be traced not to issues or positions but to how the candidates represented nostalgia for old values, past virtues, and simple solutions. Reagan dressed like a 1940s movie star (which he was!) and talked, in his charming, schoolboyish way, a homespun antigovernment line. Like Carter, much of his appeal was that he was not part of the Washington Establishment. But Carter had something else going for him: the Walton factor. Carter talked the antigovernment, traditional values, throw-the-rascals-out rhetoric, but he could also be pictured in the Walton-like setting of his origins. Plains, Georgia, offered the nation the myth of Jimmy, a kind of real-life John-Boy, growing up in a simple pastoral setting and in an extended family that bred in him the intelligence and character expected in the oldest son. The spectacle was replete with images appealing to the nostalgic mood: the peaceful little town and rural community; the Baptist "church in the wildwood"; the close-knit family of characters—the matriarchal mother, "good old boy" brother, independent sisters, and so on. Carter therefore reflected—and carefully cultivated—myths salient at that historical moment.

The Walton nostalgia was overtly nonpolitical, but politics is not a rational process. It is a stage for the dramatic presentation of qualities and values that have a covert, sometimes unconscious appeal at a mythical level. A politician or a political movement can be the emotional focus for what people would desperately like to recapture: a mythologized past that we would all like to return to, which the political leader and his setting symbolize for the moment. It is a singular fact that this impulse recurs in political history and is an important part of the politics of our time. The desire to restore or revitalize is a normal mass response to rapid change, and it is understandable why people would come to idealize a mythic past as a better, even Edenic, time. First-generation revolutionaries extol the virtues and trials of the revolution to the annoyance of later, allegedly softer, generations. Developing countries, such as Iran, undergo mass movements in order to return to the certainties of traditional values. If people cannot mythologize the future—if it seems threatening rather than promising—at least they can mythologize the past. Granted that, caught in the processes of time—as Thomas Wolfe said—"You can't go home again"; but it is a common popular feeling, and a common political manifestation, to try to re-present, and even to make live, our myths about the past.

The interrelationship between popular culture and political myth is one that deserves further exploration. The hidden agenda of a political culture, the latent ideology held by mass publics, the moods and desires pollsters don't tap: All often find expression in popular culture. In an often hidden, sometimes obvious, way, those myths we hold about politics, society, and ourselves at a particular time acquire new life for us in the creations of popular culture.

POPULAR FOLKLORE AND POLITICAL MYTH

There is a different way to talk about the relationship between popular culture and political myth. This is via *folklore,* a collection of popular expressions communicating some commonly held myth. These expressions might range from long-held folk myths that are part of the macromyths of a society or civilization to contemporary myths popularly believed. Folk myths about women (as temptresses or virgins, for instance) have taken a variety of forms in many cultures. They are frequently part of the folk culture of a community and persist over centuries in religious or simply popular imagery, perhaps passed down by word of mouth over generations. More immediate myths sometimes spring up among people in response to a current event or issue. During the energy crises of the 1970s, many people believed that the crises were the result of deliberate collusion by the big oil companies. Whether this was true or not is beside the point; the view was offered in groups—in bar talk, among workers at lunch, at gas stations—and often assented to without investigations as to its accuracy.

Such mythmaking differs from the created artifacts of popular culture discussed above. Folk myths are natural and are not a deliberate product of media organizations or artists. Richard Dorson draws a distinction between "folklore" and "fakelore": The former are myths that are authentic products of the populace; the latter are spurious and synthetic works created only to have "folkish" appeal. The former include fairy tales, folk songs, legends, and so on as products of the traditional popular culture. The latter include fabricated tales with a common appeal. The distinction is difficult to maintain. Walt Disney transformed many traditional folk tales (Snow White) into fakelore, and many traditional pieces of folklore were created by imaginative artists (Pinocchio) or were self-made legends (such as Bat

Masterson and other Western heroes). Even though, as Dorson claims, many modern tales and heroes are products of popular culture, they nevertheless constitute part of the folk culture of modern America. Indeed, in many cases they are continuations or new versions of traditional folk myths. The myth of the Superhero—the individual with "powers far beyond those of mortal men"—begins with figures like Washington; continues in the early Heroic Age with Davy Crockett, Paul Bunyan, and Daniel Boone; returns on the far Western frontier in Wyatt Earp and others; and takes on a modern, urban form with Superman, Spiderman, Wonder Woman, and so forth. If "heroic saga is the very stuff of folk tradition," then these latter-day heroes participate in a folk heritage exploited by popular culture organizations, such as Disney, that continue the process of mythmaking.[13] As Harold Schechter points out, the popularly celebrated myth of the "Eternal Child" in popular artifacts of the 1960s actually revived a mythical form literally eons old.[14]

A modern political culture such as America includes a *political folklore,* a sometimes natural, sometimes created and exploited set of myths. Some are long-lasting, others immediate and ephemeral. All can contribute to latent myths about politics held by large numbers of people. These myths may circulate through a wide range of processes and forms, but they typically involve a "shared fantasy" about politics, sometimes dramatized in an artificial setting, but usually also validated in personal contact with others who share the myth.[15] As we pointed out in Chapter 1, such myths serve several needs for people. Political folklore teaches moral lessons about politics, helps to explain things that are happening, restates settled truths, reduces anxiety, and the like. It takes many forms that, like folklore generally, are universal. Song and tale, for instance, are two types of folklore seen almost everywhere. Anthropologist Franz Boas noted that the formulas of myths and folk tales follow the same pattern, reflecting basic mythic impulses transcending cultural specifics.[16] We use mythic devices today for the same reason primitive man did: to deal with experience. What we are interested in here is the way in which we—the folk—use folklore to deal with political experience.

There is a school of thought in the study of American public opinion claiming that a relatively small proportion of Americans are informed and ideologically sophisticated citizens. The great bulk of the public relies much more on a kind of *folk wisdom* than on ideological categories ("liberal," "conservative") or informed knowledge.[17] One suspects that even informed ideologues intensely interested in politics often rely on mythical imagery and ideas more than advocates of this view want to admit.[18] Talk among the folk—the mass public—about politics is mythical, expressing some truth about politics, either unexamined or beyond examination. To illustrate, consider three forms of folk wisdom: the proverb, the tale, and the prejudice.

The *political proverb* is a mythic expression of people, an often epigrammatic popular adage that purports to tell a universal truth about politics. "The proverb," writes Hugh Duncan, "is public; it means what it does, not because an individual artist uses it or because it is indigenous to any individual group, but because it has been accepted by many groups over long periods of time. . . . When we invoke a proverb we invoke the experience of the group itself."[19] When we hear of some political scandal, we agree that "all politicians are crooks." Or we assure each other that America "is the greatest country in the world." After a frustrating attempt to get some administrative action on something, we reassure ourselves that "you can't fight City Hall." The logic or the evidential base of such generalizations is irrelevant; the function of the proverb is mythical, providing an easily available and reassuring explanation of the process underlying a specific experience. If we were to sit down and write down what we believe about politics, it might take more of the mythic form of the proverb than we would like to admit.

The *political folk tale* is a mythic form that relates a story about politics. In either a direct or displaced way, the folk tale illustrates some moral lesson or provides an explanatory framework in story form. For example, much of the so-called Lincoln lore after his death not only venerated the mythic figure of Lincoln but also celebrated social and political virtues. Myths arose about his acts of kindness or honesty. The figure of Lincoln became a mythic repository of a wide variety of virtues in the popular tales about him, which neither time nor debunking have been able to eradicate.[20] But popular folk tales can also be used to explain the political world in narrative form. A story of some past event may surface that illustrates some aspect of the political world. For example, people often attribute great powers to some past leader and underscore this with a tale in order to demonstrate the accomplishment of great deeds. After the death of Mayor Daley in Chicago, residents developed the myth of Daley's great power to accomplish things, in contrast with his successors, and illustrated his prowess with stories about what he did. Or, think of political conspiracy theories as vast folk tales that people hold and share. This helps to explain their popularity: People can accept a story form of a vast and sinister international conspiracy of such proportions and illogic because it puts in story form a tale of why politics today is the way it is. Conspiracy theories are the political folk epics of our day.

Some folk tales originally designed to convey a political message when couched in a mythical setting later become part of the nonpolitical folklore of a country. In America, the most famous example of this is *The Wizard of Oz.* Originally conceived by L. Frank Baum in 1900, it eventually became a favorite among children for decades; the 1939 movie starring Judy Garland is a perennial classic. The original Oz had an implicit political message and was indeed an extended allegory about the political situation in the United States in the 1890s. Baum was a Kansas Populist, and *The Wizard of Oz* is a folk tale designed to satirize that age: Dorothy is a midwestern Everyman and seeks help from the Wizard, who turns out to be a humbug—like President William McKinley. The Wizard lives in the capital of Oz at the end of the dangerous Yellow Brick Road, symbolic of the gold standard, a key issue in the William Jennings Bryan versus William McKinley election of 1896. Dorothy wears Silver Slippers (in the book), representing the Populist position on the free coinage of silver. The Scarecrow is, like the Kansas farmer, ignorant and in need of brains to fight the eastern establishment; the Tin Man represents labor, who rusted up, and by voting for McKinley, shows he has no heart; the Cowardly Lion is Bryan himself, bumbling and fearful, in need of courage.[21] This topical satire in the book has long since yielded to the simple delight of the story.

Political songs are a specialized form of political folk tale. Political songs—anthems, protest songs, topical songs, satirical songs—tell a story in order to teach a moral lesson or convey a message about what politics is like. The tradition of Left and Labor songs in America, for example, tell of Joe Hill and his message to "Organize!" and they tell of the "owners" and the "rich" who run politics and deprive the worker.[22]

We include *prejudice* in the category of folk wisdom because it is a prevalent and dangerous form of popular mythology. Prejudices may be expressed as proverbs ("Niggers have no morals and are lazy") or as folk tales, that is, as apocryphal stories to show prejudice toward a group. Popular beliefs supporting prejudice often rest on stereotypes not based on observation or contact with the group. Blacks or other minorities may not live in one's neighborhood, yet they are objects of considerable fear. If one member of a group relates a tale about a member of the feared minority performing an antisocial act (which he may not have observed first hand, but heard from someone else, who heard it from someone else, and so on), this soon becomes a shared fantasy and validates the myth. One person tells a tale of a sharp business deal where a sympathetic character is "taken" by a Jewish businessman, and this activates a shared prejudicial stereotype: The prejudiced group members reassure themselves of their superiority and of the true nature and inferior qualities of Jews. Such myths are common parlance in the folk culture of many countries, and it need not be stressed that they yield spurious logic and dangerous emotions.

Political prejudices often play a large role in popular evaluations of politics. A president, for example, may be disliked not for his policies or even for his style but be prejudged as bad or good because he is an Irish Catholic or a southern Baptist. If he includes blacks and women in his cabinet, this may activate prejudices about "black militants" or "pushy women who want to be men." One's attitude toward a policy—say, the Panama Canal treaty—may be colored by one's prejudice about Latin Americans: "Why, those savages couldn't possibly run the Canal." Prejudice is popular mythology, but if the shared fantasy is widespread enough, it can be mobilized into a political force of some power.

POPULAR TALK AND POLITICAL MYTH

The popular culture of a society can generate political myths in many ways, especially by various modes of *popular talk*. We distinguish popular talk from folk wisdom because types of talk are usually not purported to be universal political truths, although each is a response to social and political conditions and related to the development of folk wisdom. In any case, these forms of popular talk are ways of mythmaking: era talk, jokes, rumors, and fads.

Era talk is language usage that develops among a people in a particular time. A good example appears in Cyra McFadden's novel, *The Serial,* about the linguistic conventions of residents of rich and trendy Marin County, California. People there lead a "laidback lifestyle," are "heavily into" the "human potential movement" and "fundamental human experiences," condemn "macho power tripping," and worry about "destabilizing the environment." Era talk today is a form of the current "psychobabble" of wealthy people with leisure time who combine the pseudo-radicalism of the late 1960s with the "Me Decade" self-absorption of the 1970s.[23] There are political myths imbedded in such era talk: conterculture myths adopted by upper-middle-class professionals to prove that they are "with it" (one wealthy man says of Cesar Chavez, the leader of the Farm Worker's Union, "Cesar's my main man"); feminist myths about "herstory" and "the male ego syndrome"; and so on. People flock to political stances and figures because of seeming fashionability.

The language that develops in a particular era mirrors the political concerns of people. This language communicates to ourselves and to others political myths that reflect deep concerns about ourselves and the world. It was common in the 1970s, after the fall of Nixon and the various political tremors of that age, to hear popular talk about the ineptitude and incompetence of Presidents Ford and Carter. Ford was dogged by the image of a stumblebum of low intellect and stolidity. Comic Chevy Chase drew riotous laughter by simply falling down in parody of Ford's public gaffes. At one point (see Chapter 6), Carter emerged as a "little man," "weak," personally not capable of coping with the job. It may well be argued that this popular perception was a myth that tells us much about ourselves. It is possible that we have deep confusions and fears about the shift of power in the world and the sense that we may not, as a nation, be able to cope as we once did; also, the attribution of ineptitude to presidents may reflect widespread personal anxieties about our own personal powerlessness and inability to cope. Such political myths expressed in era talk may tell us more about our own latent political and personal doubts than it indicates an objective evaluation of presidential performance.

Similarly, *political jokes* are a form of popular talk about politics possibly expressing covert anxieties about the ambiguities and tensions of politics. For example, after the American recognition of the People's Republic of China in 1978, the anxiety level of leaders of the Soviet Union increased regarding the exact relationship between the Americans and the Chinese. There were even fears about joint attack and invasion. Russians expressed these fears in "Chinese jokes." One joke had President Carter chatting with President Brezhnev, telling him that the Americans have a new computer that foretells the future. Brezhnev asks Carter who will be in the Politburo (the Soviet ruling body) in 1990. After a pause, Carter says, "I'm sorry, Leonid. I can't read it. All the names are in Chinese."[24] The underlying grim edge of such humor clearly reveals the popular myth of Chinese invasion.

Political jokes do not always have such an ironic structure, but they still speak to some political myth. When they spoof or satirize a political figure, they tell us something of our ambivalence about authority, perceptions complicated by our intimate knowledge of the personal attributes and "warts" of political leaders as they are portrayed in the news. Thus authority is amenable to both veneration and deprecation. The joke is a way to deprecate authority safely by making fun of the personal quirks of, for instance, presidents. Serious deprecation is more socially unacceptable, since it raises questions about our mythic respect for presidential authority. The typical joke, however, does not attack the larger political myth of authority but does allow us to laugh at individual actors in authority roles.

Political *rumors* float around society by word of mouth. It is astounding what people know about politics—knowledge learned from others in everyday discourse. It is also amazing how much survival power and geographical spread a rumor can have. In the 1960s, the Paul McCartney death rumor spread all over the world; teenagers everywhere shared the myth that Beatle member McCartney was dead, that he had been replaced by an exact duplicate, and that the Beatles were trying to communicate this through their album covers. Similarly, in recent years the McDonald's hamburger chain has been beset by a persistent (and inaccurate) rumor that they use red worm meat in their hamburgers. Rumors can, of course, result in panic and hysteria and have more serious social effects. The invasion from Mars rumor that followed the 1938 *War of the Worlds* radio broadcast included panic, mobs, suicides, and so on.[25]

Political rumors can have considerable effect on both perceptions and action in politics. Presidential nominating conventions have been disrupted because of rumors developing on the floor among delegates. Indeed, politicians deliberately spread rumors to achieve some purpose, such as creating a bandwagon effect on delegates. But rumors are capable of spontaneously arising and spreading on their own. Indeed, a rumor often spreads because it activates a deeply held but latent political myth. One of the more remarkable instances of this occurred in 1963 when the U.S. Army launched "Operation Water Moccasin," an exercise at a base in Georgia to train American soldiers in counter-insurgency tactics. The exercise included observers from the militaries of foreign countries. The rumor spread among local people and right-wing groups that this was a coordinated plot to seize Georgia as a first step in a United Nations takeover of the United States and that rather than an army exercise, Georgia was under attack by 20,000 Congolese troops, supported by 30,000 Mongolian soldiers. The next step was to attack San Diego with 35,000 Chinese soldiers in Baja California. This rumor spread across the country, chiefly through the ultraconservative press and radio. Scared constituents deluged the Army and congressmen with communications. That many people would take such a rumor seriously gives credence to the latent popular myth of an international conspiracy and imminent subversion.

In other cases, of course, the rumor itself is the source of political myth, since people learn from someone else a myth about politics. A very apolitical person may hear from a trusted figure that "Carter is not really in charge; Mondale and David Rockefeller are really pulling the strings," believe it, and pass it on to others. Rumormongers are what David Riesman called "inside-dopesters": they deal in rumors, since this gives them an air of knowing what's *really* going on.[27] Rumormongers are important in the perpetuation of popular political myths because of the gullibility of people in believing the most implausible notions about politics.

Finally, *fads* are a form of popular talk that may be related to political myth. A fad is a fashionable diversion, the "thing to do" at a particular historical moment. Things "catch on," become a craze for a while, and then disappear. Hula hoops, pet rocks, Spiro Agnew watches, Disco, and so on endlessly are diversions that become popular among peer groups because "everybody's doing it." Although many fads are frivolous, they can relate to a serious undercurrent in a society. In the late 1970s, it was fashionable to watch television mini-series, such as *Roots* and *Holocaust*. But such fads reflected something of a mass desire to understand more about two great historical events, the black experience in America and the "Final Solution" in Nazi Germany. Yet, many people may selectively perceive such programs to reaffirm their myths about blacks and Jews. A fad may also reveal unconscious desires for mythical affirmation on the part of a society. The "King Tut" craze, for example, tells us something about our desire for eternal religious values; Tut became for Americans a popular symbol of timeless and transcendent truths.

Most fads, however, are not directly political, although they may suggest mass feelings that can become politically salient. The music of Bob Dylan and Janis Joplin in the 1960s was not usually directly political, but it did touch a mass nerve among the youth culture; rock music increasingly came to treat the myths of the evil Establishment and the middle class. Indeed, as the 1960s climaxed, it was the fashion in many youth circles to be "radical" and to adopt the rhetoric, clothing, posters (of Che Guevara and Mao Tse-tung), and actions of the "New Left." Although the issues that helped to create such a movement were quite real (Vietnam, civil rights), political radicalism was also a posture popularized by fad appeal. After all, everyone was doing it. The political faddism of the late 1960s appealed to young non-students, high-school kids, even older people who identified with the youth movement. It developed an elaborate political mythology, including seeing itself as the cultural wave of the future.[28] The faddishness of such political posturing was best captured in two of Tom Wolfe's essays. In one, he identified the phenomenon of "radical chic," involving trendy and wealthy New York jetsetters discovering that the fad "this season" was to be "radical" and espouse the cause of black militants, migrant farm workers, antiwar activists, Marxist revolutionaries, and so on. Thus a fundraising cocktail party for the Black Panthers took place at conductor Leonard Bernstein's condominium, and it was a society page item as to who was there. Paris designers provided expensive "radical" clothes. The "beautiful people" from Eastport to Beverly Hills adopted leftist causes. Apparently they believed that their activities were genuine and beneficial, and that they would overcome class lines and racial differences. Even though the problems of poverty, racism, and war did not go away, its fashionability did, and the beautiful people drifted into other fads, such as feminism and disco. Similarly, Wolfe notes how, in urban areas such as San Francisco, what he calls "mau-mauing the flak catchers" become a fad among the "kids"—teen-agers and even preteens. Political demonstrations at City Hall were the fun thing to do; the kids could "trash" the system directly.[29] In both of Wolfe's cases, a new political myth won acceptance and fashionability in peer groups. But each was a fad and had limited lasting ability in either belief or commitment. Today, neither jetsetters nor teen-agers are noted for political radicalism. In the 1970s, if there is a political myth perpetuated by rock music (say, James Taylor or Carole King), it is that participation is futile and that one should devote oneself to personal dynamics. The Rolling Stones' "Street Fightin' Man" has been replaced by "Staying Alive"; the teach-in by the toga party.

IN SEARCH OF HEROISM
From the Popular to the Political

This chapter pointed out some of the ways in which popular culture contributes to political mythmaking. We saw how popular mythmaking relates to identity; we distinguished the relationships between popular culture and the mythic currents of politics. It remains to speculate on the future of such a relationship.

Jerome Bruner has asserted that "we live in a period of mythic confusion that may provide the occasion for a new growth of myth, myths more suitable for our times."[30] If it is true that we need myths as guides to our past, present, and future (as we try to cope in the here and now) and that we are in a state of mythic decay, then it may be that we turn to popular sources for mythic cues for lack of any better source. Mircea Eliade thinks that we find the myths of the modern world in our entertainments—in, for instance, detective fiction. Even though reduced to the realm of social distraction—reading, watching TV, and so on—mythic forms stay alive. "In the collective life it [social distraction] sometimes reasserts itself with considerable force, in the form of a political myth."[31] Conventional myths enter a state of decay, and people go elsewhere—into cults, "electronic" churches, communes, and other particular groups. The one area of popularly shared mythic experience left is popular culture. If, for example, the institutions of the family, the school, and the church continue to decline as agencies of political socialization, young people still find common mythic experience in popular culture—youth movies, rock concerts, peer groups—and potentially draw political myths increasingly from popular culture. It is not yet the case that most popular culture creations are overtly political, nor does popular talk dwell upon political things. But one can see that if popular culture organizations—TV and radio networks, movie studios, newspapers and magazines, and so on—and new popular talk should turn political, their potential for being the key political mythmakers of the future is considerable.[32] Thus popular culture might well be the vehicle whereby a political leader, promising to redeem America and return the nation to its lost greatness, could seek power.

But what in popular culture indicates that there is an incipient desire for such a redeemer figure? In a sense, American popular culture has always had a strain in it that spoke to this desire. The "American monomyth"—the myth of the committed and incorruptible hero who single-handedly saves the community from evil—is deeply embedded in the American consciousness.[33] James Fenimore Cooper's deerslayer, the myth of the frontiersman and the cowboy, the private eye, and many other popular formulas are versions of the monomyth. However, such myth has rarely taken political form. But the myth is there, and it might acquire political salience, given the right social conditions.

Current indications of the desire for a monomythic hero appear in several popular formulas, including the comics. The comics have always been a vehicle for the expression of deep-seated social desires and conflicts. But today, comic strips, books, and Saturday morning serials stress superhero themes more than ever. Comic strips, such as "Superheroes," "The Amazing Spider-Man," "Conan the Barbarian," and "Starwars"; comic books like "Superman," "Batman and Robin," "Wonder Woman," "Captain America," and so on; and TV and movies have all been successful with a superhero theme. One sees the same phenomenon in the Tolkien books and in those of his imitators, in popular science fiction, and in children's books and games. The overarching appeal of the superheroic theme reflects the frustrations and unheroic nature of our age. In the 1970s, a period of depression, mundane and nitpicking politics, and fear of innovation, the appeal of *Star Wars,* Superman, Tolkien and the like was that they brought us a fantasy world of great adventure, heroes and heroic deeds, and the conquest of good over evil. We could vicariously participate in a romantic and fulfilling adventure that transported us to worlds beyond the present.

Such fantasy is understandable but is potentially dangerous. The bulk of the superheroes depicted get their authority to act from translegal sources that supercede normal legal precepts. Typically, they are charismatic, pure, outsiders, and they succeed because of their moral and technological power, oftentimes by violence. They are attractive because they offer a clearcut distinction between good and evil, simplify the ambiguities of life, and overcome obstacles quickly and neatly. It need hardly be added that these superheroic characteristics can take on a demonic form in political life. Napoleon, Hitler, and, to some extent, Lenin and Stalin were exalted as political superheroes who derived their authority from translegal sources; followers perceived them as charismatic, pure, outsiders (e.g., Napoleon was Corsican, Hitler Austrian); they offered simple solutions by violence; and they succeeded because of alleged moral superiority and technological skill (e.g., military and propaganda). The belief that someone can and should have that kind of power to save has had popular appeal—and truly devastating results.

If the current fad for superheroes does reflect a widespread desire for such a leader and such actions (especially among the young), then it is possible that some redeemer figure could nobilize this fantasy into a political force of considerable consequence. The Epilogue of this book deals with this mythical theme in more detail.

REFERENCES

1. See, for example, Will Wright, *Sixguns and Society* (Berkeley: University of California Press, 1975); John G. Cawelti, *The Six-gun Mystique* (Bowling Green, Ohio: The Bowling Green University Popular Press, n.d.).

2. Albert Kreiling, "Toward a Cultural Studies Approach for the Sociology of Popular Culture," *Communication Research,* 5, no. 3 (July 1978): 260-261.

3. Many of the issues are defined in Bernard Rosenberg and David Manning White, eds., *Mass Culture* (New York: Free Press, 1957); and their follow-up volume, *Mass Culture Revisited* (New York: Van Nostrand Reinhold, 1971).

4. William Blake Tyrell, "Star Trek as Myth and TV as Mythmaker," *Journal of Popular Culture,* 10, no. 4 (1977): 711–719.

5. Jerome S. Bruner, "Myth and Identity," in Henry A. Murray, ed., *Myth and Mythmaking* (Boston: Beacon Press, 1960), p. 280.

6. Tyrell, "Star Trek," pp. 712–713.

7. Susan Sontag, "Science Fiction Films: The Imagination of Disaster," in Alan Casty, ed., *Mass Media and Mass Man* (New York: Holt, Rinehart and Winston, 1968), pp. 131–142.

8. Neil Vidmar and Milton Rokeach, "Archie Bunker's Bigotry: A Study in Selective Perception and Exposure," *Journal of Communication,* 24, no. 1 (Winter 1974): 36–47.

9. George Gerbner and Larry Gross, "Living with Television: The Violence Profile," *Journal of Communication,* 26, no. 2 (Spring 1976): 173–199.

10. Arthur Frank Wertheim, "Relieving Social Tensions: Radio Comedy and the Great Depression," *Journal of Popular Culture,* 10, no. 3 (Winter 1976): 501–519.

11. Peter Rollins, "Victory at Sea: Cold War Epic," *Journal of Popular Culture,* 6, no. 3 (Spring 1973): 463–482.

12. Richard Gid Powers, "J. Edgar Hoover and the Detective Hero," *Journal of Popular Culture,* 9, no. 2 (Fall 1975): 257–278.

13. But see Richard Dorson, *American Folklore and the Historian* (Chicago: University of Chicago Press, 1971), p. 9.

14. Harold Schechter, "The Myth of the Eternal Child in Sixties America," in Jack Nachbar, *et al.,* eds., *The Popular Culture Reader* (Bowling Green, Ohio: Bowling Green University Popular Press, 1978), pp. 64–78.

15. Ernest G. Bormann, "Fantasy and Rhetorical Vision: The Rhetorical Criticism of Social Reality," *Quarterly Journal of Speech,* 58 (1972): 396–407.

16. For a survey, see Elvin Hatch, *Theories of Man and Culture* (New York: Columbia University Press, 1973).

17. See Phillip Converse, "The Nature of Belief Systems in Mass Publics," in David Apter, ed., *Ideology and Discontent* (New York: Free Press, 1964).

18. Some hint of this may be inferred from Steven R. Brown, "Consistency and the Persistence of Ideology: Some Experimental Results," *Public Opinion Quarterly,* 34 (Spring 1970): 60–68.

19. Hugh Dalziel Duncan, *Communication and Social Order* (New York: Bedminster Press, 1962), p. 431.

20. Ray B. Browne, *Lincoln Lore: Lincoln in the Popular Mind* (Bowling Green, Ohio: Bowling Green University Popular Press, 1974).

21. Henry Littlefield, "The Wizard of Oz: Parable of Populism," *American Quarterly,* 16, no. 1 (1964): 47–58.

22. Jerome Rodnitzky, "The Evolution of the American Protest Song," *Journal of Popular Culture,* 3, no. 1 (Summer 1969): 35–45.

23. Cyra McFadden, *The Serial: A Year in the Life of Marin County* (New York: Knopf, 1977); see also R. D. Rosen, *Psychobabble* (New York: Atheneum, 1978).

24. Associated Press story, "Spread of 'Chinese Jokes' in Russia," released January 3, 1979.

25. Hadley Cantril, *The Invasion from Mars* (Princeton, N.J.: Princeton University Press, 1940).

26. Tamotsu Shibutani, *Improvised News: A Sociological Study of Rumor* (Indianapolis: Bobbs-Merrill, 1966), p. 80.

27. David Riesman, *et al., The Lonely Crowd* (New Haven, Ct.: Yale University Press, 1961), pp. 180–181.

28. See, in retrospect now, Charles A. Reich, *The Greening of America* (New York: Bantam Books, 1970).

29. Tom Wolfe, *Radical Chic and Mau-mauing the Flak Catchers* (New York: Bantam, 1971).

30. Bruner, "Myth and Identity," p. 285.

31. Mircea Eliade, *Myths, Dreams, and Mysteries* (New York: Harper & Row, 1967), p. 38.

32. See Robert Jewett and John Shelton Lawrence, *The American Monomyth* (Garden City, N.Y.: Doubleday, 1977), pp. 214–216.

33. Jewett and Lawrence, *The American Monomyth, passim.*

CHAPTER 6

"And That's The Way It Is,"
Well, Might Have Been! News As Mythmaking

If opinion surveys are correct, then the most widely known, perhaps popular, and certainly most trusted person in the 1960s and 1970s was Walter Cronkite. Small wonder! It was "Uncle" Walter who comforted our shock at the assassination of a president and would-be presidents; who swelled us with patriotic pride announcing that "the Eagle has landed" on the surface of the moon; who acted as surrogate secretary of state in bringing together leaders of warring nations; who covered every important election in recent memory; and who with nightly regularity (under the sponsorship of laxatives and dental adhesives) reassured us about the past, the present, and the future. So when he proclaims "that's the way it is," Americans believe him. But do television newscasters "tell it like it is?" Do the news media report what's *really* happening?

There are several schools of thought. One is that the news media are full of nay-sayers, accentuating the negative side of politics, eliminating the positive, and ignoring any truth in between. Another, once led by a vice president of the United States, proclaims that the news media are filled with "self-appointed guardians of the liberal cause" and are hence biased and protective of leftist points of view.[1] Yet another disagrees, arguing that the news media propagate a conservative, middle-class Establishment message. Then there is the notion of the press as adversarial, as in continuing conflict with government to uncover the truth on behalf of a free citizenry. Cast in this role, say defenders of the news media, the press indeed reports bad news, but does it make sense to kill such a messenger? And, finally, there is a school that says that the news media have nothing to do with reporting, advocating, or defending or with truth as such. Rather, the news media create realities, set agendas for public discussion, stir up controversies, and elevate obscure personalities to the presidency—a sort of far-reaching *Sixty Minutes* or *National Inquirer* that touches all facets of politics. But whatever the image people have of the news media, everyone, it seems, is enamored by the "power of the press." That notion is replete with mythical implications. In this chapter, we look at myths of press power. We start with ideas about the character of news; then we explore the myths that people inside and outside the news media hold about the press; the myths that the news media create and propagate; the myth of a free press; and the newest myth of journalism, that of precision reporting.

NOW-ISM
The (D)Evolution of the Carter Myth

There is scarcely a product in the world as perishable as news. It is alive and vibrant and exciting when it is NOW, when it is the latest news you can deliver to the audience. With each passing moment it becomes more stale.[2]

News has a lot in common with gossip and rumor. All come about when something out of the ordinary happens and people want to find out what's going on. "What's happening?" is the question on everyone's lips. If the answer is restricted to a small circle of people informally talking about what happened, it's gossip. If larger numbers of people get into the act and speculations spread through informal, word-of-mouth means, we have rumors. News develops when extraordinary happenings are taken into account by formal institutions, the news media, that deem them newsworthy and convert them into stories designed to remove the ambiguity and uncertainty in what happened.[3]

Being concerned with things that happen out of the ordinary, the news media usually focus on daily occurrences, that is, "What happened today?" Even in the case of a continuing story, such as the race for the presidency in 1980, that involves unfolding events of several months duration, what happened *today* is what the press emphasizes.

Hence the news media are especially prone to "now-ism." Now-ism is the tendency to take a single happening today and discern in it a pattern, trend, or mood encompassing past, present, and future. Thus, in 1978, voters in California passed the infamous Proposition 13, a measure to limit property taxes. Within a short time, news stories labeled that happening a "tax revolt" destined to sweep the nation like an invasion of locusts. When later referenda propositions met with mixed success at the polls, news of the tax revolt faded to be replaced by another "now" and "with it" newsworthy event. In short, now-ism can be likened to "an irresistible urge to extrapolate tiny momentary changes into Necessary Historical Tidal Forces."[4]

Through now-ism, the news media act as mythmakers. In order to consider how, let us examine a case of news media now-ism that we shall call "The Search for the Carter Persona," perhaps not as intriguing as the search for the secrets of the Bermuda Triangle or the Lost Continent of Atlantis, but nonetheless one that has occupied the attention of the news media for several years.

With respect to recent presidents (see Chapter 3), there has been a strong tendency in the news media to convey an overall image or myth, if you will, about the character of each presidency or *press*idency! The administration of John F. Kennedy evoked the Camelot image of a young and handsome king, a fairy princess wife, stalwart brothers at his side, and numerous ladies of the court. The presidency of Lyndon Johnson was captured in the ride of the cowboy, part wheeler-dealer card shark and part rustler putting his brand on everything. Then came Richard Nixon as Lucifer and Gerald Ford as Bozo the Clown.[5]

The search for the Carter persona has been far more elusive. A given day's image has had about as much staying power as the garbage wrapped in the newspaper that conveyed it. Reflect on the following sequence:

☐ *The pre-'76 Carter: Jimmy Who?* News readers and viewers learned of a political unknown, announcing for president but surely really out to get on the Democratic ticket as a vice-presidential candidate.

☐ *The early '76 primaries: Jimmy the New Face!* A refreshing change, we were told: a man promising never to tell a lie, achieving early momentum—a sure stopper of George Wallace.

☐ *The late '76 primaries: Jimmy the Old New Face!* The freshness gone, no longer a "Who" from "Whoville" but the frontrunner hounded by the newest of new faces, Jerry Brown of California: this was the news portrayal.

☐ *The '76 Democratic convention: Jimmy What?* Having covered the nomination, the news media now turned to the question, "What manner of man is this Jimmy Carter?"

☐ *Campaign '76: Jimmy the Greek!* Carter appears in the guise of a standard politician, hedging his bets and making needless blunders (remember the *Playboy* interview?). As one set of stories concentrated upon Carter's rebuilding of the New Deal coalition, another explored his background, and he became the submariner, the nuclear engineer, the peanut farmer, the former governor, the southerner, and the technician.

☐ *Victory and Transition: Jimmy, Man of the Year!* *Time* magazine declared the president-elect "Man of the Year" while news articles focused upon the "Georgia Mafia" and likened the upcoming inauguration to a rerun of *Gone With the Wind.*

☐ *Early '77: Jimmy the Active-Positivist.* Speculating on what kind of president Carter would become, a national newsmagazine offered the speculation of a political scientist who predicted an active president enjoying and finding self-fulfillment in the White House.

☐ *Mid- and Late '77: Can Carter Cope?* So asked the cover story of a national newsmagazine after the earlier Carter persona of active efficiency had been (Burt) Lance(d). Serious questions were raised of Carter's capacity to govern. Was he up to it?

☐ *Mid-'78: Jimmy the Inept.* Plagued by problems with Congress, a troublesome economy, the decline of the American dollar on world markets, and other problems, the Carter persona assumed the aura of a confused, impotent, one-term president.

☐ *The end of '78: The New Carter!* Propped up by a reorganization of his advising staff, the hiring of a skilled public relations expert to fashion a new image, and buttressed by foreign policy successes regarding the Panama Canal, the Middle East, and China, Carter found a new persona in news stories—Jimmy as tough, aggressive, decisive.

☐ *Early '79: Jimmy the Cool.* Carter at mid-term took on the public image of a cool, managerial president, but lacking in charisma. Said a *Washington Post* reporter after noting Carter's accomplishments: "What he has not done, and may be incapable of doing, is to stir the imaginations and emotions of his countrymen."[6] In a mid-term assessment for *Parade,* columnist Jack Anderson described Carter as having "studious mastery of detail," being "plodding" in approach, possessing "quiet stubbornness" and a "gut feeling for simplicity."[7] David Broder, widely syndicated national political correspondent, summed up the mid-term image: "This is not a time of—or for—heroic leadership, and the president seems to know that."[8]

☐ *Mid-'79: Jimmy Who, Revisited.* After Carter's summer meetings with various national leaders at Camp David and his "crisis of confidence" speech, he took on the aspect in the media again of something of a puzzlement. Who is the "real Carter?" it was asked yet once again. By this time, there were as many Carters in the media as in the country: Carter the Candidate for '80, Carter the Beleaguered, Carter the Desperate, Carter the Wily, Carter the Laughable, Carter the Survivor. It is no wonder that people were confused about him! Media people, who like certainty as much as anyone else, found it perplexing and frustrating that they could not get a "fix" on Carter with a definite, agreed-upon myth. It seemed at this point that the media, and thereby the public, were back to square one in their evaluation of Carter.

So after four years, Carter was as hard for the news media to pin down as ever. In early March of 1979, he was labeled in columns a "stand-by President" for asking for stand-by authority to deal with the energy crisis; yet by the end of the month, he was "Jimmy the Persuader," for having arranged a treaty of peace between Egypt and Israel.

But the telling remark, almost a lament, that describes the whole futile search for the Carter persona by the news media also came from Anderson's assessment: "The remarkable thing about Jimmy Carter is the degree to which he remains an unknown quantity." For once, through now-ism, the press was hoisted on its own petard!

JOURNALISTS, LIKE MISS SHERWIN, ALSO LIVE IN GOPHER PRARIE

The news media's search for the Carter persona is hapless and futile. Perhaps the power of the press to define events, set agendas, and make and unmake presidents is overdrawn. People in the news media are, we submit, less omnipotent titans than reincarnations of Miss Sherwin of Gopher Prarie, a fictitious character created by noted journalist Walter Lippmann sixty years ago. He was trying to make a point, that is, that people live in a pseudo-environment of fictions, symbols, and images. Miss Sherwin knew that there had been a war in France, but, having never been there, or even seen a battle map, she could scarcely conceive it. Instead, like anyone trying to feel and know about an event not experienced directly, Miss Sherwin had only a mental image of things, a second-hand reality.[9]

Reporters deal in second-hand realities. They may witness events they write or talk about—although this is more rare than not—but they scarcely experience them as directly as the actors on the stage of the political drama do. What journalists do experience is a result of what they believe their jobs are about, what news is about, and what responsibilities they possess. In short, the myths that people inside and outside the news media hold about the press condition journalistic performance. Those myths are worth considering.

Contemplating One's Navel: Journalists' Self-Myths

Journalists' myths about the character of their enterprise derive from their training, background, and experience. One myth gaining widespread acceptability among news people is *the myth of journalism as a profession*. The myth derives from the efforts in the last century to formalize the education of journalists through training schools. In 1878, for example, the University of Missouri offered two courses in journalism and in 1908 opened the first recognized school of journalism. Added to the professional training movement (which in fifty years produced more than 500 schools giving formal training in journalism) were other trends: Journalism became a full-time occupation, professional associations developed, ethical codes emerged, and journalists lobbied for the legal right to control their own work. By the 1970s, a nationwide survey of people in the news media reported that "it is clear that journalists regard those aspects of work which are part of the professional work ethic much more highly than they do financial rewards or other tangible benefits which accrue from one's employment.[10] Public service, autonomy, and freedom from supervision—all professional values—were highly prized by the journalists surveyed.

But not all journalists accept the myth of professionalism in unqualified fashion. Witness the remarks of two nationally reputable political columnists: "It is necessary to emphasize at the outset that . . . reporting is not a profession, despite the complacent contrary belief of a good many reporters who have achieved the upper brackets. . . . The fact has to be faced: . . . reporting is a craft or trade, like undertaking, which it sometimes resembles."[11] A profession, as implied in this dissent, consists of more than people who call themselves professionals. It is, as one philosopher wrote, an enterprise subjected to theoretical analysis and guided by the conclusions of that analysis as a physician is guided by conclusions from scientific theory: "The antithesis to a profession is an avocation based upon customary activities and modified by trial and error of individual practice . . . a Craft, or at a lower level of individual skill it is merely a customary direction of muscular labor."[12]

Reporting about politics is surely more hit-and-miss, trial and error, than an activity based upon tested theory. True, there are vague customs and conventions about what makes a "good" news story (topicality, accuracy, comprehensiveness, conflicting motives, interesting content), but these are ill-defined catch phrases, not deduced principles. To illustrate the problems associated with professional values, consider a related myth, *the myth of objectivity*.

The most prevalent charge against the news media leveled by newspersons themselves is that news is biased and lacking in objectivity.[13] Despite the fact that objectivity is no longer the prized journalistic canon that it once was—and that it is not the cant of journalism school rhetoric it once was—there remains a mythical attraction to the notion. Whether reporters think of themselves as neutral scribes merely telling what happened, or prefer to label themselves investigative reporters, adversaries of government, or even advocates of viewpoints, few want to be charged with out and out bias. Most want to be regarded as objective. But it is the appearance that counts. And to achieve this appearance, journalists engage in a variety of rituals.[14] They offer both sides of the story, thus creating the illusion that there are only two conflicting possibilities. Or, journalists include supporting evidence by the citation of proper authorities—not just mentioning Secretary of State Cyrus Vance but "the State Department's Cyrus Vance" in order to fashion the image of unity of purpose through ownership. The judicious use of quotation marks, inverted pyramidal form to include "who, what, where, when, how" and the material facts of the story in the lead, and the labeling of "news analysis" as distinct from reporting: All leave an impression of accuracy and impartiality, even though the news story itself may be tilted considerably behind a particular point of view.

In addition to believing in their own professionalism and objectivity, journalists believe that there is a general agreement about what, on any given day, constitutes "the news." That there is some substance to *the myth of a news consensus* is apparent to anyone who compares the major stories in leading newspapers on a particular day, or closely watches all three national television network evening news programs, or sifts through the almost identical contents of *Time* and *Newsweek*. From whence springs that consensus? We suspect that there is no satisfactory answer to that question, but two emerge. One says that news consensus is a matter of "editorial judgment." Here, the good news sense of wire service editors, managing editors, network program producers, and others coincide. But overlapping news judgment is scarcely the same thing as an accepted set of guidelines derived from tested theory, and, again, we have no reason to regard a loose news consensus as evidence of professional norms.

A second answer to the question of where lies the source of news consensus comes from journalists who believe in the "journalistic pack" and the insights of its leaders. The pack consists of national political journalists, those working for the television networks, the large metropolitan dailies, and the major newsmagazines.[15] Centered in Washington, the nation's capital, pack members are close to and friendly with government leaders or aspiring leaders and have entrée to the "big" stories. They hold prestigious positions, are well paid, and are influential. But something else sets them apart: They share a common political belief system. Among its axioms have been that a policy of anticommunism led to our disgrace in Vietnam and should therefore be abandoned; that a cut in defense spending is laudable if we are to spend on much-needed domestic programs at home; that environmental policies must be advanced in order to save our air and water from spoilage; that a realigned tax structure should be adopted to redistribute society's wealth; and that a firm, no-nonsense energy policy is essential to the well-being of America. Working within a common belief system and following common leaders—James Reston of the *New York Times,* David Broder of the *Washington Post,* Dan Rather of CBS News, and other notables in the pack—it is no wonder that journalists view daily events in the same fashion and hence arrive at a news consensus.

Whether such a pack of national political journalists exists is problematical. That some reporters believe it does and take their cues accordingly might indeed help to mold an overall news consensus, but again, this scarcely documents the verity of the myth of professional journalism. We suspect that the national political journalist is as elusive as editorial judgment is in explaining why all the news that's fit to print turns out to be so often the same news for every citizen.

That there is some news consensus, whatever its source, gives rise to another journalistic myth about the press, that is, *the myth of press agenda-setting.* The power of the press, so goes the argument, lies not in telling us what to think but what to think about. By bringing items, events, problems, and issues to our attention, the news media set the agenda for public discussion. There is a considerable body of evidence to suggest that, indeed, the things people say concern them (when asked in opinion surveys) turn out to be the things emphasized in news accounts.[16] But does that mean that there is a cause–effect relationship, that the power of the press extends to telling us what concerns us? We think not. To begin with, let us face the fact that there are a lot of things that concern us—our finances, health, families, golf handicaps, bowling scores, sex lives—that do not derive from the news media. But even if we confine our attention to political matters, the cause–effect relationship is spurious, or at least far more complicated. It is just as conceivable to argue that politicians pay close attention to their constituents and talk about constituent concerns for news media consumption. In short, the news media tell people to think about what people have already told politicians to think about, a feedback analogous to a dog trying to swallow its tail. Moreover, as an increasing number of news organizations conduct sophisticated opinion surveys in order to find out what people are thinking about in order to report it, one wonders if journalists truly understand which is the cart and which the horse.

Journalists' Political Myths

We know of no comprehensive study of what journalists know about politics, that is, a sort of sophisticated civics test for working reporters. We do know that tests given entering journalism students generally expose vast areas of political ignorance, even about such basic things as the names of the three branches of the national government. Whether either through trade school or on-the-job training this ignorance is substantially reduced, we are not prepared to say. However, there are a variety of myths about politics—whether substantiated or not—that journalists hold.

The first is what we shall call the "we know how it really works" myth. This is the belief that journalists work in the real world and that politics doesn't occur as the textbooks say but as the journalist's experience suggests. Do journalists know how politics *really* works? The dominant mood of now-ism alone suggests otherwise, but there are two other qualifications to keep in mind. First, any journalist's experience—no matter how long the career or varied the assignments—is ultimately but a narrow sampling of all political possibilities. To speak of knowing a single overarching reality from such a biased and narrow sampling of possibilities is, to say the least, presumptuous. Second, notions of how politics *really* works vary from journalist to journalist. Aside from insights that in fact *do* appear in the textbooks—about bargaining, power brokers, influence peddling, and so on—there is not that much about political reality on which journalists agree. And when they do, think how often they are wrong. What year was Thomas E. Dewey elected president?

Secondly, there is the "we know what our readers/viewers really want" myth. This "pulse of the citizen" approach simply says that

journalists—unlike callous politicians and myopic social scientists—
have a feel for the political stances of readers and viewers. This intui-
tion gives rise to the journalistic license to criticize office-holders and
candidates for being—you guessed it—callous about citizens' needs.
There is actually nothing to indicate that journalists are any better informed about the needs and demands of the citizenry than are elected
politicians. Moreover, even with sophisticated polling techniques to
provide evidence about what is on citizens' minds, there is no
assurance that such concerns are politically crucial. Prior to the 1976
presidential nominating campaigns, CBS News and the *New York
Times* jointly sponsored a nationwide survey to discover the issues of
Campaign '76. Although the surveys uncovered a host of key citizen
concerns, and although the news media got each candidate to go on
record on every one of them, one of those concerns emerged as important during presidential politicking.[17]

In addition to self-delusions that they know what politics is really
all about and what politicians should do to serve constituents, there
are other myths evident in the performance of political journalists.
They believe that for every political effect there is a simple cause—
Carter won in 1976 because of the black vote; Ford lost because of a
gaffe during the presidential debates about eastern Europe; crime
arises from poverty or evil human nature; energy shortages stem from
profligate consumption or price-rigging oil companies, and so on.
And they believe in cycles—economic upturn and downturn; the rise
and fall of presidential popularity; the pendulum swings back and
forth as the public mood shifts from liberal to conservative, conservative to liberal. Moreover, politicians are of two types: The innocents
are devoured by the clever. Finally, journalists are in a never-ending
search for the elusive majority that should, or could, govern America:
the silent majority, the majority engaged in tax revolt, the emerging
Republican majority, the new Democratic majority, the independent
majority, the ticket-splitting majority, the fed-up majority, and so on.

In sum, the overriding picture of politics from the journalistic
image is dialectical: what "we" know that "they" don't, cause and effect, left and right, innocence and shrewdness, majority and minority,
and, ultimately, good versus bad. But if journalists have myths about
themselves and the polity, so too do people hold myths about the news
media.

POPULAR MYTHS ABOUT NEWS
AND THE NEWS MEDIA

Robert Cirino is a cogent critic of the news media. He has explored the sources of the power of the press manifest both in the stories published and broadcast and in those generally ignored by the news media. He implies that the press do more to prevent items being placed on the agenda of public discussion by failing to report them than by agenda-setting through news accounts.

In a provocative book entitled *Don't Blame the People,* Cirino describes sources of bias and distortion in the news.[18] He argues that low levels of information among citizens about public affairs is due not to widespread apathy but to the failure of the news media to cover all sides of all stories. In his chapter on "The Mythology of News Media," Cirino lists myths about news presented by the press. So ingrained have these myths become through repetition that we may extend Cirino's analysis and think of them as popular myths about the press.

First, the *myth of objectivity* is probably as widely believed, perhaps more so, among the citizenry as we argued it to be among journalists. As Cirino notes, numerous studies dating back decades demonstrate that bias, not objectivity, is the rule in newspaper headlines, stories, photographs, and word selection. More recent studies note that television news—although popularly regarded as the most credible of news media—also has its share of bias.[19]

But the myth of objectivity goes beyond the belief that news is unbiased, when much of it is not. The myth also extends to the view that even if bias cannot be eliminated, there is a built-in check against it—that is, all important viewpoints have an opportunity to be expressed, even if biased. This leads to a second popular myth about the news: that even if it is not objective, it is fair. The *myth of fairness* has legal status in the so-called "Fairness Doctrine" of the Federal Communications Commission, which states that, on a controversial matter, if a broadcast station presents one viewpoint, a reasonable opportunity must be afforded to the opposing viewpoint. But what is a reasonable opportunity to grant free broadcast time is at the discretion of media managers. The fact is, for instance, that few requests to respond to remarks made by a president in a televised news conference are likely to be granted.

"If not objectivity then fairness" contributes to yet a third popular myth about the press—that is, *that all sides of controversies are presented.* But *all* usually means two in the dialectical presentation of news. A story about a proposed treaty with the Soviet Union to limit strategic arms boils down to a controversy between proponents and opponents, with only cursory attention to alternative viewpoints advocating some parts of the treaty but not others, strict United Nations regulation of all strategic arms, banning of all nuclear weapons production, and so on.

The *myth that all controversies are presented* in the news is a fourth popular belief about the news. If "that's the way it is," how could it be otherwise? Nonetheless, there are conflicts and issues that scarcely surface in the news media. For instance, the federal government alone has dozens of independent agencies housing countless bureaus and offices and spending billions of taxpayer's dollars every year. Yet how much do we know from reading newspapers, magazines, or watching television about what goes on in most of them? Unless a scandal occurs, very little. Even then, once the story is history, the agency in question vanishes from the news as though nonexistent. Follow-up stories on corrective action to prevent future scandals are rare.

Two points should be noted regarding these myths about news and the news media shared by citizens. The first is obvious to the reader—that is, that journalists' self-myths are also myths held by readers and viewers. The audience of the news drama accepts the images of its leading characters. Second, how widely shared these myths are among the populace, we cannot say. We have no evidence from nationwide polls stating the percentages of people who believe the news media to be objective, fair, and comprehensive. But some polls provide hints: A higher percentage of peopie rate the job their television stations are doing as excellent or good than so rate their churches or police; a higher percentage rate the job of newspapers as excellent or good than so rate the schools or local government. One-half of those surveyed nationally believe that news programs, discussion shows, and television devote about "the right amount of time" to allowing people to express their views than "too much time" or "too little."[20]

Regardless of how widespread these popular images of the news and news media are, the ultimate question is how much faith, confidence, and trust do people place in what they read in newspapers and magazines and in what they see on television news? The answer lies partially in what journalists believe about themselves and about politics and what other citizens believe about the news media. Also crucial in fashioning an answer are the myths that the news media create and propagate to establish credibility.

"IT ISN'T NEWS UNLESS IT'S ON NBC NEWS"

The quotation has been attributed to Ron Nessen, one-time correspondent for NBC news and later press secretary to President Gerald Ford. Nessen, however, was not the first to suggest that news is precisely what people in the news media choose to make it (although he may have been the first to state so blatantly that but one news network was in the newsmaking business). If we are to believe that "the" news is what the news media says it is, the press must establish its credibility with us. It does so in three ways—by the style of presentation, by the content of news reports, and by identifying itself as the reflector of our social values. In all three respects, the news media are mythmakers.

Background Myths: Sustaining, Not Killing, the Messenger

Background myths are the taken-for-granted conceptions about the news media that the press has created and propagated in order to foster credibility. They arise through the press manner of presenting the news. Uppermost is the impression of *omniscience* conveyed in the style of news presentation. With the exception of the "happy talk" formats of local ABC outlets in the early 1970s, viewers and readers learn that news is serious business. Whether it be the sober-sided sophisticated essays of columnists like George Will, James Reston, or David Broder; the tragic sense of "all the news that's fit to print" in the *New York Times;* the triumph of trivia reported in national newsmagazines; or the comforting Walter Cronkite, professorial John Chancellor, and dour David Brinkley, the message is the same: We know all, see all, hear all, tell all. Even when there is a lighter side of the news, the contrast with the pathos and import of what wise, professional journalists report is apparent and comes as a relief!

Omniscience appears in another guise—that is, the labeling and language of news accounts. Journalists are inside dopesters quoting personages that only wise, powerful reporters could know. Hence we get "unnamed sources," "a reliable White House spokesman," reports from "background briefings," and "knowledgeable informants." Added to source labeling is the stylistic device widely employed by academicians, the passive voice: "It was learned today," "It was reliably reported," or "It is expected that." Who learned? Who reported? Who expects? Only the grand viziers of the press can say for sure.

But the press employs its omniscience (it implies) not for selfish gain but on behalf of all of us who have a guaranteed First Amendment right of freedom . . . of the press. Journalists are each *citizen's sentinels,* serving the right to know. Aside from the fact that, like a peep show, investigative reporting titillates and sells, the current post-Watergate fashion of going behind the scenes and revealing the governmental backstage is a clear message to readers/viewers to have confidence and faith in the press to do the right thing on their behalf. Trust us, it says, to be fair, responsible, and reliable, for we uphold the standards of the First Amendment.

Styles of presentation also leave lingering impressions in people's minds regarding what is true and real in politics. The *news is news; it is true and real.* The new face, new revolt, new controversy, new plan, new solution—all are newsworthy; old problems, programs, and conflicts grind on but scarcely get reported. Small wonder that politicians dress up conventional ideas with "now" terminology—New Freedom (Wilson), New Deal (Roosevelt), New Foundation (Carter). Even an old political face, such as perennial heir-apparent to the Camelot myth, Teddy Kennedy, must appear as a "new" threat to an incumbent president or throw down a "new" challenge to old bosses. In fact, however, the necessities and demands of the news business often render news stale and old. Feature articles and background stories for major newspapers may be researched for months before reaching print. National newsmagazines, such as *Time, Newsweek,* and *U.S.*

News and World Report, must have considerable lead time in planning a given issue's weekly contents. And producers of televised news shows master a variety of techniques: They shoot and store film from various locales, edit and reorder the sequence, and hold it until something occurs that makes such canned, prefabricated accounts appear as live, topical events taking place in the here-and-now.[21] As long as people believe that the account and the events depicted are new, the result is true and real.

Moreover, *what is reported is true and real,* what is not is not. In 1968, the vote-count winner of the New Hampshire Democratic primary was Lyndon Johnson on a write-in candidacy, but for the press, the true and real winner was Eugene McCarthy. He was the story. In 1972, Edmund Muskie won a plurality of votes in the New Hampshire Democratic primary, but in press accounts, George McGovern—by getting more votes than expected and by preventing a Muskie majority—was the true and real winner. In 1976, Gerald Ford won the New Hampshire Republican primary by 1,500 votes over challenger Ronald Reagan, scarcely indicative of a true and real winner at all. Yet press reports wrote an early end to Reagan's candidacy, despite the close vote. This was a clear case of now-ism, for Reagan's challenge later almost unseated the president.

The *now-ism* syndrome itself serves as a background myth that, strangely enough, offers an aura of credibility—even though the predictions based upon the new and now in the press often go awry. Now-ism generates an impression that journalists are readers of tea leaves, capable of gleaning national moods and trends. Nowhere is this more apparent than in the writings of syndicated columnists and in the utterances of television commentators. For years, Eric Sevareid made a career out of a few minutes commentary on the CBS nightly news. Facing the camera so that only his head and upper torso were visible, Sevareid seemed to all the world like the bust of Pericles emanating wisdom to the masses. His counterparts on the other networks, David Brinkley on NBC and Howard K. Smith on ABC, looked less like Pericles but were not less pundit-like in their pronouncements on the past, the present, and the future.

The myth of *representativeness* also helps to build press credibility. Journalists continuously search for the typical to represent and illustrate the whole—the typical voter, the average American community, the normal taxpayer, the ordinary driver lined up at the gas pump, or the middle-class consumer hit by inflation. By reporting on the typical, the news media personalize the news, making it not only easier to grasp seeming complexities but yielding the illusion that the press reports about each of us. We believe because we know what it is like to vote or not vote, pay taxes, suffer from gasoline shortages, and tire of paying high prices. If what the press says about *us* is true and real, then it must be so about other things as well.

Two other key background myths flow from the way the press reports the news. Everybody likes a good show. A good show is more believable than a bad one. Hence the *dialectical mode of news reporting* emphasizes conflict and drama as essential ingredients of what is true and real in life. News accounts conform to the melodramatic imperative.[22] This is especially so for television news, with its emphasis upon visual action, but is essentially the case with written news stories as well. The melodramatic imperative states that the elements of a news story must satisfy the time and/or space requirements of the news media. In short, the account must (1) emphasize symbols and images readily understood; (2) be entertaining and *not* boring; (3) tell a story with a beginning, middle, and end; (4) portray rising action, falling action, and denouement; (5) demonstrate conflict in content and structure; and (6) offer leading and supporting characters, preferably as winners and losers, good and bad, rich man and poor man, the have and the have not. These same elements, of course, are precisely those that comprise the basics of mythology (see Chapter 1). Small wonder that the news media are key mythmakers in our society.

Finally, the emphasis on news reporting through the major media is upon the *national political picture*. Although America has no national press—not in the sense that a single or a few newspapers have nationwide mass circulation, as in Great Britain, France, West Germany or other Western nations—the style and presentation of most political news yields a national news picture nonetheless. No matter what the total number of daily local newspapers, wire service accounts from Associated Press and United Press International appear with little variation in most of them. Newspaper chains with ownership of dailies in major metropolitan areas provide homogenized fare regarding political stories. Three national circulation weekly newsmagazines dominate the market. CBS, NBC, and ABC offer nationwide morning and evening televised news accounts, and the MacNeil-Lehrer report airs nightly on the public broadcasting network. Even local radio news depends heavily upon national wire services. The overall impact of making political news national is to convey the image of a government far removed and remote from the average citizen's daily life. Controversies, issues, personalities, and events cannot be directly experienced. We must have others—that is, journalists—do it for us and tell us about it. Out of default if for no other reason, the news media are our eyes and ears on an abstract, distant national political scene. W. C. Fields may have said, "A man has to believe in something, and I believe I'll have another drink," but it is today more apt to say that we must believe in something and that there is no choice but to believe in the news media as observers, reporters, and soothsayers.

Substantive Myths: Fantasy Building Through News Content

Coverage of the 1968, 1972, and 1976 presidential primaries in New Hampshire typifies how the news media have options in how to tell *the* story. In each year, the press could have emphasized different features to tell a different story—in 1968 of a Johnson victory or that both hawks and doves voted for McCarthy, in 1972 of McGovern's survival not victory, in 1976 of a dismal showing for an incumbent president. Since in telling stories about issues, events, and persons there is nothing inherently true and real for the news media to say—only choices—journalists engage in mythmaking. They do so by initiating a process of *group fantasy.*

When members of a group share the same dramatic messages as stories, narratives, or anecdotes, the messages act as fantasies—that is, inventive works with "characters, real or fictitious, playing out a dramatic situation in a setting removed in time and space from the here-and-now transactions of the group."[23] A news story is a dramatic message with precisely such characteristics of fantasy, characteristics shared with mythical accounts—dramatic structure, interpretative content, and credibility. As members of a group share the same fantasy, the fantasy "chains out" in person-to-person communication. In this respect, a news story is a vital part of chaining out as the vehicle for fantasy transmission because it serves as the dramatic tale, which the participating people share.

There is evidence that chaining out of news fantasies begins with the journalist. Studies reveal that in writing stories, journalists imagine the kinds of audiences who read or view them. If they imagine an audience supportive of what they are writing, they write one way; if they imagine a critical audience, they adjust to that. Thus, "the variable is the writer's flow of associations which appeared to influence most markedly what he wrote was the affective relationship that he conceived to exist between himself and his imaginary interlocutors." For instance, "the reporter himself may be a shy man, but behind the protective moat that separates him and his piece of paper from the world, he can indulge in fantasy about overcoming all sorts of toils and troubles and ending up with love or with triumph."[24]

It is not necessary to search far for myths created and propagated via fantasy chaining in news. American involvement in the Vietnam War in the 1960s and 1970s is one of many examples. During the buildup of American forces in Vietnam, journalists accepted and reported official explanations of United States intentions. War correspondents were part of the "American team" that reported the effort to "contain" communism and prevent a Chinese "takeover" in Indochina. Good guys and bad guys were clearly demarcated, and the fantasy was a simple tale of good and evil. But after 1965, the plot thickened. Reporting produced a "living room war," as scenes from battlefields appeared nightly on network television news shows. This produced a problem. As night after night Americans saw fighter planes swooping in on villages of old men, families, and children, a question emerged: Who is the enemy?

The fantasy in reporting the Vietnam War was essentially the continuing effort to answer that question. The search for an answer proved as hopeless as the press quest for the true Carter persona in the 1970s. By the mid-1960s, the bad guys in the Vietnam drama had been variously labeled "Communist guerrillas," "Vietcong raiders," "Hanoi's forces," "Communists," or simply "Reds." The implication was always the same—that is, that the enemy was alien, a threat not native to the region but aided and abetted by outside forces. By the early 1970s, however, news accounts recognized that the enemy in Vietnam was not, in fact, alien to the country but came from within. Hence, labeling shifted to "Vietcong" and to "North Vietnamese." The drama that unfolded was now the "South Vietnamese" (good guys) versus the "Vietcong and North Vietnamese" (bad guys). Then, as South Vietnam was overrun and portions of the population did not even support the war effort, news accounts turned to the only designation left: "the enemy."[25]

A key event in the Vietnam War was the Tet offensive in January–March of 1968. The "enemy" launched surprise attacks on every city, town, and vital military installation in South Vietnam. As an offensive, Tet was a military setback for the enemy. But, as reported in the media, the fantasy was different. Tet came across to Americans not as a military victory but as a defeat; for many antiwar groups, it was the turning point of the war. It was not until ten years after Tet that a serious debate over news coverage of that battle put in perspective the fantasy chaining role of the press. Whether Tet was either a military or psychological victory for anyone in the Vietnam War is open to question. That the mythmaking role of the news media was paramount in creating images of enemy victory of some type, however, has considerable credence.[26]

There are many other instances when the press makes myths through the process of fantasy chaining. In reporting events in the Middle East, think how often the labels Palestinian "terrorists" and Israeli "commandos" appear. Or think how passage of a single referendum item in a single state limiting property taxes (California's infamous 1978 Proposition 13) became an overnight "tax revolt." When what had previously been a relatively unknown religious sect engaged in mass suicide/murder in 1978, the news media warned of cultism as an evil in civilized societies.

In focusing upon fantasy chaining through news stories, however, we are not arguing that the press engages in a conscious effort to mislead, distort, and contort. Rather, we are saying that the nature of news reporting lends itself to mythmaking. Television news is one of the most obvious cases in point. A study of network and local television news programs conducted in 1978 uncovered a number of interesting things regarding the mythmaking qualities of television news. For one, 70 percent of television news coverage dealt with preplanned events—governmental investigations, hearings, meetings, and the like—rather than spontaneous events. In such coverage, government is the dominant actor. Governmental activity revolves about decisions, decisions linked to suffering, to catching villains, to injustice, to corruption, and to tests of strength. The study concluded that the mythical image of our society portrayed in television news is simple and straightforward: "In the place of sirens, demons, sensations of flying or falling, we have a new narrative: political leaders as an omnipotent elite, beyond both marketplace and law, struggling with each other to determine the rules under which the rest of us must live. The Greek gods on Mount Olympus were no less remote and only slightly more powerful."[27]

Continuing Myths: America Through the Lenses of the News Media

The portrayal of our society as a war of the gods (i.e., political elites) is a substantive myth that arises from how television covers the news. It is also a continuing myth, a stereotype about ourselves that we accept after its constant repetition in the news. There are other such stereotypes. Some deal with relatively limited situations, events, or single institutions. To the news media, for instance, California is a bizarre place, filled with all kinds of strange people doing weird things. Or, consider press stereotypes of our governing institutions: The presidency swings back and forth from the "imperial" to the "impotent"—either having too much power or not enough; Congress investigates but does not initiate; the Supreme Court arises as the "final arbiter"; the states are, at best, "junior partners."[28]

Aside from these more limited images, however, there are some that emerge from the news media that provide long-term myths about ourselves as Americans and about the kind of society we have. Sociologist Herbert Gans has made a careful study of the "enduring values" implicit in the news over the last two decades. Looking at the way the news describes actors and activities, the tone of news stories, and the connotations of words in the news, Gans has identified eight clusters of what, from our standpoint, are eschatological myths (see Chapter 1, page 26) that project the nation's destiny on the basis of past and present.[29]

Ethnocentrism is the myth that America is a superior nation to be valued above all others. Although news stories frequently criticize faulty domestic conditions, such domestic problems and crises are deviant cases that prove the rule. Hence, as we saw in Chapter 2, both the Civil War and Watergate prove that the system works. In wartime, as we saw in Vietnam, news stories seek to identify the enemy. As

Gans notes, the news media wrote of the end of that war as "the fall of South Vietnam" rather than as a "liberation" or simply a change in governments. *Altruistic democracy* is the myth that politics in America should be based on the public interest and service. Implicit in that myth are prescriptions for how government should be conducted: Politicians, whether winners or losers, should be honest, efficient, and dedicated to the public interest; merit—not "pull," "contracts," or "patronage"—should guide the selection of public officials; "waste," "paperwork," "deals," and "red tape" are all to be rooted out. The consequence of this portrayal of altruistic democracy is to emphasize stories of financial corruption and bureaucratic bungling but to ignore violations of civil liberties or problems faced by the powerless in achieving political access.

The myth of *responsible capitalism* is the belief that the business community acts to increase prosperity for all without seeking unreasonable profits or exploiting workers or consumers. The myth accepts unions and consumer organizations as healthy counterbalancing forces, economic growth as good, government intervention (but not government subsidies) as bad, and government welfare programs for the "deserving" (but not the "cheaters") as tolerable.

Small-town pastoralism is the continued focus upon the mythical rural, anti-industrial America of Thomas Jefferson as the ideal society. Even in an era when many small towns have all but vanished, they are celebrated in the news. CBS's *On the Road,* with Charles Kuralt, glorifies the goodness of small-town pastoralism. The suburbs, where so much of America lives, were castigated in news stories in the 1950s and 1960s as hotbeds of boredom, blandness, and adultery, whereas urban areas carried the image of poverty, crime, and racial strife. The pastoral myth prizes smallness for its own sake. The evils of contemporary America lie in being too big: big business, big labor, big government, and big bust.

Individualism is a holdover from the Jacksonian era of "rugged individualism" and "self-made men." Contemporary news prizes individuals by stressing the threat posed by technological developments. Computer technology contributes to anonymity, television to dehumanizing, data banks to snooping. Not only news media but even pop culture gets into the act; for example, the comic strip, "Dick

Tracy,'' in 1979 carried a long tale about a computer killer who went around town blasting computers with a shotgun in order to avenge an error that left him jobless, homeless, and penniless.

The belief that extremism is bad contributes to the myth of *moderatism*. Middle America is prized—middle-of-the-road politics, evolution not revolution, and moderation in ، 'l things. Moreover, deviants are suspect: The cultist is no more mainstream than the atheist, the bland speaker must be condemned along with the demagogue, and ambition must at all times be tempered with a aose of altruism.

The myth of *order* insists that the natural state of things is peace and tranquillity. It should be preserved. But it is a particular type of order—that is, the social and political order of public, business, and professional upper-middle classes, the middle-aged, and the white-male sectors of society. Protests, demonstrations, riots, and the like are news precisely because they are out of the ordinary. Stories announce their culmination with the ritualistic phrase, "Order was restored."

The myth of *leadership* reflects the tendency of the press to personalize politics by focusing its stories on public figures. Controversies, issues, and events revolve about a few key leaders, and, if there appear to be no such figures, then the news media aid in creating leaders—as, for instance, in the civil rights movement of the 1960s. Implicit is a theory of society that views progress as flowing from what leaders do through their charisma, political and managerial skills, and sheer gall. The leadership myth, of course, revolves primarily around the American president—what he can do to exercise political and moral leadership, whether he inspires or not, whether he is imperial or impotent.

For Gans, these eight enduring values or myths portrayed in the news add up to an overarching picture of politics that is closely akin to the ideal of government contained in the Progressive and Liberal ideology of this century. The myths of this ideology include honesty, meritocracy, and efficiency; they disparage politics, demagogues, and weak leadership. Like the Progressive mythology, they emphasize the preservation of an upper- and upper-middle class with strong ties to a responsible capitalistic establishment. There is the same preference for small rather than big business, for craftsmanship rather than technology, for pastoral ways over urbanism run amuck. Thus, although the developmental myth of Liberal progressivism has been dead for half a century, its eschatological form has been preserved in the news as the ideal embodying America's past, present, and future.

THE NEW MYTH
Precision Journalism and the Pollsters

To strengthen the justification for "that's the way it is" and to reinforce their self-myth that as journalists they know what people really want, reporters have turned to a new technique of finding out what's happening. They have adopted the methods of the opinion pollsters. Once limited to buying the syndicated columns of pollsters, such as George Gallup and Louis Harris, many newspapers, newsmagazines, and broadcasting networks now commission or conduct their own polls in order to feel the public pulse. They include not only news organizations attracting a national audience (*New York Times*, CBS, *Washington Post*, Knight-Ridder newspapers, Associated Press, and NBC) but even smaller ones, such as the *Dubuque Telegraph Herald,* an Iowa paper with a circulation of 40,000.

The rationale for the new fad of precision journalism is simple. Said one newsman, "If we can find out what people are thinking in basic, simple terms on clear-cut issues and no longer have to be captives of politicians and others who spout off, it is a device, when done right—which is not easy—that allows us to make broad, sweeping generalizations with confidence, something that an individual reporter has one hell of a time doing."[30] Contained in that statement, however, are features of polling that offer journalists not so much the promise of the pollenium as the potential for mythmaking.

This is not the place to describe why it is problematic that any poll will be "done right" and that valid and reliable polling "is not easy." The reader will find numerous critical assessments of the art and science of opinion polling.[31] Rather, our concern is with making "broad, sweeping generalizations" on the basis of "what people are thinking in basic, simple terms on clear-cut issues."

First, we must recognize that "the poll, though a scientifically shaped instrument, cannot be a neutral construct. . . . To inquire about a group's views for *any* reason, suggests the initial mind-set of the polltaker and implies a promise of future action or, no less significantly, inaction somewhere in the societal decision-making apparatus."[32] Although a pollster regards issues as clear-cut, the fact is that the polltaker, in selecting some items for attention while ignoring others, thereby defines the domain of public issues. To the degree that those issues are *not* important to those polled or that people are ignorant of them, the polltaker creates an agenda of mythical issues. Granted that the issues might be important to some persons polled or might even become important *after* the pollster raises them, this is no demonstration that they were clearcut when selected. Take, as an example, the polls conducted from 1975–1978 on the question of America's negotiating a new treaty regarding the Panama Canal. For most people, the Panama Canal treaties were simply not an issue until the middle of 1978. Instead, people were ignorant of the matter, misunderstood what was going on, and could not anticipate what was going to happen. When the issue did become salient, the treaties—which passed the United States Senate—were opposed by a five to three majority.[33]

If it is not possible in advance of a poll to know what is a clear-cut issue, it is even less so to "find out what people are thinking in basic, simple terms." Different opinions flow from differing ways to ask questions. Opinions do not lie around like eggs in a chicken coop to be gathered by anyone who opens the hatch—be it farmer, fox, or egg-sucking dog. Instead, opinions are *created through the opinion-gathering process.* Word two questions on a single issue in different ways, and different opinions emerge. As a case in point, consider the issue of whether or not to adopt a policy of public financing of candidates in elections for congressional offices—the House of Representative and the United States Senate. In the same week in 1979, two polling organizations sampled Americans' views. The samples were comparable in representing a cross-section of adults. One organization, the Gallup Poll, asked:

It has been suggested the federal government provide a fixed amount of money for the election campaigns of candidates for Congress and that all private contributions from other sources be prohibited. Do you think this is a good idea or a poor idea?

Fifty-seven percent of those sampled said it would be a good idea, 30 percent said it was a poor idea, and the remainder had no opinion. Surely this finding would permit a journalist to "make a broad, sweeping generalization with confidence" that Americans favored public funding of congressional campaigns. But wait a minute. Another polling firm, Civic Service, Inc., asked "Do you approve or disapprove, and how strongly do you feel, of the proposal to use public financing, tax dollar support, to pay the costs of congressional elections?" Only 11 percent had no opinion, 22 percent favored the proposal, and 67 percent were opposed![34] Why the difference? People respond differently, and more positively, to such cues as "fixed amount of money" and prohibitions on "private contributions" than to public financing as "tax dollar support." Where does a true reading of public opinion lie? We suspect that no true public opinion exists, only opposing myths that are neither true nor false but simply credible, depending upon which body of evidence one wishes to select.

The mythmaking potential of news polling combines with nowism in a most striking way when the press predicts the outcomes of major elections. Although the Gallup Poll claims a record of accurate performance in nationwide elections (having an average error of a percentage point from predicting the final outcome in each election since 1950), the fact remains that election forecasting remains soothsaying. Even Gallup, in 1952, found the presidential election "too close to call" when, in fact, Eisenhower received over 55 percent of the votes cast. The dreary record of news media polls was highlighted in 1978: The *Topeka Capital-Journal* and the *Kansas City Star* and *Times* carried late polls showing the ultimate winner in the United States Senate race, Nancy Landon Kassebaum, as the probable loser; The Minnesota Poll, published by *The Minneapolis Tribune,* called two of three statewide races wrong; *The Des Moines Register* gave Senator Dick Clark a ten-point lead two days before the election, but he lost; and the *Detroit News*–Market Opinion Research Poll rated the Michigan gubernatorial race too close to call, yet the winner received 56 percent of the votes. Granted that some press polls proved accurate in 1978, yet the overall record suggests that, like Jimmy the Greek, election forecasting provides entertaining mythmaking rather than useful reporting.[35]

THE POWER OF THE PRESS
Fourth Branch of Government or Griot?

People fret about the power of the press. Spiro Agnew viewed it inimical to good government. Richard Nixon thought the press out to get him. And liberals see in the press a conservative cabal, whereas conservatives see a liberal conspiracy. We suggest that the power of the press is a myth. To be sure, the news media are key channels of political information, opinions, and judgments for Americans. This is not to say, however, that the press is so powerful that it tells us what to think about and what to think, makes and unmakes presidents, moves faster than a speeding bullet, is more powerful than a locomotive, or leaps tall buildings at a single bound.

Many would disagree. For them, the press is "the fourth branch of government."[36] That branch, made up of diverse news organizations staffed with equally diverse personnel, serves as the citizens' representative—watching and uncovering what goes on in the executive, legislative, and judicial branches; investigating beneath the surface; advocating alternative points of view; and acting as an adversary of wrongdoing in public office. The image is attractive, especially to journalists. However, it lacks an authentic ring. Although the investigative and adversarial roles of the press are highly publicized and romanticized, for every Jack Anderson, Mike Wallace, or the legendary Edward R. Murrow, there are hundreds of what can be called the "journalist as bureaucrat."[37] The fact is that most journalists depend upon official sources for their livelihoods—for tips, leaks, advance announcements, interviews, and so on. In return, they perform a valuable service for the public official—that is, they provide free publicity in a government run by publicity. Journalists do not reside in an independent fourth branch of government but are, for the most part, handmaidens in each branch, going about routine, bureaucratic roles of filing stories.

Given such partnership between government and the news

media, one might ask, "Is the free press also a myth?" In the sense in which we have defined myth, it is. The story of a free press fighting for the unfettered right to serve the citizen as adversary is dramatic, appealing, and credible—but provable as neither true nor false. Certainly the American news media are more free to investigate, report, and advocate than the press of many other nations. But does it always maximize that freedom? Journalists in their partnerships with politicians and flacks do not; acting as popular entertainers to hype sales and ratings (sensational news, yes; bad news, no) is also not maximizing freedom. Moreover, the press, not government, is often a major censor of news. In 1978, a panel of news media critics selected the top stories censored by the news media in the previous year—that is, each story that had been published in an obscure place and ignored in the national press, although it was important in social and political consequences, controversial, and topical. Among the stories were the failure of blacks to make social progress despite government reports to the contrary, the failure of the national "all-out war" on cancer (costing 4 billion dollars), Jimmy Carter's connections with the Trilateral Commission (a policy-making organization connected with the Rockefellers), serious problems raised by the decommissioning of nuclear power plants, massacres in Cambodia and Vietnam, acidity in rainfall, and the plight of illegal aliens.

If the press is not all powerful; not a fourth branch; not adversarial, investigative, advocative, or precision-minded, then what is it? We have argued that the press simply makes myths. In his widely acclaimed novel, *Roots,* Alex Haley describes how in Africa he found a *griot* to assist him in his search for his African ancestors. A *griot* living in the present narrates facets of the past, without repeating himself. In the process, the past takes on a mythical character. Nobody, not even the *griot,* can prove how the past really was.

The news media are the *griots* of our civilization. They narrate what has happened and, as practitioners of now-ism, accentuate that the *new* is true and real. They make and transmit myths, also trying not to repeat themselves for fear of boring and thereby losing their audiences. But it is news, not truth, that is their stock in trade, and, as Walter Lippmann once wrote, "News and truth are not the same thing."[38] He also argued that the press cannot organize and report public opinion, but that "public opinions must be organized for the press if they are to be sound, not by the press as is the case today."

Who should do this if a mythmaking press cannot? Lippmann had an answer he was later to retract: "This organization I conceive to be in the first instance the task of a political science that has won its popular place as formulator, in advance of real decision, instead of apologist, critic, or reporter after the decision has been made."[39] But is political science free of mythmaking? Let us see in the next chapter.

REFERENCES

1. The remarks of former Vice President Spiro T. Agnew can be found in Edward W. Knappman, ed., *Government and the Media in Conflict/1970–74* (New York: Facts on File, 1974), p. 9.

2. Walter Cronkite, CBS new release, 12 July 1979.

3. Tamotsu Shibutani, *Improvised News* (Indianapolis: Bobbs-Merrill, 1965).

4. Quoted in Everett Ladd, Jr., Charles Hadley, and Lauriston King, "A New Political Alignment," *The Public Interest,* 23 (Spring, 1971): 48; coinage of the term "now-ism" is credited to Kingman Brewster in an interview published in *The Manchester Guardian Weekly,* December 4, 1977, p. 1.

5. William A. Rusher, "'Artists' Add Final Touch to Carter Image,'" *Knoxville News-Sentinel,* October 26, 1977, p. 15.

6. Edward Walsh, "Mr. Carter's Cool Competence Leaves Him Vulnerable," reprinted from *The Washington Post* in *The Manchester Guardian Weekly,* February 4, 1979, p. 15.

7. *Parade,* January 14, 1979, pp. 4–7.

8. "Attaining Modest Goals," reprinted from *The Washington Post* in *The Manchester Guardian Weekly,* February 4, 1979, p. 15.

9. Walter Lippman, *Public Opinion* (New York: Macmillan, 1922), pp. 22–23.

10. John W. C. Johnstone, Edward J. Slawski, William W. Bowman, *The News People* (Urbana, Ill.: University of Illinois Press, 1976), p. 110.

11. Joseph Alsop and Steward Alsop, *The Reporter's Trade* (New York: Reynal and Co., 1958), pp. 3–4.

12. Alfred North Whitehead, *Adventures in Ideas* (New York: New American Library [Mentor Books], 1933), pp. 64–65.

13. Johnstone, et al., *The News People,* p. 121.

14. Gaye Tuchman, "Objectivity as Strategic Ritual," *American Journal of Sociology,* 77 (July 1972): 660–678.

15. Robert D. Novak, "The New Journalism," in Harry M. Clor, ed., *the Mass Media and Modern Democracy* (Chicago: Rand McNally, 1974), pp. 1–14.

16. Donald L. Shaw and Maxwell E. McCombs, *The Emergence of American Political Issues: The Agenda-Setting Function of the Press* (New York: West Publishing Co., 1977).

17. See James David Barber, ed., *Race for the Presidency* (Englewood Cliffs, N.J.: Prentice-Hall, 1978) and Edwin Diamond, *Good News, Bad News* (Cambridge, Mass.: The M.I.T. Press, 1978).

18. Robert Cirino, *Don't Blame the People* (Los Angeles: Diversity Press, 1971).

19. See Edith Efron, *The News Twisters* (Los Angeles: Nash Publishing, 1971) and C. Richard Hofstetter, *Bias in the News* (Columbus, Ohio: Ohio State University Press, 1976).

20. Burns W. Roper, *Changing Public Attitudes Toward Television and Other Mass Media* (New York: Television Information Office, 1977).

21. David L. Swanson, "And That's the Way It Was? Television Covers the 1976 Presidential Campaign," *Quarterly Journal of Speech,* 63 (October 1977): 239–248.

22. Edward Jay Epstein, *News From Nowhere* (New York: Random House [Vintage Books], 1973).

23. Ernest G. Bormann, "Fantasy and Rhetorical Vision: The Rhetorical Criticism of Social Reality," *Quarterly Journal of Speech,* 59 (October 1972): 397.

24. Ithiel de Sola Pool and Irwin Shulman, "Newsmen's Fantasies, Audiences, and Newswriting," in Lewis Anthony Dexter and David Manning White, eds., *People, Society, and Mass Communications* (London: The Free Press of Glencoe, 1964), p. 145.

25. Edwin Diamond, *The Tin Kazoo* (Cambridge, Mass.: The M.I.T. Press, 1975), pp. 113–122.

26. On the nature of the debate regarding news media mythmaking in Vietnam, see Peter Braestrup, *Big Story: How the American Press and Television Reported and Interpreted the Crisis of Tet in 1968 in Vietnam and Washington* (New York: Westview Press, 1977); Noam Chomsky, "10 Years After Tet: The Big Story that Got Away," *More,* 8 (June 1978): 16–23; Peter Arnett, "Tet Coverage: A Debate Renewed," *Columbia Journalism Review,* 16 (January/February 1978): 44–48; Philip Knightly, *The First Casualty* (New York: Harcourt Brace Jovanovich, 1975), pp. 373–400.

27. Robert Rutherford Smith, "Mythic Elements in Television News," *Journal of Communication,* 29 (Winter 1979): 82.

28. Epstein, *News From Nowhere,* pp. 239–257.

29. Herbert Gans, *Deciding What's News* (New York: Pantheon, 1979).

30. The quotation from the *Washington Post's* director of polling, Barry Sussman, is in Dom Bonafede, "Polling," *Washington Journalism Review,* 1 (September/October 1978): 34.

31. See Michael Wheeler, *Lies, Damn Lies, and Statistics* (New York: Liveright, 1976); Leo Bogart, *Silent Politics* (New York: Wiley, 1972); and Lindsay Rogers, *The Pollsters* (New York: Knopf, 1949).

32. Herbert I. Schiller, *The Mind Managers* (Boston: Beacon Press, 1973), p. 105 (italics in original).

33. Bernard Roshco, "The Polls: Polling on Panama—Sí; Don't Know; Hell, No!" *Public Opinion Quarterly,* 42 (Winter 1978): 551-562.

34. The Gallup Poll, "Public Funding of Congressional Election Campaigns, March 25-28, 1979," *The Gallup Opinion Index,* Report No. 166 (May 1979): 12; Roy Pfautch, *Attitudes Toward Campaign Financing,* March 1979 (St. Louis: Civic Service, Inc., 1977).

35. Barry Sussman, "Pre-Election Polling," *Washington Journalism Review,* 1 (January/February, 1979): 24-25.

36. Douglass Carter, *The Fourth Branch of Government* (New York: Houghton Mifflin, 1959).

37. Tom Bethell, "The Myth of an Adversary Press: Journalist as Bureaucrat," *Harper's,* 254 (January 1977): 33-40.

38. Lippmann, *Public Opinion,* p. 358.

39. Lippmann, *Public Opinion,* p. 32.

CHAPTER 7

Brother, Can You Paradigm?
Political Science and Political Mythmaking

Nobody takes political science very seriously,
for nobody is convinced that it is a science or
that it has any important bearing on politics.
WALTER LIPPMANN, A Preface to Morals

Heretofore we identified a variety of mythmakers—political persuaders, persons who make or participate in popular culture, and newsmakers. We specified different reasons why these people are, wittingly or not, political mythmakers. Mythmakers, of whatever occupation, rarely *admit,* when challenged, that they communicate myths about politics. Campaign managers retreat into rhetoric about how they are really engaged in presenting their client-candidate in his true light. Reporters repeat the myths about the news that they learned in journalism school. No one likes to think of himself as the perpetuator of untruths; mythmakers prefer to believe instead that they are clearing up false notions about politics.

With this in mind, we turn to our last group of important political mythmakers: political scientists. This may cause some readers to think, but aren't political scientists those learned men who "scientifically" study politics? Would not they, above all groups, be immune from the disease of mythifying? Science, after all, involves the accumulation of a body of knowledge that tells us universal truths about the subject matter. Is not political science a discipline that has developed a body of knowledge—validated and universally shared—about its subject matter?

POLITICAL SCIENCE AS MYTHICAL KNOWLEDGE

Both laymen and political scientists are confused, we believe, about the nature and limits of social science and about the thin line between science and myth. Political science, like any other academic discipline, occurs in time. As a discipline operates in time, it develops a paradigm, or overarching image and language, that provides a satisfying world-view for a community of scholars. In many ways, a paradigm is a myth, a symbolic reality created and shared by people who communicate with each other. Paradigms reign chiefly because they offer a working myth, a set of assumptions and images to guide research and to provide a comfortable feeling that the community of scholars is undertaking significant work and solving significant problems. But because of the persistence of anomalies—nagging insoluble problems—or simply because of generational change and the appearance of other competing paradigms that are more appealing to the young or satisfying to the skeptical, paradigms change or are discarded. Paradigms succeed each other, but there is no necessary historical progress or constant accumulation of knowledge. Time works changes in the imaginative myths a discipline holds and in the data base it manipulates, but there is no guarantee that a discipline progresses toward final definitive answers.[1]

Growth of a Discipline: Confusion to Clarity or Clarity to Confusion?

Political science is a case of the succession of paradigmatic myths throughout its history. Indeed, if we take the broadest view of the study of politics in the course of Western history, we find monumental changes in conception as to what politics is all about and as to what paradigm is appropriate to describe and explain it. The twelfth-century writer John of Salisbury, in his handbook on medieval good government, *Politicratus,* used the microcosmic myth to describe the political order. The work characterizes "body Politic" with the Prince as the head; the senate is the heart; peasants are the feet; "treasurers and warders" are "like the belly and intestines, which if they become congested with excessive greed and too tenaciously keep what they collect, generate innumerable incurable diseases, so that ruin threatens the whole body. . . ."[2] If this organic image made sense to the twelfth century, why should we assume that the images of politics we hold are any more free from temporal revision and innovation?

It is the same with political language, the words we use to describe and explain politics. E. E. Schattschneider pointed out that political language changes over time. By simply looking at the definition of words in earlier and current dictionaries, he finds that some political words we commonly use now either were not used two centuries ago or had a very different meaning. Also, what was of political interest at those past times is different than what is of interest today; thus the words that went into dictionaries related to the big issues of the time.[3] In today's rapidly changing political world, it is obvious that the language of politics changes quickly. Political science as an academic discipline is as subject to such language change as the popular vocabulary of politics. Not only do changes in politics and common political parlance affect political science, but there are also changes and innovations in the academic language of the discipline. After all, political scientists manipulate symbols to communicate, just as do laypersons. Scholars introduce concepts and distinctions aimed at illuminating political affairs. But to the layperson and politician (and to future times), the current language and imagery of political science is likely to seem like esoteric jargon that obfuscates rather than illuminates. Outsiders who read the sentence, "Where articulation, aggregation, and decision making are not differentiated from one another, it is difficult to specify what degree of fragmentation is introduced or reduced at the aggregation stage," quickly realize that they are not initiated to the lore of the scholarly tribe.[4] If a reader glances at the index of the book bearing the preceding quotation, one sees terms such as "conversion functions," "access channels," "subsystem autonomy," and so forth. But if a reader consults a political science book in the same general field published in 1948, there appear instead terms like "Law," "Election," and "Parties, political."[5] It is not that political scientists do not use the latter terms still, nor that the former are meaningless generalizations, but that concepts go in and out of fashion and use.

That there is change and confusion as to the appropriate vocabulary of political science was demonstrated recently in an American Political Science Association publication. A project called "The California State University Political Science Concept Inventory" compiled 21,927 terms "drawn from forty-six political science dictionaries, encyclopedias, textbooks, master indexes, and similar sources." A panel of ten qualified political science judges rated the terms to indicate which ones undergraduate majors in political science should know well, be merely aware of, or need not know. The project was derived from a notion that "ability to communicate in a common technical language is fundamental for effective teaching and learning." Common vocabulary gives the "newcomer" an "immediate, authoritative, valid, and convenient sense of the breadth and general orientation of the political science discipline." Why the language is "technical" and by whose authority it is said to be valid and common is not clear.

But one thing is clear: The results are astounding. What emerges as more or less important to know might well puzzle the outsider. It is most important to know terms such as "empirical method" and "political theory, classical," but less important to know "modern society" and "mass communications"; it is more important to know "House of Representatives," but less to know "Senate"; it is vital to know "dependent variable," but less crucial to know "totalitarian state"; it is more important to be able to identify "Machiavelli, Niccolo" than "Stalin, Joseph" or "Mill, John Stuart"![6]

This exercise tells us something. Political scientists are probably not going to agree as to what is important to know among themselves, and they are even less likely to agree with laypersons. In other words, perceptions of the proper priority of ideas, even among those in the academic discipline, vary substantially. Similarly, there is no common agreement on the definition of concepts: definitions of "power" and "influence," for example, abound.[7] The language of political science enjoys insufficient consensus to command the kind of attention a respected science does from policymakers and the public.

In the past, political theorists communicated imaginative political myths that pervaded the political thinking of an age. John of Salisbury, John Locke, Karl Marx, and others invented a language—ideas and images—that commanded considerable vogue and power among political leaders and followers. Today, however, political science is a discipline in search of a mythical paradigm. It is an amalgam of past and present terminologies, theoretical approaches, and metaphors. It possesses no common language. Instead, political scientists retreat into obtuse wording, expand into new and fashionable areas only to abandon them for others, and borrow and beat to death contemporary metaphors. The discipline flounders from grandiose theorizing to detailed trivia in anarchistic splendor. It does not now have any dominant figure or paradigm around which a shared disciplinary myth could rally. Research and teaching have no common ground, and consequently it is difficult for politicians, administrators, or ordinary citizens to take the discipline seriously. The power of a shared myth is such that if a community of scholars communicates to the outside world that it agrees that "this is reality," people take them seriously. Noting the confusion, uncertainty, and triviality in scholarly pronouncements, many people conclude that political scientists do not know what they are talking about.

A glance at the development of American political science yields insight as to why there is no agreed-upon myth. In the past, there were paradigms, or widely shared metaphors, terminologies, and ways of doing research, but they were challenged by successive generations of scholars flacking new paradigms. American political science developed first a romantic vision of political order, based on German Hegelianism: for example, the myth that political reality resides in the institutions and formal documents of the constitutional order. There was something called "The State." This institutional image did not later disappear; rather, it faced challenge from a realist myth: that political reality lies in the political facts of life, in the *Realpolitik* behind institutions and laws. Thus political scientists rushed to discover the reality of the economic forces and social bases of politics. This paradigm yielded later to the new science of politics focusing on the study of individual political activity, a movement that culminated in the behavioral revolution. New researchers discovered political reality by statistical and psychological studies of votes cast in elections, in legislatures, or through opinion surveys. These were the observables of political behavior. Such microstudies were to provide the scientific base of an empirical discipline. The behavioral persuasion and its paradigmatic assumptions assumed a dominant place in the discipline only to face challenge itself in the late 1960s by a postbehavioral revolution, hawking radical, antibehavioral, and policy-oriented perspectives.[8] By the 1970s, political science had become a chaotic mishmash of concepts, terms, distinctions, methods, approaches, perspectives, data, formulas, theories, and paradigms. The subdisciplinary categories of the discipline proliferated. The editors of a recent multivolume *Handbook of Political Science* admitted that "Early in his career, the fledgling political scientist learns that his discipline is ill-defined, amorphous, and heterogeneous" and that their effort was an effort "to give a warts-and-all portrait of a discipline that is still in a process of becoming."[9]

What it is becoming is not clear. Political scientists, like many other communities of inquiry, believe much—almost desperately—in the myth of scholarly accumulation. Despite the historical experience cited above, affirmations abound in the literature of political science of the growth of the discipline. Out of the healthy pluralism of the present will someday emerge knowledge grounded in evidence, universal in generalizations, certain, and scientific. Further research will refine and expand the grasp of political truth. This faith ignores the disturbing fact that the history of inquiry, in both the sciences and the humanities, is strewn with the ruins of intellectual edifices once thought surely to stand forever as final answers to intellectual problems. Within the short history of American political science (the American Political Science Association came into existence in 1930), paradigms, methods, explanations, and data have come and gone. Most books and articles on American politics written over twenty years ago have been forgotten. Similarly, the finished products of contemporary political science will be largely forgotten in the future. What political scientists do now may well be the thing to do at the time, but future times may look back on their efforts as naive at best, hilarious at worst. The historical growth of the discipline has meant the survival of the discipline, not a guarantee of the accumulation of knowledge culminating in revealed and sustained generalizations.

Myths of Method

The belief in the progress of the discipline is observable in recurrent enthusiasm for new methodologies or new approaches. The penchant for labeling techniques, approaches, and analytical modes "new" is almost as great as the politician's to harp on the New Freedom, New Deal, New Frontier, or New Foundation (see Chapter 3). The obsession with sophisticated methodologies (statistics, mathematical models, etc.) belies, as often as not, anxiety about what political scientists should be doing, so that "we are forever perfecting how to do something without ever getting around to doing it even imperfectly."[10] The myth of methodology espouses that if political scientists can but hit upon the right method, then the elusive core of political truth will yield its secret.

The myth of methodology almost seems to stem from a Pythagorean belief in the magic of numbers; for example, truth is quantifiable because the basic structure of the world breaks down into units that correspond with mathematics. In recent years, political science journals have published an inexhaustible supply of articles based on positive theory, sophisticated mathematical models beyond the understanding of most political scientists and certainly beyond most policy makers. Yet many of these works are in policy areas, although their relevance to policy is seldom explained. Consider the probable reaction of a defense department official dealing with defense appropriations upon reading an article on defense expenditures in the September 1978 *American Political Science Review:* "... To determine the effect of war, z_{1t}, on congressional appropriations, the following equation is estimated:

$$y_{3t} = (b_{31} + a_{31}z_{1t}) \, y_{2t} + (b_{32} + a_{32z1t}) \, x_{5t} = u_{3t}$$

where b_{31} and b_{32} represent the impact of y_{2t} and x_{5t} on y_{3t} in the absence of war while $(b_{31} - a_{31})$ and $(b_{32} + a_{32})$ represent the impact of y_{2t} and x_{5t} on y_{3t} in the presence of war. If a_{31} and/or a_{32} are different from 0.00, there is evidence that the parameters of the policy-making rule are temporarily altered as a result of the existence of war. Furthermore, the sign and magnitude of each a_{ij} provide a measure of the change in behavior brought on by changes in either international or domestic environments."[11] Arcane perhaps, but is such a statement of help to policymakers? The article and statement deal with vital questions of war, peace, and appropriations. But those involved in the rough-and-tumble of international and budgetary politics may reel at the reality created by political science modeling. As one observer notes, "Personal experience in politics will quickly disabuse political scientists of the notion that the most important factors in making the system work can be fitted into equations."[12]

Paralleling the myth of numerology is that of metaphor. Modern-day political theories develop different imaginative perspectives on politics, employing conceptual languages based upon a root metaphor.[13] It is nothing new, of course, for a social science to employ such conceptual languages, for they help to organize pictures of the world. Our claim here is simply that such languages do not correspond to any discovered or discoverable political reality. They are no better or worse than imaginative metaphors used in other times.

Metaphorical usage, inevitable though it is, rests on a myth. The myth is that the metaphor is timeless and that it, in some sense, corresponds with political reality. Yet metaphors are the product of an historical age and of the climate of opinion of a time. Contemporary political science generates root metaphors based on ideas of politics as a "system," as "communication," and as "exchange." It is no accident that such metaphors arise in the age of complex organizations, the communications revolution, and in a capitalist-market economy. David Easton, Karl Deutsch, and Peter Blau, the respective purveyors of these three metaphors, are the Johns of Salisbury of our time.[14]

It is questionable that such metaphors possess ontological status—that is, that they really exist out there to be gathered like rose buds when ye may. Attributing ontological status to a political "system," "learning net," or what have you is an academic fiction because it abstracts a political reality into a credible, fixed schema. But a static, linguistic reality is not the same as the dynamic, active reality out there. The political "system" is hauntingly familiar to "the State": Both conjure up ideas and images about politics, but one cannot go out and find either one. They are hypothetical constructs, convenient fictions that organize perceptions of politics. There is always a danger of reifying the metaphor: Political scientists often forget that their created realities—their metaphors and intellectual constructs—are not permanent parts of a fixed real world of politics. As one of the great metaphor-builders, social theorist Talcott Parsons, recently said, ". . . Analytical thought itself is mythologization."[15]

Indeed, the biological metaphor of a society as possessing structures that perform essential functions (much as the heart pumps blood or the digestive system processes food), developed by Parsons and borrowed for political science by Gabriel Almond and his colleagues, illustrates another aspect of the use of metaphor for mythmaking: the possibility that unconscious motives underlie analytical thought and that these include covert ethnocentrism and political wishes. By covert ethnocentrism we refer to the tendency of many intellectual constructs, on the face, to appear to be universalized and neutral but on closer inspection to possess biases toward a single political milieu, and, implicitly, associated political goals. In the case of Almond's structural-functional model, he posits the idea that political systems tend over time to develop from undifferentiated structures to highly differentiated structures performing a set of complex functions. These functions include political socialization, interest articulation and aggregation, political communication, and governmental rule making, rule application, and rule adjudication.[16] The cover enthnocentrism in the Almond construct is that the developed regimes are Anglo-American, with school systems; plural interest groups who are free to agitate; mass media; and separation of powers between the legislature, executive, and judiciary. Further, there are hints of a political wish in Almond's scheme: that all political orders are developing toward such a complex system and that they will be good and stable when they most resemble England and the United States.[17] The abstractions of such an intellectual construct thereby turn out to be second-order myths, myths created to prove another, more basic myth, a first-order myth, stemming from implicit cultural biases and individual wishes.

Finally, there is another sense in which specific and descriptive political studies, regardless of methodological purity, involve myth-making. The Greek term *mythos* implied "a tale told by the mouth," which gave a narrative and dramatic quality to the community story. Political scientists tell stories about American politics by the way they structure what is important in their research and writing. Not that the stories are not in some way true, but the way the political drama is set up—who the important actors are, what is at stake, and so on—offers a mythical political reality. By necessity, the political scientist doing a study of, say, Congress, must select, choose, and amplify some aspect of the political world that omits many other elements. One political scientist dramatizes American politics as a setting for heroic presidential action; another narrates a tale of the dramatic clash of plural institutions and interests. Where one study sees consensus and community, another sees conflict and fragmentation. Not only is there disagreement over who the heroes, villains, and fools of the political drama are, there is no agreement even on who the relevant actors and factors are. Each mythical construct tells us something of the entire story of American politics, but political reality is perhaps simply too vast, inchoate, and changing for mere language and scholarship to grasp in the magnitude of its entirety.[18]

With all of the above said, there is another thought about political scientific mythmaking. The fundamental problem with the conduct of inquiry in political science is not just the magnitude of the diversity and richness of politics, or the tyranny of words and metaphors, or the lack of intellectual consensus. Rather, it may be that political science rests on a fundamental myth, the myth of an ordered and discoverable political reality. Politics occurs in time and is an ongoing process of constantly changing actors, situations, languages, ideas, accidents, and happenings. Many political scientists operate on the myth that the reality they purport to study is field-invariant and thus subject to universal generalization and laws. Perhaps, in fact, the world of politics is field-dependent, an eternally changing mix of relationships.[19] The myth that one can build a science of neat, simple, mathematically stated, universal statements about politics flies in the face of the contextual and temporal nature of the subject matter, politics. If there is, as some claim, a severe separation of the discipline from the realities of politics and policy makers, such is a possible source of the credibility gap.

POLITICAL SCIENCE AS A MYTHMAKING COMMUNITY

Political science is a loose community of scholars, an academic subculture with its own history, values, habits, and routines. The conduct of inquiry occurs in the context of that community, with all of the external, organizational, and personal features that shape the enterprise. The product is normal science, ideas and images about politics reflecting participation in community life—not, be it noted, participation in politics, for politics is another community conducting another enterprise. The myths about politics held by political actors are the result of communication in one community; the myths about politics held by political scientists are the result of communication within quite another community. The reality created in either only incidentally relates to the other.

In broadest terms, political science is a disciplinary speech community with a language and style of its own. One enters that speech community by mastery of its language and acceptance of its style and fashions. This does not mean that there are not disagreements, conflicts, schisms, and newly emergent ideas and images. It does mean that there is a widely shared community of values on which substantial portions of members taking part in the community agree. Political mythmaking derives in part from the existence of a sense of community (or communities) among political scientists.

One basic way communities perpetuate themselves is through *so-*

cialization into the values of the community, including *overarching myths, folkways, and routines.* The novice political scientist goes to graduate school to learn the language of the community and the history and folklore of American political science, the canons of research and norms of action, and perhaps most importantly, how one conducts oneself in the dramas of the profession—publishing, reading papers at professional gatherings, mastering a literature, and developing a reputation. Socialization communicates to the student not only myths about what political science is but also what political scientists are supposed to do, as well as approved ways of doing it. The fledging political scientist acquires a mythic grounding that offers membership of good standing in the Order. Through contact with the profession, in courses, conventions, books and journals, and personal contacts, the initiate enters the gates of the mythic community.

Overarching Myths

At the most basic level, the novice learns the overarching myths of the political science discipline. These include myths about the profession's past and the heritage of that past. Like any other endeavor of long standing, American political science has mythologized times, events, processes, and people from the past. For example, like residents of rural villages, academicians point to those among their very own who went on to glory in an endeavor other than the academic discipline of their origin. *P.S.,* a news-and-issues publication of the American Political Science Association (APSA), recently published a long list of political scientists who went on to become university presidents and chancellors.[20] And to venerate political scientists who demonstrate the discipline's relevance to the subject it studies—politics—there is considerable awe for those who become advisors to the King: Henry Kissinger, Zbigniew Brzezinski, Samuel P. Huntington. This is supportive of the academic myth that the sage wisdom of the learned is welcome at court. But ultimate veneration is reserved for the political scientist who *became* King: Woodrow Wilson.

Similarly, histories of political science identify key events, groups, and processes—the Great Moments in History. Thus the Somit and Tanenhaus recounting of the origins and development of political science says, "From its very inception, the profession was committed to the pursuit of truth and to the propagation of demo-cratic values and practices. . . . 1921 . . . was the first year of Mer-riam's momentous effort to move the profession toward a 'science of politics.'. . . The ultimate nature of American political science, we need hardly say, will be profoundly influenced by the fate of the be-havioral movement.[21] The dramatic and sweeping tone of such state-ments gives the history of an academic discipline much more impor-tance than it probably deserves. It is in retrospect that history acquires meaning and order, and the extent to which the political science pro-fession was "committed," Merriam's efforts "momentous," or "fate" a force in shaping the discipline's future is questionable.

A favorite pastime is creating the discipline's usable past (recall Chapter 2), the game of Top Ten. Top Ten involves naming and rank-ing the Immortals: the Great Names, the Great Books, the Great De-partments. One study of the profession's character actually has a chapter entitled "Political Science's Hall of Fame." A survey asked political scientists to name the Immortals (the table is entitled "Rank-ing of Great Men"): Charles E. Merriam heads the pre-1945 list (named by 37.4 percent of respondents), whereas V. O. Key, Jr., heads the post-1945 list (named by 36.6 percent of respondents). Harold Lass-well, on both lists, drops from second to fifth, betraying some loss of greatness.[22] An even more popular sport is ranking the prestige de-partments of political science in colleges and universities wherein, one assumes, the Big Guns of the profession are doing the Great Books. This sort of thing appeals to the American achievement mania about "We're Number One," a cultural mythos in which people have an inex-haustible interest. By being Number One or in the Top Ten, a depart-ment then proves its greatness; the myth has been validated by their peers (rather than by sportswriters). But the competition is stiff, and the National Championship must constantly be defended. In the latest poll, Harvard and Yale are neck and neck (32 percent rank Yale Num-ber One; 29 percent rank Harvard in that place), so undoubtedly this enhances their reputations and perhaps even puts pressure on their faculties to try harder.[23] It is striking how important such rankings are and how much Americans believe in the democratic myth that great-ness emerges by ballot. Also, such hierarchies of greatness stem from our desire to create myths about founts of wisdom: We can, by believ-ing in their intellectual greatness, look to them for leadership. It is no secret that people from the elite schools tend to dominate the profession, and some of the deference and expectation of leadership paid them derives from the myth.

Another way to mythologize the discipline's past for the new political scientist is to explain that (s)he is part of a Great Tradition. One of the major functions of Great Names, Great Books, and so on is to demonstrate that tradition exists. The student of the role of interest groups in politics learns of the great tradition of the group approach that includes luminaries like Robert Dahl, David Truman, Arthur Bentley, and even John C. Calhoun and James Madison. Each subfield in political science uses a review of the literature for this purpose, to guide the new student along the correct path of normal science in that field by invoking the Greats of the Past whose work initiates humbly carry on. The myth of such cumulative traditions inspires amazing rhetoric. In his presidential address to the APSA in 1966, Gabriel Almond heralded the historical triumph of the behavioral movement, to the effect that "while an older generation—Herring, Shattschneider, Odegard, and Key—saw a new land on the horizon, a new generation—Truman, Easton, Deutsch, and Dahl—have been moving across the Jordan to possess it."[24] Such Biblical imagery conjures up visions of being part of a grand, glorious, honorable, and triumphant enterprise.

But the most ardently held myth of a Great Tradition exists in the field of political science called normative political theory or the history of political thought. Herein, one learns that to be part of a great and higher tradition than any of the other mere political scientists, an aspiring political scientist studies the "Great Conversation," the accumulated wisdom of the ages that it is our duty to defend, cherish, impart, and glean. From the metaphysical subtleties of Plato to the empirical utilitarianism of Mill, the intricate continuity and the Perennial Questions are part of an historical and philosophical fabric that takes the scholar a lifetime to master. However, one political theorist has called the enterprise "the myth of the tradition." "Over the years," he writes, "by academic convention, a basic repertoire of works has been selected, arranged chronologically, represented as an actual historical tradition, infused with evolutionary meaning, laden with significance derived from various symbolic themes and motifs, and offered up as the intellectual antecedents of contemporary politics and political thought."[25] The history of political thinking, then, acquires an organic structure and cumulation that it does not possess.

But why have political theorists done this? Because they derive a sense of belonging to a mythical community, a philosophical elite that continues through the present adherents. "What is presented," Gunnell says, "is not so much intellectual history as an epic tale, with heroes and villains, which is designed to lend authority to a diagnosis of the deficiencies of the present. The past is often used in very much the same manner as a dramatist might use events of everyday life to construct the world of the play."²⁶ The organic unity of the Great Conversation is a myth, but it serves the needs of a present community by supporting solidarity, helping to undergird the group feeling that we value the significant knowledge, study the true tradition, are doing the significant work. Also, it supports the sense that we are the ones who will move across the Jordan to possess Zion.

So the house of political science has many mansions. They all seem to have a vision of their mythic mission and future. Such subcommunities bound together by common symbols and effort want to believe in the myth of progress. Responding to that desire, frequent rhetorical addresses by significant figures in the discipline appeal to communal longing. APSA presidential addresses include rhetoric conjuring up notions of Our Common Task. In the Almond address cited above, he concludes with the image of "our own unborn Joseph" that "is passed on to us inescapably by our past and imposed on us by our present division of labor." Recommitment to "our special professional culture" ensures that we will have "a significant part in the solution of the ultimate problem of man's enlightenment."²⁷

Similarly, any article, anthology, or book speculating on Our Common Task often ends with mythic statements. Even the hard-nosed and much revered Harold Lasswell ended his *The Future of Political Science* with "The need for a world-wide system of public order—a comprehensive plan of cooperation—is fearfully urgent. From the interplay of the study and practice of cooperation we may eventually move more wisely, if not more rapidly, toward filling the as-yet-mysterious potentialities of the cosmic process."²⁸ And a collection from various subcommunities of the discipline on the theme, "What should political scientists be doing?" includes an array of stirring finales:

> "Know thyself" can then be understood as a call to moral consciousness and to political consciousness. To help each other

and our students to heed that call, and to keep relating it more rationally to our expanding political knowledge, surely should be a key responsibility on our part as political scientists.[29]

... [T]he truth is often missed because it is so seldom sought. Let each seek it from his own perspective, bound together by a common commitment to employing reason in the development of political knowledge.[30]

The ordering of existence in accordance with the truth insofar as men are given to know it in experience is the end of politics as both art and science. It is therefore equivalent to the obligation of Everyman to live justly within his powers.[31]

Indeed, the recurrent question of what political scientists should be doing raises such anxieties and so reveals the fragility of the overarching myths of the discipline that it spurs sporadic attempts to provide clear-cut goals. The APSA has sponsored studies of Our Common Tasks, such as the "Goals for Political Science" study published in 1951. (There had been two before, in 1914 and 1930.) The 1951 report focused on teaching, emphasizing the goal of "citizen education": "The need to make citizens better informed and better participants is more widely felt today, when free political and economic institutions are on trial in their struggle with antithetical forces, than ever before in American history. Amongst political scientists in the United States, training for intelligent citizenship is the predominant interest and emphasis."[32]

The goals report restates the democratic myth of The Alert and Informed Citizenry and reconfirms the myth that political scientists were (or are) primarily interested in citizen education. It is a fine-sounding goal, but it is one that is far from the everyday doings of the profession. A 1964 survey asked political scientists what contributed to "career success": "Volume of publication" was ranked first; "teaching ability" was ranked tenth![33] In a 1976 survey, fully two-thirds of the American political scientists said that doctoral programs stressed research at the expense of training effective undergraduate teachers![34] The goal of citizen education is valued neither in graduate training nor in career goals. Although the faithful may remain within the church, they are not moved by the spirit of revivalism enough to repent.

A 1976 survey of political scientists revealed that a significant number said that if they had it to do over again, they wouldn't go into political science at all! (Thirty percent were definite; 11 percent weren't sure.)[35] Much of this may reflect a feeling that the overarching myths taught in disciplinary socialization are not valid. That feeling has probably contributed to the fragmentation of the discipline and to the vigor and continuity of the various subcommunities mentioned above. A sociologist who has surveyed the ways of political scientists, S. M. Lipset, claims that a big factor that contributes to low morale among political scientists is that it is not so much of a field as a "category of subgroups"; as a result, there is little "sense of discipline" among the members.[36] But the subgroups do acquire a mythic structure of their own as a substitute. In fact, a subcommunity of the discipline is often the object of intense devotion and outsider groups the object of intense derision. Labels attach to such subcommunities: the Straussians in political theory, the Rikerian positive theorists, the Survey Research Center (SRC) group, the Caucus for a New Political Science, the behavioral Establishment. Groups even form around a methodology or a common school background. Each such group possesses a shared fantasy (see Chapter 6): Myths are shared and reinforced by the like-minded within the group, myths that develop a sense of community and superior values to undergird mythic devotion. Given the intensity and the holier-than-thou air that can emerge in such subcommunities, it is no wonder that there are conflicts and little communication between them. In some respects, these subcommunities in political science are cults. A cult, after all, is a community that forms around a charismatic leader (like a Leo Strauss or a William Riker), develops and shares a myth about itself and the world, insulates itself from outside influences and denigrates other faiths, engages in gestures of cohesion and gestures of differentiation, and sees itself as the bearer of a truth that puts it above the rest of humanity.[37] This is not to suggest that such factions in political science need to be deprogrammed, but simply to point out that the existence of these subcommunities and their respective myths are antithetical to the myth of a transcendent scientific community and free communication within it, values many political scientists profess to share.

Folkways

Learning how to "do" political science involves induction into *folkways.* Folkways are simply the common ways of doing things, the ways of the folk. Every group, be it political, academic, tribal, or whatever, has its "unwritten rules of the game, its norms of conduct, its approved manner of behavior."[38] Large organizations of long standing, for example, develop power relations, habits of decision making, networks of informal communication, rites and ceremonies, time schedules, *modus operandi,* and *modus vivendi.* When an outsider enters an organization, that person must get used to things; learn where the bodies are buried; who has the paper clips; what the special language and hierarchy of the group is; and, all in all, adjust one's thinking and acting. Folkways support myths within a community, since they reaffirm the organizational hierarchy and group norms, the guardians or carriers of the myths. Folkways initiate the new members into the structure of the community and recruit respect and deference for it and, by implication, for its myths. Experience with folkways gives the individual contact with the consequences of myth in the structure and actions of the community during the time he or she is part of it.

We mentioned above that socialization of the graduate student in political science includes learning the overarching myths of the discipline and/or the myths of a subcommunity within it. This involves mastery of the language of the group, the agreed conceptual terminology that defines the subject of inquiry and provides the parameters for normal work. Scholarly communities, like other communities, provide opportunities for the novice to demonstrate mastery of the language and, by implication, acceptance of the community standards and structure. This is especially apparent at the culmination of the typical graduate career when the aspiring political scientist takes comprehensive examinations, writes a dissertation, and defends it before a faculty committee. These rites of passage give the would-be Ph.D. an opportunity to show his familiarity with the language and to pledge loyalty to traditions of the community or subcommunity. The ordeals do as much to validate community or subcommunity standards and structure as to show the student's originality and contribution to knowledge. Comprehensive examinations, for example, turn out to be rehashes of myriad tests the student managed to survive in courses, being less comprehensive and demanding of imagination than rewarding the capacity for rote learning of an endless series of approaches, relevant variables, approved solutions to disciplinary problems, and demonstrations of technical sleights of hand ("What assumptions enter into the use of chi square?" rather than "What is the cause of causal modeling?''). Dissertations must show proper respect for the Great Names of the past, for the developed language of the field, for approved methods of inquiry—all in all, the lore of the Tribe. Defense of the Cherished Document is a symbolic act gaining the novice passage to community membership by demonstrating his grasp of community myths and scholarly folkways. Such rituals serve an important socialization function for the community by ensuring the acceptibility of the candidate. The whole process of writing a dissertation—selection of topic, the obligatory review of the literature, citation of the Great Books, confinement to approved issues and results, attention to form of presentation, use of method—helps to shape the mind-set of the new generation of scholars and to ensure the continuity of organization folkways and underlying mythology.

A similar process occurs with the preparation of journal articles and convention papers. The quality, topics, and procedures of such papers are controlled by what communications theorists call "gate-keepers," established members of the political science community and its subdisciplines who read and approve or reject papers. Now it is true that there are valid grounds to screen papers, but the point is that it is established scholars who keep the gates—who decide what are unimportant or insignificant contributions, methodological shortcomings, theoretical problems, and canons of presentation. Journal editors sometimes exercise editorial discretion and do not submit papers for review at all, but this "buck stops here" procedure is rare.[39] Such gatekeeping may eliminate the unworthy, but it also may favor pieces most readily conforming to existing myths and operating most comfortably within the confines of established work. There are recurrent accusations of favoritism, that editors and reviewers tend to favor pieces that support their own personal or subcommunity myths. However, from a larger perspective, one can argue that the reviewing process is functional for the continuation of the discipline, since it helps to conserve myths of both a theoretical and procedural nature long valued in that community. It also tends to lead young political scientists who are breaking in to tailor what they write so as to defer to reigning conventions of what is going to get through the gate and what is not. Since the new generation of scholars is dependent upon earlier generations for scholarly approval, it should be expected that eagerness to please the elders contributes to concentrating on topics deemed safe. A glance at lists of dissertation, article, and book titles over the past few years gives the outsider a sense of the repetition of topics and the redundancy of insights. Even seeking to publish a book with a commercial publishing firm does not permit escape from community pressures, since the manuscript is almost always sent for review to respected academic experts in the field, who earn their honoraria reviewing fees by calling for endless rounds of revisions.

Awareness of the pearly gates to the profession tends to channel young political scientists into fairly predictable and typical career lines. Socialization processes and career choices appear much like those political scientist Donald R. Matthews found in the United States Senate. Matthews argued that the Senate had a set of folkways that pressured senators into forms of behavior demanded by the institution. These were apprenticeship, legislative work, specialization, courtesy, reciprocity, institutional patriotism, and conformity.[40] With slight modifications, one can observe the same process occurring in many political science careers. Freshmen senators, Matthews notes, learn quickly that they are supposed to serve an apprentice period on the Hill and that they occupy a subordinate status in the Pecking Order of the Senate.[41] Similarly, political scientists serve a long apprenticeship, both in graduate school and as junior faculty. They usually cleave unto a senior professor or leader of a subcommunity and are pegged as "having studied with" or as a "student of" such-and-such, much like an apprenticeship in a medieval guild. Apprenticeship inculcates the myths of the master or the group into the novice, who carries them on. Such apprenticeship is functional both for the senator and the political scientist, since it provides sponsors who teach the ropes and open doors and makes initiates acceptable to the other members of the community.

In like fashion, hard work is a valued trait in both institutions. Political scientists, to use a term quoted by Matthews, can be "show horses or work horses."[42] The show horse puts in many appearances but does little real work; the work horse conforms to one of the basic myths of the profession: the lonely scholar who grinds out the hard and detailed studies that are the heart of the discipline. The latter usually assumes acceptance of the folkway of specialization, focusing work on a few subject matters within one or two subcommunities of the discipline.[43] After all, political scientific knowledge is so vast that it is impossible anymore to be a generalist; anyway, the really valuable knowledge emerges from narrowly focused, detailed studies. Political scientists understand that career success is often dependent on such a specialist norm and structure their work accordingly. What results is an inexhaustible supply of microscopic studies, many linked to the parochial myths of the subcommunity that identify a particular scholar's special approach and cant.

This emerges strikingly in academic hiring: Departments do not advertise to hire a political scientist but rather a comparativist-European or a judicial behavior person or a normative theorist. In large departments, specialization reaches amazing proportions. In 1977, responding to student complaints, the political science department of the University of Chicago sought not only a specialist in American politics but someone who could "combine creative interpretations of American politics with mathematical models."[44] In other departments, one professor will teach nothing but "Soviet Politics" or "Executive-Legislative Relations in the United States." Some scholars spend virtually their entire careers studying Marsilius of Padua or the French Communist Party. It is not that these subjects are unimportant and should not be studied in detail. Rather, it illustrates a marked emphasis on specialization as essential on the path to knowledge and career success. But specialization can isolate political scientists in pigeonholes and so fragment the discipline that it is all too common for scholars in one field to have little idea of what is going on in another—nor do they care.

As courtesy and reciprocity are key folkways in the Senate, so are they in political science.[45] Courtesy includes playing the game like a gentleman, and reciprocity includes willingness to do things for others. Both are manifest in respect for other political scientists' myths. One scholar listens to another's myths in exchange for equal time to expound. Even disagreements (at, for instance, a convention panel on political party reform) fade in the face of these norms. Most such encounters are standoffs, ended by the panel chair uttering homilies about "need for further research," "agreeing to disagree," and "let a hundred flowers bloom." Disagreements are further muted by institutional patriotism, in much the same sense as among United States Senators.[46] Since disagreeing scholars at a conference panel are usually part of the same subcommunity, they share the belief that theirs is the most important field and that they are doing the most important work. Such settings offer membership in a mutual admiration society, with courtesy and reciprocity accorded insiders, even in debate. All assent to the bottom line: "While we may have conceptual and methodological disagreements, we are bound together by the great task of building the science of international relations." This is a normal way for groups to maintain cohesion, but is intellectual camaraderie necessarily synonymous with full commitment to the pursuit of truth? Received notions of a subcommunity may be challenged, but more often from without than within, a practice frequently resulting in added fragmentation, the creation of a new specialization.

A final folkway, conformity, also leaves a mark.[47] Social psychologist Solomon Asch long ago discovered that group consensus affects many people's perceptions of reality.[48] A kind of drive toward consonance occurs in subcommunities of political science and, in some measure, across the discipline as a whole. This is not to say that, like the United States Senate, there are no Mavericks, Show Horses, and Ideological Rebels in political science. As in any other group, rugged individualists exist and are tolerated. Such scholars have typically undergone the normal socialization process to accept the norms and mythical constructs of the discipline or field, but they later rebel, for a variety of reasons. If they are not eminent or from elite school backgrounds, the established subcommunity politely tolerates or ignores them. If they are eminent scholars or products of prestigious Ph.D.-granting departments, they may be something of an embarrassment. One such Maverick amuses himself (and many others who turn out at convention panels to see him in action) by trashing panels in his field, as well as the overarching and data myths generated by others. He tears up papers, verbally (and once, physically) assaults panel members, stalks out. Among Show Horses are few cynics and opportunists who do not believe in the myths of the academic community but who cultivate elite ties and fashionable research paradigms in order to enhance their careers. Exploiting the discipline is one way of "showing." A more serious problem for the discipline has been the appearance of a new community of Ideological Rebels, a group that does not share the myths of the discipline and that puts forth an alternative myth. For example, the Caucus for the New Political Science, which emerged in the late 1960s with a New Left mythology, argued that the APSA should become relevant, should take stands against war, racism, and poverty. The Caucus charged that the intellectual mythology of the APSA Establishment was sterile and biased, favored stability over change, and avoided value questions. In order to restore a modicum of conformity, the Association attempted, and in some measures succeeded, to co-opt the rebels by capitulating to some of their demands, by showing deference and respect for their arguments, and by attempting to adjust established myths with Caucus myths.[49] By the late 1970s, the conflict was largely defused, and mythic consonance was restored. The Caucus mythology had been legitimated as an extant subcommunity with a point of view.

Analysis of the folkways of political science reveals nothing more spectacular than the fact that the community has a social structure. Like any other organization the discipline has the familiar communications networks: Pecking Orders, Elders of the Tribe, Big Names, Gurus and Disciples, Old Boy Networks, Old School Ties, and the like. Individuals and groups act as community guardians, perpetuating myths held officially by the discipline, the subcommunity, or an elite. Social structures serve the function of mythic continuity. Control of the mechanisms of the organization by an elite helps to guard the myths held by the group or, at least, by the established inner circle. So it is important who becomes president of the Association or editors of professional journals; what is published in the journals; what the topics of convention panels are; and who gets what, when, where, and how. The dramaturgy of mythic assertion is a major activity in the discipline, reaffirming not only myth but also the social structure that supports it. Much of this is manifest in the routines of the discipline.

Routines and Rituals

Like most people, political scientists settle questions of value quickly (or suppress troublesome questions) and proceed to routine work. The young corporate executive or lawyer rationalizes and accepts certain values about the organization he or she works for early on and does not go through a daily value crisis. Political scientists, as professionals, accept certain academic and intellectual values, usually in graduate school when they affiliate with a particular subcommunity, and do not agonize over values thereafter. Once accepting a set of myths, most political scienitsts proceed with their work and do the jobs they are trained to do: teaching, researching, consultation, writing, government service, and so on. What they do usually supports the myths previously accepted, including those of the discipline and each scholar's subcommunity. In Kuhn's terminology, once a paradigm is accepted, most practitioners do "normal science" within that framework. The mythic paradigm defines political reality or the political reality of, say, international relations. Normal science is work limited to questions that the paradigm admits as real. Since the mythical questions have been answered, the tendency is for normal science to affirm the paradigm's reality. Findings clarify and validate the myth. Questions that are threatening—or anomalies—are not addressed.[50]

The routines of normal science dominate the work of political scientists for two reasons. One, as part of an academic community, scholars adopt the myth of that community. Two, to advance or even to get along in that community, they use the myths of the community. From the point of view of the typical political scientist, normal science serves career goals. The community structure demands that most people do normal science. Most young political scientists follow the line of least resistance and use rather than challenge the social structure, folkways, and overarching myths of their profession.

The benefits of community, however, do have a price. Not only does normal science encapsulate the perspective and innovativeness of political scientists, but it tends to reduce what they do to a ritual. To be sure, humans are often creatures of habit, reducing daily routines to rote. But the work of political science—so the graduate student hears —is creative, not repetitive ritual. Yet, in teaching each aspiring political scientist the method of normal science, graduate departments pass on ritual. The method consists of approved ways of designing research and reporting results. In speaking of the method, however, we are not denoting canons and standards of scientific research; rather, we are speaking of the catechism of scholarly procedure. The method is a form of scholasticism, an exquisite and esoteric exercise in the manipulation of trivia. Method is so important that criticisms of scholarly articles and papers typically center not around substantive findings but on whether researchers adhered to the method. The method serves mythmaking by creating the illusion that a given piece of research was actually conducted *as designed* and *as reported*. Political scientists are very strict about what must enter into the design of research—a clear, precise statement of a research problem; unequivocal statements of working hypotheses and testable hypotheses;

specification of data gathering techniques, sampling plans, analytical modes, and rationales for employing all qualitative/quantitative techniques. They are no less compulsive about how research results should be reported. A typical article begins by presenting conflicting theories, judiciously citing Big Names and Legends in the field. The report is structured in an appropriate sequence, a kind of academic liturgy that includes such titillating sections as "Statement of Problem," "Research Objectives," "Measures," "Data Base," "Procedures," "Results," and "Discussion" (with an obligatory denial that the study was anything more than "Exploratory" and, hence, that there is a need for "further research"). Numerical and conceptual tables frequently abound (political reality, after all, is a 2 × 2 table). Data or ideas are developed, but only to the most parsimonious limit. The prayer for "further research" appeals to the myth of accumulation. By obeying the dictates of the method, the research becomes a litany.

The problem with all of this is that rarely is the research ever conducted as designed or reported. Doing research demands all varieties of adjustments to exigencies never dreamed of in the research design. For example, people refuse to be interviewed, unthought of hypotheses emerge, tests of reliability turn out badly, and so on. Yet these practicalities of doing research never appear in either its design or report. Instead, the final report provides a picture of an orderly, sequential planned inquiry, as though everything went off without a hitch. Obviously something so well reported must have been well executed. Hence, why quibble over substantive results? Only the method must be put to test. If the method is flawless, the substantive conclusions must be the truth. Such a view reminds one of the line from Herman Wouk's novel about the navy in World War II: "The navy is a master plan. Designed by geniuses for execution by idiots."[51] Political scientists should not be charged with idiocy, but neither should ritual reign in the form of the method.

This goes to the core of political mythmaking in the discipline. Political science is, in many ways, isolated from the world of politics. The conceptions of politics developed are the province of the academic community, not the product of close contact with or experience in the political world. It is not unfair to say, for the charge has been made, that political science is severely alienated from the reality it purports to study.[52] The routines of political science assume and produce a reality validated by reference to myths shared in the academic community. Could it be that the political knowledge of political scientists is "book-wise," whereas the knowledge of politicians and political activists is "street-wise," and that the two are very different things?

POLITICAL SCIENCE AS A SERVICE INDUSTRY

There is another area of political science mythmaking. The one way the discipline does touch the world of politics is through development of ties with government and many private groups. These political interests demand myths, and political science supplies them. Political science is a service industry meeting the demand for messages that people want to hear and are willing to pay for. The discipline is part of the knowledge industry, consisting of all those groups that generate ideas, images, and facts for consumption by other groups. Political scientists work for a wide variety of clientele groups, both political and nonpolitical. Some critics charge that the profession is dominated by these outside clients. Theodore J. Lowi writes that " . . . the intellectual agenda of the discipline is set by the needs of the clientele, not by the inner logic of political science." Political science, like many other areas of academic knowledge, is put to use by social institutions. Lowi uses the image of the service station: Political science provides technical and legitimating myths that fuel the activities of external groups.[53]

If it is true that external clientele set the agenda for many political scientists, that agenda includes mythmaking. The impulse to buy knowledge from political science at all stems from the myth of the expert. Nonacademics often feel that what they do is more valid if it receives the *imprimatur* of a certified expert, someone with academic credentials. There is a pervasive belief that academics have a monopoly on technical and philosophical expertise or, at least, that one must legitimate an activity by consultation with the learned professions.

A few examples illustrate how this symbiotic process works. The Defense Department is an established governmental institution that performs various military functions for the United States. It is also in politics to further its point of view. Policy makers have definite ideas about what kind of defense posture and weaponry should be used.

The Pentagon and the defense industries around it search for ideas to support their notions of preferred policies. It is typical for policy makers in government or elsewhere to have preconceptions about what is to be done and *then* to search for supportive ideas. Sometimes, of course, an academic generates an idea that catches the eye of policy makers, but it is likely that the idea simply articulates what the policy makers were leaning toward in the first place. In any case, academics who expound ideas that policy makers want to hear are often rewarded with fees, access to policy-making networks, paid conferences, free books, and so on. Indeed, the entire international relations establishment in their discipline brings political scientists into contact with decision makers as high as the president. Political scientists Henry Kissinger and Zbigniew Brzezinski became academic advisors to presidents because they shared and articulated views that presidents-to-be wanted to hear.

This is not to say, of course, that such academic advice always results in wise or successful policies. Since academic advisors often tell policy makers what they want to believe, there is a possibility that the shared fantasy does not conform to reality. Irving Janis notes the phenomenon of "groupthink"—that is, that decision-making groups hold to illusions about what the world is like and what their policy is likely to accomplish. Since policy makers like to have around themselves like-minded men, there is the danger that the shared illusion will not be penetrated by any disconfirming messages.[54] Political scientists in advisory roles are as capable of such mythmaking as anyone else. Some critics allege that the American government did not anticipate what was to happen in Iran in 1979 because experts (some were political scientists) kept telling policy makers what they wanted to believe.

This is only one example of a political science service industry. These various myth industries create myths for political purposes. This is not to say that political scientists or other intellectuals do so cynically, although clearly some do; but it does mean that the holders of congenial myths find each other. If the scholarly view coincides with the interests of the institution, ideology, or politician, then the perpetuator, no matter how sincerely he believes his myth, accepts the prospect of lucrative rewards and applause. Co-optation is easier to handle under such circumstances. For example, political scientists and other intellectuals espousing a neoconservative ideology and policy alternative in the 1970s found their interpretation of American society and defense of corporate capitalism embraced by elites with resources to reward such conclusions. Thinktanks funded by the powerful and rich, such as the American Enterprise Institute, sprang up to provide funds and a forum for neoconservative ideas, which not incidentally supported the political and economic views of their patrons.[55]

It is singular that such intellectual forums are a major source of recruitment for advisors to significant politicians and parties. For example, in 1973 David Rockefeller, head of Chase Manhattan Bank, started a policy-making group called the Trilateral Commission that had as its purpose the coordination of economic policy among the three Western areas of the world—Japan, the United States, and Western Europe. It was an elite thinktank that generated studies of how to deal with international economic and political problems. It included not only intellectuals but also politicians, such as Georgia Governor Jimmy Carter. When Carter became president in 1976, he chose for top positions in his administration many of the people connected with the Trilateral Commission: Zbigniew Brzezinski, Cyrus Vance, W. Michael Blumenthal, Harold Brown, Andrew Young, and so on. It is likely that Carter found these people congenial to his own political myths, or perhaps membership in the Commission helped to develop a myth among Carter and his cohorts while all were a part of it. In any case, over fifteen of his most important appointments went to members of the Commission, including the political scientists who were (or are) part of it. Thus elite myths developed and shared in that forum help to shape public policy and political decisions.

There are many other industries related to politics and involving political scientists. Their technical expertise emerges in such service industries as campaign management and public opinion sampling. Political scientists frequently serve on teams formed to make myths about a candidate. But they also serve as consultants for public opinion polling firms hired to make myths about politics. Organized interest groups commission public opinion surveys that, even though they obey the canons of survey sampling, come up with data that support the position of the sponsor. It is possible to so load questions that the direction of public response can be sharply changed. An interviewer can ask, "Do you agree or disagree with the following statement: Before we sign any SALT treaty with Communist Russia, we had better be sure that it doesn't so weaken our defenses to the point that they will be tempted to try a sneak attack on us." The images of "Communist," "weak defenses," and "sneak attack" conjure up a complicated political myth, dating from Pearl Harbor and the Cold War, which is likely to color many people's response to it. A more neutral wording might bring out a different response, and indeed several different responses on the issue may be expected. The interest group can then select which piece of "data" to use in, for example, congressional hearings on the SALT treaty. Since the methodology of the entire survey may have been supervised and certified by political scientists, it carries more weight with policy makers, since it reflects public opinion. But in reality the aggregate opinion is a myth shaped for political purpose; political scientists, wittingly or not, add legitimacy to deliberate mythmaking.

Perhaps the major industry with which political science is linked is the publishing business. Political scientists produce books to sell to profit themselves and the publishing company. More often than not, the books are compilations of myth about politics that political scientists believe in. But the myth held by the political scientist makes its way into print only if it meets the approval of editorial personnel at book companies who make decisions about what to publish. Editors usually rely on political scientists paid by the company to evaluate book proposals. If reviewers do not share the myth that the book proposal wishes to present, then it may not get published. Also, the company wants to sell books and has some idea of the potential audience. Therefore, there is an impulse to publish books palatable to the myths held by a potential audience, usually one composed of still other political scientists and undergraduate students.

The most obvious example is the American government textbook designed for adoption in introductory American government classes at the college level. There is an enormous potential audience, and book companies vie for this highly competitive and lucrative market. Political scientists compete to publish such texts, since they stand to gain, too. Aspiring authors typically propose texts with a "theme," "perspective," or "position" to run through the book, each reflecting biases, interpretations, and values. The theme that organizes the book is likely to be a myth that, again, there is a political reality whose nature I (the author) have discovered and which can be explained in terms of the concepts that organize this book. One book claims that American politics can be understood as a "polyarchy"; another sees politics as "conflict resolution"; another evaluates American politics by how much gap there is between "promise" and "performance"; others take a Marxist approach; another focuses on "elites"; still others have vaguer themes, or none at all.[56] In any event, the approach, a particular way of looking at things, is supposed to give the student an inclusive handle on political reality now and for all time. American government texts also perpetuate myths by presenting the author's pet interpretations of political objects. In one text, the Congress is the pivotal political institution; in another, the presidency. In one, change is the central issue; in another, stability is stressed. For some, the American political system is benevolent; for others, it is sinister. Some have chapters on political objects that others do not. This reflects not only the lack of consensus among political scientists on what is vital to know among political scientists but also the fact that authors can convince publishers that they can gain a share of the college market with their particular gimmicks.

Even in books for upper-division courses or in academic books there is a tendency for myths to pervade a field. On a particular political subject, a measure of mythic consensus appears in texts. Thomas E. Cronin has criticized what he calls the "textbook presidency," perpetuated by political scientists, book companies, and the mass media. In this myth, the president is the personal hero who single-handedly moves and shakes history; he is attributed power and virtue; he has almost mystical powers because he walks in the shoes of giants; he is the dynamic center of American politics; and so on. Cronin argues that one of the sources of the myth of the presidency is the commercial and political goals of textbook authors.[57] Patriotic, political, career, or simple pecuniary goals may thus affect the myths written and published about a specific topic. One writer may want students to believe in the institution of the presidency; another may believe that the presidency is the locus of political changes he would like to see; a scholar may elaborate a fashionable myth to advance his own career; or someone else may discern that mythifying the presidency simply sells books.

If one looks at the range of political science textbooks produced for mass college audiences, recurrent mythical elements pervade their structure. First, they tend to oversimplify political reality. Oftentimes, politics and political institutions are reduced to personal terms. A complex institution like the presidency reduces to the men who have occupied it, and stories are told about their great deeds. Or the intricacies of legislative politics appear in flow charts of how Congress enacts a law. The student is left with the impression that this *is* presidential or legislative reality. Secondly, textbooks reify political reality. They attribute structure and permanence to what is process and change. The history and nature of, say, elections emerges as part experience, and the elements of elections are eternal and fixed. It is true that one has to rely on the past and pick out what one thinks are the key elements; but if one does not admit that the future will likely be different, one implicitly perpetuates the myth that this is a marble statue of elections. Finally, textbooks mythify by overdramatizing political reality. A lot of politics is exciting, but there is a recurrent tendency in textbooks to treat all of political reality as dramatic, as the clash of either personal heroes and villains or of reified forces.

This last point requires elaboration. Since political science texts are for popular consumption, it should not surprise us that the publishing business favors entertaining books. Thus political science textbooks display in their content the entertainment values that students will read books that are entertaining—with dramatic storytelling; engaging lead-ins; pithy quotes; case studies; and visual aids, including pictures, tables and charts, and cartoons. The writing cannot be too academic. So American government texts are often a combination of myths brought by the political scientist and filtered through a popular presentation style expected by the company. The result is often breezy reading, and indeed some authors and publishers have made the introductory textbook into a popular art form of high quality. But it can be a fictional art form, a dramatic, reified, simplified product that has only a mythical relationship with the political world it purports to describe. The political order of textbooks is negotiated between academic political scientist-authors and publishers, and this order is not the same as that of the extant political world.

There are many other services that political scientists perform for outside clientele, too numerous to mention here. They crop up in all sorts of settings, as if there were a greater demand nowadays for political myths. It is possible to see political scientists on news programs (such as the CBS Morning News) to explain to a deferential newsperson exactly what is going on in China. Even though the area specialist called upon is a professor at a distinguished university and knows all of what he thinks he knows about Chinese politics from books and the *New York Times,* reporters listen solemnly while he tells them what is going on in less than three minutes. The distinguished political scientist appears in the role of sage, pontificating in other forums about his ideas on virtually every imaginable political subject. Journals that appeal to middlebrow educated myths—*Psychology Today, Harper's, New Times,* and so on—constantly have pieces by well-known or well-placed political scientists that discuss some subject of mass audience interest. James MacGregor Burns, a political scientist who has sage status, recently was interviewed in *Psychology Today* on the subject of true leadership, on which he had written a book. Burns has previously written biographical studies of Franklin Roosevelt, John F. Kennedy, and Edward Kennedy, and he has close ties with Eastern Liberal Establishment circles. It is not therefore surprising that true leadership resembles very much these types of men and their orientations. But dictators, we learn, are not true leaders. Hitler and Lenin, for example, were not! Neither, as we might expect, are Jimmy Carter and Howard Jarvis. But we have the hope that there is a "leadership corps in exile" in the land, and we may be "on the threshold of a period of political reform and excitement that could rival the Progressive Era, the 30s, and yes, the 60s."[58] Sageness apparently does not free the political scientist from mythmaking—defining leaders as those one agrees with and imposing one's desires about politics and who one would like to see in charge in a mythical future. However, such a myth might have great appeal to the readership of such a periodical.

There are many other service areas we could discuss, but the above is sufficient. Political science is connected to a network of industries that want mythic messages, and scholars serve them by creating and communicating such messages. Those that want certain messages and those capable of producing them usually find each other, but what emerges is often enough the illumination of a myth that both producer and consumer can comfortably share.

A FINAL COMMENT ON DEMYTHOLOGIZING POLITICAL SCIENCE

Our argument has been simple but severe: Political science, a learned discipline, makes myths. It makes myths through the knowledge it develops, because of norms and pressures in the academic community, and because it is also a service industry. Such mythmaking is likely to continue. When one possesses a mythical knowledge or belongs to a community that shares a myth or serves an industry in which it is lucrative or rewarding to communicate a myth, it is difficult to give up the habit. The uncertainty of political knowledge is such that the search for new, more satisfying, myths is likely. We expect revisions in what we know about politics, in how we should approach politics, and in what methods we should use to uncover truths about politics. Political scientists, like many of us, are incapable of admitting that the realities they create are their own and not necessarily an immanent property of some reified political world. Nor are they likely to admit that they are affected in their views by membership in a subcommunity or by service to an external industry. The tragedy is that such work habits tend to trivialize politics and that the drama of politics becomes lost in esoteric language and numerical exposition.

The question remains: Can political science demythologize itself? The renowned philosopher of science, Karl Popper, wrote that "what we call 'science' is differentiated from a myth, but by being accompanied by a second-order tradition—that of critically discussing the myth."[59] This is precisely what political scientists need to recognize. If our argument in this chapter is accurate, then political science needs to understand at least that the political reality it has created is mythical. It needs to understand that political reality is not as real as it looks. It needs to develop a language of metamyths, which would allow it to study and recognize its own myths.[60] Perhaps political science can never fully demythologize itself, but if it understands its role in political mythmaking, it has taken a long step in self-knowledge.

REFERENCES

1. See Thomas S. Kuhn's celebrated *The Structure of Scientific Revolutions* (Chicago: University of Chicago Press, 1964); and Martin Landau, "Objectivity, Neutrality, and Kuhn's Paradigm," in his collection, *Political Theory and Political Science* (New York: Macmillan, 1972), pp. 43–77.

2. John of Salisbury, quoted in Ewart Lewis, ed., *Medieval Political Ideas* (New York: Knopf, 1954), Vol. I, p. 225.

3. E. E. Schattschneider, *Two Hundred Million Americans in Search of a Government* (New York: Holt, Rinehart and Winston, 1969).

4. Gabriel Almond and G. Bingham Powell, *Comparative Politics: A Developmental Approach* (Boston: Little, Brown, 1966), p. 110.

5. Frederick Austin Ogg, *European Governments and Politics* (2nd ed.) (New York: Macmillan, 1948).

6. Ralph M. Goldman and DeVere E. Pentony, "The Language of Politics," *News for Teachers of Political Science* (Fall 1978): 19-21.

7. David V. J. Bell, *Power, Influence, and Authority* (New York: Oxford University Press, 1975), Appendix A, "The Poverty of Political Science Concepts," pp. 111-115.

8. For a sampling, see George J. Graham, Jr., and George W. Carey, eds., *The Post-Behavioral Era* (New York: McKay, 1972).

9. Fred I. Greenstein and Nelson W. Polsby, "Preface," to *Handbook of Political Science* (Reading, Mass.: Addison-Wesley, 1975), p. vii.

10. Abraham Kaplan, *The Conduct of Inquiry* (San Francisco: Intext, 1964), pp. 24-26.

11. Charles W. Ostrom, Jr., "A Reactive Linkage Model of the U.S. Defense Expenditure Policymaking Process," *American Political Science Review,* 72, no. 3 (September 1978): 954.

12. Michael Nelson, "What's Wrong with Political Science," *Washington Monthly* (September 1977), p. 20.

13. A good survey is in Michael A. Weinstein, *Systematic Political Theory* (Columbus, Ohio: Merrill, 1971).

14. See the discussion in Martin Landau, "On the Use of Metaphor in Political Analysis," *Political Theory and Political Science,* pp. 78-102.

15. Talcott Parsons and Charles Ackerman, "The Concept of 'Social System' as a Theoretical Device," in Gordon J. DiRenzo, ed., *Concepts, Theories, and Explanation in the Behavioral Sciences* (New York: Random House, 1966), pp. 25-26.

16. Almond and Powell, *Comparative Politics,* pp. 73-189.

17. William T. Bluhm, *Theories of the Political System* (2nd ed.) (Englewood Cliffs, N.J.: Prentice-Hall, 1971), pp. 157-162.

18. Jerald Washington, *The American Political Drama,* Ph.D. diss., University of Tennessee, 1976).

19. Stephen Toulmin, *The Uses of Argument* (Cambridge, England: Cambridge University Press, 1958); John G. Gunnell, *Philosophy, Science, and Political Inquiry* (Morristown, N.J.: General Learning Press, 1975), pp. 84-96.

20. *P.S.,* Fall 1978 (Washington, D.C.: American Political Science Association, 1978), XI, 4, pp. 534-536.

21. Albert Somit and Joseph Tanenhaus, *The Development of American Political Science* (Boston: Allyn & Bacon, 1967), pp. 47, 87 and 288.

22. Albert Somit and Joseph Tanenhaus, *American Political Science: A Profile of a Discipline* (New York: Atherton Press, 1964), p. 66.

23. Everett C. Ladd and Seymour M. Lipset, "New Grades for America's Colleges," reprinted from *Chronicle of Higher Education* in the *Chicago Tribune,* February 4, 1979, section 2, page 2.

24. Gabriel A. Almond, "Political Theory and Political Science," in Ithiel de Sola Pool, ed., *Contemporary Political Science: Toward Empirical Theory* (New York: McGraw-Hill, 1967), p. 12-13.

25. John G. Gunnell, *Political Theory: Tradition and Interpretation* (Cambridge, Mass.: Winthrop Publishers, 1979), p. 68.

26. Gunnell, *Political Theory,* p. 68.

27. Almond, "Political Theory and Political Science," pp. 18-19.

28. Harold D. Lasswell, *The Future of Political Science* (New York: Atherton Press, 1963), p. 242.

29. Christian Bay, "Thoughts on the Purposes of Political Science Education," in Graham and Carey, *The Post-Behavioral Era,* p. 99.

30. George G. Graham, Jr., "Reason and Change in the Political Order," in Graham and Carey, *The Post-Behavioral Era,* p. 123.

31. Ellis Sandoz, "The Philosophical Science of Politics Beyond Behavioralism," in Graham and Carey, *The Post-Behavioral Era,* p. 305.

32. *Goals for Political Science,* Report of the Committee for the Advancement of Teaching, American Political Science Association (New York: William Sloane Associates, Inc., 1951), p. ix.

33. Somit and Tanenhaus, *American Political Science,* p. 79.

34. Ellen K. Coughlin, "Many Political Scientists Are Unhappy About their Jobs, Salaries, Students," *Chronicle of Higher Education,* September 11, 1978, p. 9.

35. Coughlin, "Many Political Scientists," p. 9.

36. Coughlin, "Many Political Scientists," p. 9.

37. These symbolic actions were discussed by Joseph Gusfield in *Symbolic Crusade: Status Politics and the American Temperance Movement* (Urbana, Ill.: University of Illinois Press, 1966), pp. 171-72.

38. Donald R. Matthews, *U.S. Senators and Their World* (New York: Vintage Books, 1960), p. 92.

39. See Charles M. Bonjean and Jan Hullum, "Reasons for Journal Rejection: An Analysis of 600 Manuscripts," *P.S.,* Fall 1978, (Washington, D.C.: American Political Science Association, 1978), xi, 4, pp. 481-482.

40. Matthews, *U.S. Senators,* pp. 92-103.

41. Matthews, *U.S. Senators,* p. 92-93.

42. Matthews, *U.S. Senators,* p. 94.

43. Matthews, *U.S. Senators,* pp. 95-97.

44. Chicago *Maroon,* Richard Biernacki, "Fewer Courses, Large Class Sizes Stir Poli Sci Student Complaints," November 18, 1977, pp. 1-2.

45. Matthews, *U.S. Senators,* pp. 97-101.

46. Matthews, *U.S. Senators,* pp. 101-102.

47. Matthews, *U.S. Senators,* pp. 102-103.

48. Solomon Asch, "Effects of Group Pressure upon the Modification and Distortion of Judgement," in H. Proshansky and B. Seidenberg (eds.), *Basic Studies in Social Psychology* (New York: Holt, Rinehart, and Winston, 1965), pp. 393-401.

49. See Theodore J. Lowi, "The Politics of Higher Education: Political Science as a Case Study," in Graham and Carey, *The Post-Behavioral Era,* pp. 11-36.

50. The notion of "anomaly" was developed by Kuhn, *Structure of Scientific Revolutions.*

51. Herman Wouk, *The Caine Mutiny* (Garden City, N.Y.: Doubleday & Co., 1952), p. 97.

52. Paul Von Blum, in a review of Frank Smallwood, *Free and Independent* (Stephen Green Press), in *The Chronicle of Higher Education,* September 13, 1976, p. 20 cited by William Siffin, "Portents and Prospects: Graduate Study and the Profession," *P.S.,* 10, no. 1 (Winter 1977), p.11.

53. Theodore J. Lowi, "The Politics of Higher Education," in George J. Graham, Jr., and George W. Carey, eds., *The Post-behavioral Era* (New York: David McKay, 1972) pp. 32, 36.

54. Irving Janis, *Victims of Groupthink* (Boston: Houghton Mifflin, 1973).

55. See Peter Steinfels, "The Reasonable Right," *Esquire,* February 13, 1979, pp. 24-30.

56. Consult Robert A. Dahl, *Democracy in the United States: Promise and Performance* (Chicago: Rand McNally, 1976); Dan Nimmo and Thomas Ungs, *Political Patterns in America: Conflict Representation and Resolution* (San Francisco: Freeman, 1979); Richard A. Watson, *Promise and Performance of American Democracy* (New York: Wiley, 1978); Kenneth M. Dolbeare and Murray J. Edelman, *American Politics: Policies Power and Change* (Lexington, Mass.: Heath, 1977); Edward S. Greenberg, *The American Political System: A Radical Approach* (Cambridge, Mass.,: Winthrop Publishers, 1977); Thomas R. Dye and L. Harmon Zeigler, *The Irony of Democracy* (North Scituate, Mass.: Duxbury Press, 1978).

57. Thomas E. Cronin, *The State of the Presidency* (Boston: Little, Brown, 1975), p. 37.

58. James MacGregor Burns, interviewed by Doris Kearns Goodwin, "True Leadership," *Psychology Today* (October 1978), pp. 46-58, 110 (quote is on p. 110).

59. *Conjectures and Refutations: The Growth of Scientific Knowledge* (New York: Basic Books, 1962), p. 127.

60. A sobering place to start is the symposium, "Social Science: The Public Disenchantment," *American Scholar,* 45, no. 3 (Summer 1976), 335-359.

EPILOGUE

Sin, Suffering, Sacrifice, and Salvation
American Style

In the preceding chapters, we did a number of things. We described the nature of political myths and explored a variety of them, especially foundation, sustaining, and eschatological master myths and contemporary myths about political figures, groups, institutions, and ourselves. Moreover, we looked at the people who make and circulate those political myths—politicians and their flacks, the purveyors of popular culture, the news media, and political scientists. The careful reader will note that the variety of political myths and mythmakers notwithstanding, certain themes keep cropping up. In this epilogue, we make those themes explicit and explore the religious-like undertones that hold American political mythology together.

THE MYTH OF THE AMERICAN EDEN

In an entertaining and informative work, two scholars, one in religious studies and the other in philosophy, describe what they call "the American monomyth."[1] Their argument is that running through a variety of pieces of popular entertainment—movies, television series, comic strips, novels, and so on—is a recurring plot, that of a community threatened by evil but redeemed through heroic acts. Thus the Lone Ranger brings law and order to the American West; Superman fights for truth, justice, and the American way; and Luke Skywalker rids galactic space of the evil Darth Vader.

Our political mythology bears striking similarities to the American monomyth, especially in that "the American monomyth begins and ends in Eden."[2] From the time of their settlement, the American colonies of the New World became the New World became the New Eden. The Edenic myth—the belief that America was paradise—has had a captivating appeal to generations ever since. Even before America's settlement, as far back as five centuries ago, Columbus wrote of the New World as a terrestrial paradise, as the place for a millenial kingdom. Those that followed were no less optimistic. For Cotton Mather in the 1690s, the Puritans in America were passing through the wilderness to the promised land. And as settlers pushed westward, each advance was but another step into "The Garden of the World."

In the preceding chapters, we have witnessed the recurrence of the Edenic myth many times. The idea of Americans as God's chosen people expresses it. The agrarian democracy of Thomas Jefferson, the frontier democracy of the nabobs, and manifest destiny all testify to the strength of the Edenic myth, a master myth of eschatological appeal. The myth of small-town pastoralism still propagated by the news media is no less Edenic. And even the thrust of political science, seeking all the variables that cause human behavior, marches on to a distinctly American dream of a promised land of validity, reliability, and progress through scientific truth. All political mythmakers, no matter what their calling, offer us residence in the City on the Hill, the American Eden.

But the Edenic myth has another facet to it. The Edenic community of hard-working Americans living in peace, harmony, and tranquillity, faces recurring threats from alien forces. Sometimes these are from outside Eden—a communist conspiracy in the here and now, a King with a "history of repeated injuries and usurpations" in 1776. In other instances, they come from within—a house divided against itself" at one time; "pushy niggers," "pushy broads," or "beatniks, hippies, and queers" at another; heretics outside the mainstream of political science at yet another; and, *always,* the politicians. In the words of a song from the hit Broadway musical and movie, *The Music Man,* "We've got troubles right here in River City," not merely because of technical breakdowns or human flaws but because of an alien force of evil in our midst. In the myth of the American Eden, consensus is the norm, conflict the detested exception that must be stamped out at all costs.

Since we formed the Eden theme repeated implicitly in our

earlier accounts of American political myths, we need only pause to jog our memories to see how much of our political mythology repeats the paradise lost theme. If Eden was threatened by a tyrannical King, then the founding fathers (superheroes certainly) banished the serpent from the garden and restored paradise with the Constitution. And, as we saw, Lincoln returned to the theme at Gettysburg. In contemporary guise, we find it in the search for the enemy in Vietnam, the flack attacks of any election campaign, the portrayal of the Eastern banking establishment as evil in *The Wizard of Oz,* the stereotypes held by journalists of politicians, and political scientists' theories of elites who direct democracy for self-serving interests.

The Edenic myth, then, has been part of American political mythology for centuries. Combined with it are two other overriding master myths of considerable political relevance—the myth of the Fall and the myth of the Hero's Quest.

THE MYTH OF THE FALL

Anyone familiar with the Book of Genesis knows well the myth of the Fall: The Lord God created Adam, Eve, and the Garden; bid them eat the fruit of any tree but that of the knowledge of good and evil; tempted by the serpent, Eve did eat of that fruit and gave it also to Adam; "and the eyes of them both were opened, and they knew that they were naked." The Lord God found out and banished Adam and Eve from the Garden, promising "in sorrow shalt thou eat of the herb of the field," leaving Adam to till the ground from which he was taken.

The story is short, simple, and direct. Yet it "carries more weight per line than any other literary document one can think of."[3] But what does it have to do with politics? A great deal. Implicit in the myth of the Fall is a cycle of sin, suffering, sacrifice, and salvation that echoes again and again in the American political drama.[4] To understand that cycle and its political implications, we must look more closely at each facet of the overall myth of the Fall.

To begin with, consider Adam and Eve before their grapple with the apple. Here are two innocent persons in a wilderness paradise, very much like the Eden populated by the American colonists. It is a land unburdened with history, traditions, or ancient cleavages of class or social standing. Indeed, it has—in the sense we outlined in Chapter 2—no usable past. In this respect, "because the story emphasizes youth, because Adam and Eve are in a verdant Virgin Land, without the weight of an historical past, without social forms and traditions, the Adam story and the myth of the Fall become *the* American story."[5]

Adam, Eve, Americans—all are innocents. Innocents are ignorant, that is, not stupid and unable to learn but simply unaware of ideas and experiences that they can know but do not as yet know. Think of it as childlike innocence. An encounter with knowledge changes all that. In the story of Adam and Eve, the encounter is with the forbidden fruit; sin is the eating of it. In the recurring American cycle of sin, suffering, sacrifice, and salvation, the encounter has taken many forms. Were we once so innocent as to believe that American presidents do not lie? The encounter with Watergate made us more knowledgeable. Indeed, so knowledgeable that Jimmy Carter running for president in 1976 promised never to lie to the American people, employing a phrase reminiscent of that given to America's first Adam figure, George Washington, "I can't tell a lie, Pa" (see Chapter 2). But there have been other American encounters with sin—the My Lai massacre in Vietnam, dropping of nuclear bombs in World War II, the collapse of middle-class America in the Great Depression, the Civil War, the War of 1812, and on and on.

The Fall is thus a transformation from innocence to experience. It carries with it pain and suffering. For Adam and Eve, it was the fulfillment of the Lord God's promise of "sorrow." The recurrent falls from the American Eden have been no less painful and traumatic. American political mythology is replete with symbols of suffering—at Valley Forge, Gettysburg, the Argonne, and the Battle of the Bulge in wartime; in the Critical Period, Reconstruction, the Great Depression, and Watergate in peace.

But the primary consequence of the Fall is to provide Adam and Eve with the knowledge of good and evil. Painful though it is, there is hope of promise and fulfillment. For after the Fall, there is a vision of Hell, the prospect that "man's nature *is* fallen, morally weak, flawed, degenerate, selfish, aggressive, hostile, fuller of hate than love" and that "the social community in which man lives must reflect this nature."[6] Balanced against this vision of evil is one of goodness—that love, charity, kindness, and benevolence can and do prevail in human affairs *if people are willing to sacrifice* for it. For Adam, the sacrifice was to "till the ground from whence he was taken." For Americans, the vision of Hell and sacrifice to avoid it has taken many forms. In 1979, for instance, following the cutoff of Iranian oil, the vision of Hell faced by most Americans was the prospect of being rationed only two gallons of gasoline per day if they did not adopt conservation practices. Few found the vision sufficiently plausible to sacrifice.

The call to sacrifice reverberates throughout America's political past, be it Nathan Hale's "My only regret is that I have but one life to give to my country" in 1776 or John F. Kennedy's "Ask not what your country can do for you; ask what you can do for your country" in 1961. One of its most profound statements, however, came from an American president who was viewed not so much as an Adam figure but as a Messiah come to break the cycle of sin, suffering, sacrifice, and salvation. Consider the words of Abraham Lincoln's Second Inaugural Address. First the sin—that is, that of slavery and "wringing bread from the sweat of other men's faces." That sin had evil consequences: "These slaves constitute a peculiar and powerful interest. All knew that this interest was somehow the cause of the war." Next, the suffering: "Woe unto the world because of offenses, for it must needs be that offenses come, but woe to that man by whom the offense cometh." For God "gives to both North and South this terrible war as a woe due to those by whom the offense came." Now sacrifice: "Fondly do we hope, fervently do we pray, that this mighty scourge of war may speedily pass away. Yet if God will that it continue until all the wealth piled by the bondsman's two hundred and fifty years of unrequited toil shall be sunk, and every drop of blood drawn with the lash shall be paid by another drawn with the sword, as was said three thousand years ago, so still it must be said, that the judgements of the Lord are true and righteous altogether." And, finally, salvation:

> With malice toward none, with charity for all, with firmness in the right as God gives us to see the right, let us finish the work we are in, to bind up the nation's wounds, to care for him who shall have borne the battle, and for his widow and his orphans, to do all which may achieve and cherish a just and lasting place among ourselves and with all nations.

So there is a choice. The Fall offers either evil or good. Which form of knowledge is it to be? With sacrifice it is to be good—hence, salvation. For Adam and Eve, this could never mean a return to the Garden: "So he drove out the man; and he placed at the east of the Garden of Eden cherubim, and a flaming sword which turned every way to keep the way of the tree of life." Americans, however, raised in a tradition of happy endings to their stories, want full pardons and redemption. Nothing less than a restored Eden will do, an Eden whose fruits can be shared with all parts of the globe, whether it be through the manifest destiny of making the world safe for democracy, the promise of human rights (morality), technological know-how and Yankee ingenuity (technology) and American culture for everyone, or Pepsi Cola for the Russians and Coke for the Chinese. The flaming sword guarding the garden must be overcome. For that, there must be a hero.

THE HERO'S QUEST AND AMERICAN REDEMPTION

A hero is one of great strength of character and of courage who transcends human frailties and limitations in order to perform bold exploits—exploits that can redeem a society from its sin, suffering, and sacrifice if people will but heed and follow. The hero appears in many guises—as Hercules of Greek and Roman mythology; as Superman of comics, television, and movies; as Dorothy of *The Wizard of Oz;* as Gary Cooper in *High Noon* or as Buford Pusser in *Walking Tall;* as Sir Gawain in King Arthur's Camelot; as Jack climbing a beanstalk; as *Alice in Wonderland;* as Huck Finn. The roll call of heroic characters of song and story is almost endless.

Certainly America has had its share of politicians who emerged either as heroes or hero pretenders—George Washington, Thomas Jefferson, and all the founding fathers; Abraham Lincoln; Teddy and Franklin Roosevelt; Woodrow Wilson; John Kennedy; Martin Luther King; even a Richard Nixon in China or a Jimmy Carter in Cairo. What typifies these mythical heroes of real life typifies those of fiction as well—that is, each one sets out on a quest destined to produce risks, anxieties, threats, and dangers. Thus "the hero of myth must abandon all and be abandoned," for the hero "enters, of necessity, the pit, the labyrinth, the cavern, the ark, the wilderness; the symbolic nether-world or 'tomb' . . . in *order to find the path, follow the path, be the path.*"⁷ In American political mythology, it is the recurring Hero's Quest that provides an ever-renewed hope of redemption from evil and a promise of restored Eden.

Both the hero and the quest, as portrayed in mythology, have clearly identifiable features. Each is apparent in American political mythology.⁸ First, the hero is often one *of obscure and mysterious origin*. Be he Huck Finn, the Lone Ranger, Robin Hood, or Jesus Christ, the hero's origins are strange, hidden, and miraculous. The American version of this element in the mythical paradigm of the Hero's Quest is the log cabin myth. Reflect on how many aspiring politicians point to their humble origins. The most famous was Abraham Lincoln, and the Lincoln legend owes much to the obscurity of his origins. Four states—Indiana, Kentucky, North Carolina, and Tennessee—have claimed him as a native son. Fifteen different places offer the actual locale on which stood the cabin in which Lincoln entered this life.

Today, even if the origins are not so obscure and mysterious, the fledgling political hero setting out on an historic quest must still lay claim to a humble upbringing. Whether it be Harry Truman from little Lamar, Missouri, Lyndon Johnson making myths about his youth on the Pedernales River in Texas, or Richard Nixon extolling the small-town pastoral qualities of Whittier, California, the message is the same: "My origins are humble, what I have today I achieved through true grit; therefore, my struggle was heroic." Lest one think that the syndrome is vanishing from American politics, consider the following passage from a once little-known author named Jimmy Carter: "My life on the farm during the Great Depression more nearly resembled farm life fully 2,000 years ago than farm life today. . . . We lived in a wooded clapboard house alongside the dirt road. . ., a house cool in the summer and cold in the winter. . . . There was no source of heat in the northeast corner room where I slept. . . . For years we used an outdoor privy."⁹ And what hero was on his quest fully 2,000 years ago?

A hero *hears the call,* that is, the hero takes up the quest out of urgent necessity. Often it is with sore reluctance that the hero sets out. Clark Kent might rather be with Lois Lane, but there is crime in the streets, and, as Superman, he must pull himself away to fight for "truth, justice, and the American way." As a hero, it is his manifest destiny. So too the political hero heeds the call. Thomas Jefferson wanted nothing more than to retire and tinker around his beautiful, pastoral Monticello, but Madison helped to coax him out of retirement and a second career began—as ambassador, secretary of state, vice president, and president.

To be sure, many a politician is most eager to advance and thus to undertake a quest for higher office or a special crusade. Yet surface reluctance at least is the keynote and urgent necessity the motivating force, not self-serving ambition. So Jerry Brown, a year after his re-election as governor of California and with an eye on the White House, journeyed to New York City where he met with politicians, labor leaders, spokesmen of the Jewish community, representatives of black organizations, and so on. Backstage conversations might have revolved about unseating Jimmy Carter, but the onstage performance spoke of the urgency of re-establishing America's technological superiority; developing human and technical resources; and preserving the land, water, and atmosphere of the planet. Whether from Krypton to Metropolis or from Sacramento to the Big Apple, urgent necessity carried the day.

Heroes are *neither fools nor invincible.* Yet they may adopt the fool's disguise. Abraham Lincoln was famous for his self-deprecating homilies and homespun humor. But the stories always had a telling point, and few mistook his simplicity for clownishness. The authentic fool—or one who appears as such—has no heroic possibilities. Hence Ron Nessen, press secretary to President Gerald Ford, fumed at press coverage of Ford's spills on the ski slopes or of the times when he bumped his head on a helicopter door or tripped walking down a corridor. A sense of humor is desirable in a hero (at least, an American style hero); an image of the clown is defeating.

But no matter how powerful the hero, there is some human weakness. Achilles' heel made him vulnerable; Superman is helpless in the face of kryptonite; even the Six Million Dollar Man had to have an occasional lube job. So it is with political heroes, revered or aspiring. Washington had ill-fitting false teeth; Lincoln was gangly and ugly; Teddy Roosevelt wore thick glasses; Franklin Roosevelt could not walk; John Kennedy had a roving eye; Jimmy Carter admitted to lust in his heart. If not carried to extremes, these human qualities go far toward convincing the populace that, although the hero is set apart because he transcends most human limitations, nonetheless a weakness here or there makes him a man of the people and thus able to respond to their call.

The hero has a *goal.* It may be holy, as was that of Jesus Christ. It may be fanciful, as was Huck Finn's to sail to Cairo where his black friend, Jim, would be free. It may be simple, as for Dorothy in *The Wizard of Oz* to get home. In any event, it is the purpose of the journey, of following the path down the yellow brick road. The goals of American political heroes have been equally diverse, depending upon time and circumstance. Washington's was to win a war of independence, Lincoln's to end the suffering but preserve the union, Wilson's to assure "open covenants openly arrived at," and Eisenhower's to lead a "crusade" against the sins of "crime, communism, and Korea." The refrain is unending as would-be heroes set out on their quests, as exemplified in 1979 by an Associated Press dispatch datelined Washington, D.C., and describing Jimmy Carter's journey to Cairo and Jerusalem: "His fervent desire to be the peacemaker between the Arabs and Israel," said the dispatch, was "driving him to the Middle East this week on what appears to be an enormously risky trip."

But all *heroic quests are risky.* Dangers, loneliness, and temptation abound along the way. Captain Kirk and Mr. Spock, in their five-year mission aboard the U.S.S. Enterprise in *Star Trek,* are heroic figures facing countless physical dangers from alien beings, the loneliness of sexual renunciation (even Kirk's occasional escapades were to save his crew and ship), and temptations (in one story, aliens promise them Eden if they will but obey; instead, they destroy the Edenic planet).

Risks in political quests are an accepted part of the heroic life. Martin Luther King, Jr., faced physical danger throughout his career and ultimately died by an assassin's bullet. And the myth of the presidency as a lonely place where "the buck stops here" has become an accepted part of American political folklore. Certainly, there are always temptations—to go on the take, to foresake the journey, to compromise principle, to pander to public opinion, or to take advantage of office secretaries. Surely the entire sorry Watergate episode was a drama of a presidential administration that employed heroic rhetoric in public but whose chief figure yielded to both temptations and human frailties behind closed doors.

Although possessing a goal and setting out on a journey to reach it, *the hero's way is not always clear to him.* It took the mythical Greek hero Odysseus ten years of sidetracks and detours to reach his goal, that is, returning to his home. Jesus wandered to and fro across the countryside in pursuit of his holy goal. Or consider Captain Ahab's often aimless search for the white whale, *Moby Dick.* (Although some might consider Ahab more antihero than hero, the hero's quest was still apparent.) The path for political heroes is also unclear and indirect. Abraham Lincoln, in his farewell address at Springfield, Illinois, as he set out to Washington for his inaugural, expressed his uncertainty but knew that a "duty devolves upon me which is, perhaps, greater than that which has developed upon any other man since the days of Washington," and he asked for prayers to the Almighty Being "without which I cannot succeed, but with which success is certain. Similarly, other aspiring heroes have been unsure or have taken indirect routes to their goal: Franklin Roosevelt was soundly defeated when running for the vice presidency in 1920, Richard Nixon's political obituary came after defeats for the presidency in 1960 and for the governorship of California in 1962, and even Jimmy Carter lost in his first try for the governorship of Georgia in 1966.

Perhaps because the way is uncertain and full of risks, most tales of the hero's quest provide *friends, servants, or disciples* to travel with the hero. Sometimes these serve as a *guide* or *guides.* Jesus had his twelve disciples, Huck Finn had Jim, Tonto accompanies the Lone Ranger, and *Gunsmoke's* Matt Dillon first had Chester and then Festus as deputy marshal. As we saw in Chapter 4, politicians have all manner of hacks and flacks surrounding them in their pursuit of heroic goals. Guides and confidants about: Washington had Hamilton; Jefferson had Madison; Franklin Roosevelt had Louis Howe; John Kennedy his brother Bobby; and who can forget that remarkable trio opening vistas for Richard Nixon—John Mitchell, Robert Haldeman, and John Erlichman. Certainly no telling of a saga of Jimmy Carter from statehouse to White House is complete without the touching story of how Carter and Jody Powell (later to be his press secretary) traveled many a lonely mile, driving long into the night across the highways and byways of Georgia, Iowa, and other states.

What makes the hero's quest an epic tale is that at some point in the journey, *the hero descends into darkness.* In this respect, then, the hero suffers a crushing blow of some type that symbolizes the same sin that the Edenic community has gone through with the fall from grace.

It is in the darkness that the hero faces the ultimate test of traveling alone to a dreaded place and, if successful, redeeming the community as well as himself. In many quest sagas the dreaded place is Hades or is Hell-like; in others, it is simply a place of unending torment. No matter what the hour or the place, it is the terrible loneliness and fear that makes the experience dreadful—Christ's torment on the cross, Jonah's being swallowed by the whale, Dorothy chased by the wicked witch in *The Wizard of Oz,* or Gary Cooper stalking the streets awaiting his enemies at *High Noon.*

The politician projecting a heroic image also publicizes a descent into darkness in order to prove that he fits the heroic mold. The myth of Washington falling on his knees at Valley Forge is but one example. Lincoln was reputed to have kept a lonely vigil in the White House late at night, suffering over the human sacrifices of the Civil War. Franklin Roosevelt descended into darkness when he contracted infantile paralysis, which left him a cripple during the whole of his later career. Richard Nixon recognized the role played by the descent in projecting a heroic image and wrote a volume of memoirs entitled *Six Crises* before he became president. And, again, Jimmy Carter has recounted the torment suffered after his loss the first time he sought the governorship of Georgia in 1966.

But truly heroic figures survive these lonely descents to *emerge from the darkness transformed.* The hero usually comes away from the ordeal a wiser, calmer, more sober, more mature, more spiritual person. Sir Gawain was transformed from a boy into a man after his fight with the Green Knight; Ebenezer Scrooge survived his ghastly visit from the Ghost of Christmas Yet to Come to emerge as a totally new, loving, generous human being (the ruin of a good man, say some cynics).

Politicians also emerge transformed from their confrontations with evil and defeat. Few have suffered more widely publicized descents and emergences than the heir to the Camelot throne of American politics, Edward "Teddy" Kennedy. The assassinations of John and Robert Kennedy alone represent crushing encounters, but the descent into darkness (both figuratively and literally) that helped to transform a career occurred in July, 1969, when Teddy Kennedy drove a car late at night, carrying a female companion off a bridge and into a creek. Kennedy admitted leaving the woman, swimming away, and then returning after seeking help. The woman was killed in the accident. Kennedy emerged from that experience and from the earlier loss of two brothers to assassins' bullets, chastened and transformed, projecting a new image as the responsible head of the Kennedy clan; a hard-working, knowledgeable, courageous United States Senator; and a loyal and indefatigable party worker. Having undergone such heroic transformation—from playboy to statesman—his stature as a potential presidential contender increased throughout the 1970s.

Suffering not only transforms the hero but *purifies* him. Being chastened, tested, or tempted and overcoming these obstacles, the hero proves worthy of his quest and is therefore able to meet the challenge set for himself. Jesus is tested in the desert by Satan, Ulysses tempted by Circe, Scrooge chastened by the Ghosts. Similarly, the American Adam has his Eves, his scourges, and his temptations: Women, money, drink, satisfaction, and enemies all materialize to prevent him from the completion of his quest. But if he is of true heroic stature, he overcomes these obstacles, and his purity aids in the completion of his task. He may suffer wounds, doubts, diversions, and the like, but such experiences purify and temper him into strong steel, thus preparing him for completion of the heroic task.

In the American heroic drama, testing takes a variety of forms, but in almost all cases, the hero overcomes a flaw, doubt, enemies, or something that proves heroic devotion and makes for stronger character. Devotees of Edward Kennedy claim that the Chappaquiddick experience matured, that is, purified, him. Perhaps Jerry Brown, like Lancelot, will resist being detained in his heroic task by the luscious temptation of Linda Ronstadt; only the pure can balance the budget. Certainly Jimmy Carter, like Nixon, Wilson, and others before him, believes in the purity of his motives and will continue to do so since he was purified by overcoming defeat, doubt, and disappointment when he was born again.

The hero and his quest are *vindicated* in either victory, defeat, or death. If the hero's quest is completed and a symbolic victory obtained then the hero can claim vindication. His quest has been justified, the community redeemed. Troy falls, the dragon is slain, death and evil are overcome. Yet the hero may be vindicated even in defeat or death. The hero who dies for the community shall not have died in vain. Those defeated in their quests are often accorded eventual apotheosis. King Arthur was vindicated by the nobility of his quest, even though it failed. Tragedy revolves around the theme of heroic failure, but there is also a measure of justification of the heroic quest.

American political heroes experience both types of vindication.

Successful presidential candidates feel vindicated in victory, electoral or otherwise. The heroic quest for peace in the Mideast in 1979 vindicated Jimmy Carter, at least for the moment. Witness the language of news dispatches covering his trip to Egypt and Israel in March of that year: "President Carter returned from his Mideast odyssey," "his quest for a Middle East peace agreement often close to failure"; and "President Carter returned to a hero's welcome," saying, "'I believe that God has answered our prayers.'" But even those who die are defeated and often vindicated by the unfulfilled promise of death or the tragedy of defeat. Robert Kennedy became for his admirers the lost president whose bright promise was tragically cut down. Senator Joe McCarthy was vindicated in death by his admirers as one who cried in the wilderness only to be ignored and scorned but whose quest was not in vain, since he was right all along. Hubert Humphrey received the vindication in illness and death that was repeatedly denied him as a presidential candidate. Thus even if heroic figures fail to redeem the community, they can redeem themselves through the agony of defeat. The Kennedys, Humphrey, and McCarthy were all purified by death. Sometimes vindication is the hero's in both victory and death. Lincoln, the classic prototype, was vindicated by victory in the Civil War and purified by tragic death ("Now he belongs to the ages").

These, then, are the basic features of the myth of the Hero's Quest. It is important to be clear about what we are saying. Simply put, the saga of the questing hero is a dramatic tale with a distinctive sequence and logic. Although that drama has emerged in numerous epics, ballads, and pieces of fiction, folklore, and fantasy, it reappears so often that it has a life of its own. As witnessed by popular movies, including *Superman, Star Wars, Close Encounters of the Third Kind,* and *Rocky* or perennially favorite television series, such as *Star Trek, Bonanza, Gunsmoke,* or *Battlestar Galactica,* it is a drama that people never tire of retelling.

Being a hardy and viable tale, the myth of the Hero's Quest (and the overlapping myths of Eden and the Fall) offers an interpretative framework for standing in the present and looking both backward and forward. In the political realm, we have constructed myths about America's past that combine over and over again the fantasies of Eden, the Fall, and the Hero's Quest. Whether compiled, for example, by American historians or by the general population, any list of the Great Presidents contains those with heroic qualities—Washington, Lincoln, Wilson, the Roosevelts. For the less heroic, but often successful, presidents, only Near Great can be awarded—Polk, Truman, and so on.

Politicians and their flacks, purveyors of popular entertainment, journalists, even political scientists recognize—sometimes instinctively, sometimes from research, and sometimes from reading Machiavelli's *The Prince* or Shakespeare's *Henry V* and *Richard III*—the enduring appeal of the myths of Eden, the Fall, and the Hero's Quest. Given that appeal, these mythmakers adapt to it. Politicians and flacks couch presentations of self in heroic terms; movie and television producers, novelists, and other creators of popular fare cater to public expectations; journalists write dramatic accounts of America's sins, sufferings, sacrifices, and salvations; and political scientists explore alienation, the crisis of authority, charisma, images, and political attitudes —scholarly versions of a concern with America's loss of Eden and the Heroic quest to restore it.

What we are suggesting, then, is that life not only imitates art, just as art imitates life, but that we conduct ourselves in accordance with the dramatic logic of three overriding master myths—those of Eden, the Fall, and the Hero's Quest—that combine to form an attractive, seductive, political supermyth. It is primarily through that supermyth that we know our political past, present, and future. For it is from the present perspective of that supermyth that we project visions of what has happened, of what is going on, and of what will (as well as should) occur in the future.

AMERICAN POLITICS
Idyllic or Idolatry?

In sum, because as Americans we believe in a political supermyth, we *need* to feel as God's chosen, to restore Eden, and to wash away our sins. And for that, we *need* heroes. The mythmakers labor to supply them. We have suggested a number of examples of who they are and how they do so, but there is one whose career spanned several decades. We single him out not for criticism but to illustrate how persons possessing the best of intentions to "tell it like it is" end up making myths.

Following each presidential election from 1960 through 1972, Theodore H. White, a noted and reputable journalist, wrote a book entitled *The Making of the President*. They were absorbing, entertaining, insightful volumes that established a new genre and school of inside reporting of politics. But in 1976, as he set out to chronicle another presidential election, he found that he could not do it. Why? White might disagree, but a reviewer of another of White's books offers a possible explanation. The reviewer writes that "From Kennedy to Nixon, White's books enshrouded reality in romantic mythology, the good king mystically selected to lead, battling heroically against the fates, enlarged by his territorial responsibilities to a heroic dimension, unifying the nation by his goodness." But sadly, the review reports, "each of White's heroes failed on the throne, for every modern president since Eisenhower has disappointed the unreal expectations implicit in White's myth of heroes." In sum, White faced the evidence "that he had been wrong—wrong about four presidents, wrong about the presidency itself, wrong about beloved America and where it was headed in history."[10]

But if White was proved wrong and if he became disillusioned, he is not alone. He simply succumbed to the American state of collective consciousness when thinking about politics—that is, unquestioned acceptance of the cycle of sin, suffering, sacrifice, and salvation and the belief that after our fall from Eden, only a hero can lead. We submit that idyllic as the notion of an Edenic America might be, it never did, does, can, or will exist. No Fall took place. No heroes have redeemed us. But believing in an idyllic past, present, and future and unable to restore the nostalgic Eden, we search endlessly for heroes to do so. Thus has a mythical idyllic state yielded to an American brand of idolatry, a worship of the notion that someone or something will make our world right again—will end dissension, restore America as the world's "Number One" power, clean up our air and water, assure an unlimited supply of gasoline, and guarantee a glorious future.

The Idolatry of Heroic Redemption

Idolatry, in part, takes the form of redeemer figures—mythic heroes who intervene to save the community. Redeemer figures offer hope in victory, and if they fail, they become the objects of our blame. We transfer our anxieties and guilts onto them. American politics includes at least four major types of redeemer figures, appealing to different myths, audiences, and moods of the moment but nevertheless recurring in the American political drama. These are heroes who quest to restore the idyllic state or lead us to the promised land.

The first is the *Heidi redeemer*. This heroic type is "a superheroic figure who miraculously saves individuals or communities by psychological manipulation or other nonviolent means."[11] Usually salvation manifests itself as an appeal to moral transformation brought about through the good offices of a morally pure exemplar. Heidi redeemers implore us to "reason together," to "look deep into the human heart," to transcend interest and calculation for principle. Moral conversion rather than power is the path to community redemption. This has always been a key theme in evangelical Protestantism, as well as in politics. It appears as a mythic theme in the careers of such Heidi redeemers as William Jennings Bryan, Woodrow Wilson, and Jimmy Carter. Each endeavors to tap wellsprings of goodness is us all and thus to redeem the community by appealing to individual morality. Thus, announced Jimmy Carter in seeking the presidency in 1976, America must have a government " as good as its people." Critics of the Carter administration, not enraptured either by the Heidi-like president or by Carter policies, feared that might be precisely the kind of government he provided!

Secondly, American politics witnesses the recurrence of the *royal redeemer*. This is the mythic hero who, because of noble background or accomplishment, saves the community by the dint of leadership. Even though we have no hereditary king, we do have a tradition of *noblesse oblige*—that is, that aristocratic background or bearing infuses some chosen few with talents to redeem the community. It is thus the duty of the privileged to do so. Hence, the Roosevelts, the Rockefellers, the Kennedys, the Harrimans, and others enter public service as "to the purple born." Through institutional management—that is, keeping the Ship of State and the values it carries on course—they strive to redeem. They govern not through moral conversion but through deference to their aristocratic right to rule.

There are various versions of the royal redeemer myth. For example, there is the Lincoln scenario, that common men naturally arise from the democratic mass to greatness and a right to rule. They are not originally aristocrats but are nonetheless of royal character sufficient to rise above the herd. They assume royalty by proving their heroism in gaining office and successfully exercising power. Not only Lincoln but other "common men," such as Harry Truman, fit this type. They acquire the mantle and the ruling style (and connections) of institutional managers. Second, there are paths to royalty other than politics, most notably soldiering and business, which offer proof of heroism to be later carried into politics. Eisenhower proved his heroism in the crusade in Europe and thus had credentials that were transferable to political royalty. Successful business magnates make a claim to political royalty on the argument of their business experience and management expertise. But in all cases, royal redeemers claim that the benevolence of an elite is our path to salvation.

A third kind of figure that recurs is the *technocratic redeemer*. He does not appeal to moral transformation, nor does he have elite claims. But he does claim that some engineering problem—be it constitutional, institutional, or legislative—is the way to community redemption. A constitutional amendment to balance the budget, a change in presidential power, a law to commit us to full employment, the advice of the knowledgeable: All are techniques urged as the answers to our problems. Technocratic projects, such as those in sending a man to the moon, emerge as ways to solve earthly problems, such as poverty. The myth is that political problems are really questions of technique and that they can be solved through the concerted efforts of scientists, engineers, and other experts. Jerry Brown, among contemporary politicians, is a clear example of this type of proffered redemption. The country, he argues, will be saved by fiscal and environmental balance, the kinds of balance that can be brought about only by technocratic engineering. The problems are not those of morality or leadership but those involving the mastery of technique.

There is a fourth type of redeemer figure that has been hitherto fairly unsuccessful, although not absent, from America: the *demonic redeemer*. Moral, royal, and engineer redeemer figures fall within the American democratic tradition and thus are limited by that tradition in what they can do. But sometimes, especially during periods of crisis and change, there is a call for someone more elemental, more vindictive, more aggressive. The primal impulse is for a redeemer figure who is not limited by the democratic tradition, who does not appeal to morality, and who is not an elite member. The desire is for solutions, not via the usual heroes, but instead from someone messianic and vengeful who can mobilize hate and fear, identify scapegoats, and promise a restored Eden of community, security, and authority.

The appeal is demonic in that there are no limits, moral or institutional, placed on the hero's quest. The desire is for vengeance, purgation of the community through violence, and final purification. The hero represents a punitive principle, and his ferocity and even diabolic actions are justified by the gravity and threat of the evils that beset us. We have noted in chapter 5 that this is a theme in contemporary popular culture. We might also note that American life has not been devoid of such figures, from Puritan witch-hunters to contemporary death cults. Indeed, the great American epic novel, Melville's *Moby Dick,* has as its central character the sharply drawn symbol of a demonic redeemer, Captain Ahab. Ahab's quest is demonic: He leads his crew into a ferocious and unlimited search for the White Whale, abandoning land values and the fear of God. Ahab becomes a satanic god-figure, and his diabolic hatred and purpose are gradually shared by many of the crew. His single-minded cosmic aim is vengeance, which implicitly rids the world of the menacing force of the White Whale. He and the crew are ultimately destroyed by the very force they set out to destroy, the whale.

Ahab's demonic quest has been muted in American politics, not as yet bearing the power and ferocity of other famous demonic redeemers: Hitler, Lenin, Robespierre, Mussolini. But there have been figures here who were on the fringe: Thaddeus Stevens, Huey Long, Joe McCarthy, George Wallace. They wanted vengeance; they identified scapegoats; they saw the quest as having an importance beyond the normal political restraints. The call for a demonic redeemer is especially tempting in an era of American decline as a nation. Sensing that we are drifting ever further away from the dream of the American Eden, people seem dissatisfied with the other, more traditional redeemer figures, and they sometimes display a depth of hate, fear, and frustration that could be mobilized into a massive political force. The world created by the moralists, the royal institutionalists, and the engineers may be rejected for a simpler, more primitive world, an Edenic community secure from the threats of aliens by the demonic authority of the redeemer figure.

Idols of American Politics

But idolatry is deluding. Over three and one-half centuries ago, the English philosopher Francis Bacon wrote of the four classes of idols that beset our minds, each replete with mythology.[12] First, he said, are the Idols of the Tribe. They stem from the belief that the "sense of man is the measure of things." We recognize these idols in the reverence people pay to common sense—that is, all those things we are somehow supposed to know just because we are human. Common sense tells us that we don't light matches near open gasoline tanks, that we don't play with rattle snakes, that wealthy men don't run for public office unless there is some financial gain in the offing, and that we can't remove poverty by giving money away. The problem with the idol of common sense, however, is that it is indeed common sense—that is, a sense widely held and believed, but rarely tested. To be sure, smoking cigarettes around gasoline fumes would probably prove common sense correct, but would common sense prove to be a useful guide if we could find out all of the motives for why the wealthy seek public office? It was once common sense to believe the earth flat, the sun revolving about the earth, and the moon made of green cheese. The point is not that some common sense might be right and other common sense wrong. Rather, we seldom bother to test our taken-for-granted world. Hence, we believe in the mythical Idols of the Tribe.

Idols of the Cave are the self-myths each of us accept as individuals—myths about ourselves, about others, about the world. "For everyone," wrote Bacon, "has a cave or den of his own, which refracts and discolors the light of nature; owing either to his own proper and peculiar nature or to his education and conversation with others; or to the reading of books, and the authority of those he esteems and admires; or to the differences of impressions, accordingly as they take place in a mind preoccupied and predisposed or in a mind indifferent and settled; or the like."[13] How often we have seen these self-myths at work in politics! Recall the self-myths, the cave idols, generated by journalists: that they have standards, are fair and objective, know what politics is really like. Or think of the self-myth of political scientists—that is, that they don't make myths.

Idols of the Market place derive from the give-and-take of open discourse. The words we use to describe and explain things serve as labels, and the labels themselves become myths. To label the presidency "imperial" is to make a myth. To call Congress "unruly" is to do the same. Or consider the following labels used by the news media (principal sculptors of the Idols of the Marketplace) in stereotyping presidential candidates in 1976: "soft-talking, evangelist-sounding peanut farmer," "former actor," "refreshingly pleasant former college football player and congressional insider." Only a moment's thought brings to mind Carter, Reagan, and Ford as the objects of such imagery.

Finally, Bacon wrote of Idols of the Theater—that is, philosophic dogmas, "received systems," and idols entering men's minds "from wrong laws of demonstration," including "many principles and axioms in science, which by tradition, credulity, and negligence have come to be received."[14] In the political realm, these are the idols and myths derived in large measure from a political science that has become overly concerned with its own search for community, pastimes, rituals, and games rather than for the substance of politics it purports to study. To the degree that political science produces Idols of the Theater (and we have argued in Chapter 7 that to a large degree it does), then it has long since replaced economics as "the dismal science."

CONCLUSION
Escaping from Flatland

By now the reader must wonder, "Is everything myth?" In the words of singer Peggy Lee's ballad, "Is that all there is?" Not necessarily, but as we pointed out early in Chapter 1 and have argued since, most of what passes for popular knowledge of politics is mythical. The more important question is not how much of political knowledge is mythical but rather, must it be so? We think not. At least it need not be *if* we are willing to *substitute possibilities for certainties.* Recall our definition of myth: a credible, dramatic, socially constructed representation of perceived realities that people accept as permanent, fixed knowledge of reality while forgetting its tentative, imaginative, created, and perhaps fictional qualities. *It is when re-presentations become certainties and all other possibilities vanish that myths command.*

The best illustration of our concluding point lies in a little novelette written almost a century ago by a schoolmaster, *Flatland: A Romance of Many Dimensions*. [15] The world of Flatland is two dimensional, a land of length and breadth but no height—much like a table top—and inhabited by triangles, squares, rectangles, and other two-dimensional figures. Although the inhabitants can move freely on the two-dimensional surface, they cannot rise above it or even imagine the possibility of a three-dimensional, that is, a Spaceland, world.

In the story, the narrator, a Flatland inhabitant, has a dream. In it he travels to Lineland, a one-dimensional world. All residents of Lineland are either dots or lines. Linelanders are free to move back and forth along a line but can move neither to right nor left. Traveling in such space is an unthinkable possibility to a Linelander. The Flatlander dreams that he tries to explain to the Lineland King, who is the longest line in Lineland, about such things in order to enlighten the King's ignorance. The King takes umbrage and calls an attack on the Flatlander (who is a Square), but the latter awakens from his dream.

Later that day, a strange thing happens to our Flatlander. A visitor arrives claiming to be from Spaceland, a three-dimensional world. He tries to explain to the Square what three-dimensional reality is all about, but, like the King of Lineland, the Square cannot fathom it. The Spacelander reasons with the Square, but to no avail. The latter will have none of the Gospel of Three Dimensions. The Spacelander loses patience: "Ha! Is it come to this? Then meet your fate: out of your Plane you go. Once, twice, thrice! 'Tis done!"

Driven from his Garden of Edenic Flatland, the Square is horrified. He describes a "darkness, then a dizzy sickening sensation." He shrieks in agony, "Either this is madness or it is Hell!" But to the Square's interpretation of the Fall, the Spacelander replies, "It is neither; it is Knowledge; it is Three Dimensions: open your eye once again and try to look steadily." Soon the Square sees and having seen is overwhelmed with curiosity. He begins to inquire of the Spacelander about four, five, and six dimensions. "There is no such land," responds the Spacelander and throws the Square back to Flatland. Needless to say, the Square tries to preach the Gospel of Three Dimensions to his fellow Flatlanders. But they will have none of it. Such things are not possible. The Square receives a sentence of perpetual imprisonment.

It is for the Square thereafter a life of unending vexation. Having the possibilities that lie behind certainty, myths never again provide the comforting balm they once did: "All the substantial realities of Flatland itself appear no better than the offspring of a diseased imagination, of the baseless fabric of a dream." In short, there is a price to pay for surrendering our myths, for leaving the garden of political realities and certainties and entering a political world of many dimensions, many possibilities. An idyllic American politics is a chimera. An idolatrous political life, although perhaps more comforting, is no better. Only acceptance of and tolerance for uncertainty will open the mythical world of idylls and idols to inquiry.

REFERENCES

1. Robert Jewett and John Shelton Lawrence, *The American Monomyth* (Garden City, N.Y.: Doubleday [Anchor Books], 1977), p. 169.

2. Jewett and Lawrence, *The American Monomyth,* p. 169.

3. F. Parvin Sharpless, *The Myth of the Fall* (Rochelle Park, N.J.: Hayden, 1974), p. 2.

4. Jerald Washington, *The American Political Drama* (Unpublished PH.D. diss., University of Tennessee, 1976), *passim.*

5. Sharpless, *The Myth of the Fall,* p. 3 (italics in original).

6. Sharpless, *The Myth of the Fall,* p. 10 (italics in original).

7. Dorothy Norman, *The Hero: Myth/Image/Symbol* (New York: World Publishing Company, 1969), pp. 5-6.

8. The discussion of aspects of the hero's quest relies in large measure on features described in Peter R. Stillman, *Introduction to Myth* (Rochelle Park, N.J.: Hayden, 1977) pp. 26-32.

9. Jimmy Carter, *Why Not the Best?* (Nashville, Tenn.: Broadman Press, 1975), pp. 7-8.

10. William Greider, Review of "In Search of History: A Personal Adventure," by Theodore H. White, *The Manchester Guardian Weekly,* September 17, 1978, p. 18.

11. Jewett and Lawrence, *The American Monomyth,* p. 249.

12. Francis Bacon, *Novum Organum,* in Edwin A. Burtt, ed., *The English Philosophers from Bacon to Mill* (New York: Random House [Modern Library], 1939), pp. 24-123.

13. Bacon, *Novum Organum,* p. 35.

14. Bacon, *Novum Organum,* p. 35.

15. Edwin A. Abbott, *Flatland: A Romance of Many Dimensions* (New York: Barnes & Noble Books, 1963).

Index